Claris Em@iler™ Companion

Claris Em@iler™ Companion

Thomas Dell

AP PROFESSIONAL
AP PROFESSIONAL is a Division of Academic Press
Boston San Diego New York
London Sydney Tokyo Toronto

AP PROFESSIONAL
1300 Boylston St., Chestnut Hill, MA 02167
An Imprint of Academic Press
A Division of Harcourt Brace & Company

United Kingdom Edition published by
ACADEMIC PRESS LIMITED
24–28 Oval Road, London NW1 7DX

Dell, Tom.
Claris Em[a]iler companion / Thomas Dell.
p. cm.
On t.p. "@" in "Emailer" appears as an at sign.
Includes index.
ISBN 0-12-208865-4 (alk. paper)
1. Electronic mail systems—Computer programs. 2. Claris Emailer.
I. Title. II. Title: Claris emailer companion.
TK5105.73.D45 1997
005.7' 1369—DC21

97-14007
CIP

Printed in the United States of America

97 98 99 00 IP 9 8 7 6 5 4 3 2 1

Dedication

To my son, Garret Thomas.
May email bring us closer together.

Contents

Introduction

If email is important to you, you have made a wise choice in purchasing Claris Emailer. If you have one email account, you will appreciate the way Claris Emailer enables you to organize the email you receive. If you have several email accounts, you will love the fact that you can now control all of them with this one efficient little application. If you travel, you will depend on Claris Emailer's ability to accept and memorize different configurations for different locations. For must of us, Claris Emailer is the only email application we will ever need!

In this book I will attempt to make you comfortable with the set up and use of Claris Emailer. I will also show you a few tricks along the way so you can get more out of it.

Conventions Used in This Book

When I want to alert you to something special, you will see one of three symbols:

NOTE *This is information that adds depth to the topic at hand.*

tip *This is an idea or procedure I think you will find helpful.*

WARNING! *This is an important fact that is vital to the topic at hand.*

How This Book Was Written

My original drafts of this book were all created on a Macintosh PowerBook using ClarisWorks. That includes all text and art.

About The Author

I am a former newspaperman who left mainstream journalism to become a computer networking consultant, corporate trainer, and of course, an author of books. As president of Scion Networks in San Francisco, I help some of the world's biggest firms communicate on the Internet. In addition to this book, my writing appears in newspapers, trade publications and half a dozen other AP PROFESSIONAL titles including *AppleShare IP 5 Clearly Explained, Macintosh Crash Course,* and the six-volume *Network Frontiers Field Manual Series.*

I am proud to be a member of the Society of Professional Journalists.

The easiest way to contact me is, of course, via email: trdell@scionnet.com.

Acknowledgements

Thanks to: Joan Hiraki, for being my principal contact at Claris Corp.; Dave Marandino, for making sure I had the Claris Emailer 2.0 beta software as fast as it was ready; Robert Perrier, for reviewing my rough drafts and giving me useful suggestions; Cass Kovel, for her friendship and for her skill in editing and formatting this book; Juliana Dell, for her loving support and insightful editing, and Katie Mulligan, Jeffrey Pepper, Gael Tannenbaum, and Jacquelyn Young of AP PROFESSIONAL, for their patience and support on this and other projects.

1

How Email Works

Electronic mail, or email, can be defined simply as a form of text-based communications delivered over a computer network. This communication can take place in a variety of ways, and we will look at several of them here.

The Evolution of Email

When I was a kid I exchanged email with students in the midwestern United States from my small school in rural Minnesota. Desktop computers were not yet common, let alone email applications that permitted computers to serve as facilitators of human conversation. Instead, my classmates and I used a terminal about the size of a half-height refrigerator that connected us to a then little-known education network called the Internet. This machine was essentially a typewriter with a modem attached, and it was painfully slow. Nevertheless, it was a thrill to exchange notes with other students, some of them as far as 60 miles away!

Today my son, about half the age I was then, can use email from his own bedroom and from a Macintosh no bigger than a bread box. He can communicate with me, some 2,000 miles away, almost instantly. He can exchange messages with other students in Mongolia, Sweden, Argentina, or Nigeria as easily as he can with students in the next town. When he reaches my age he probably won't remember a time when email was not a regular part of day-to-day communications.

Email started innocuously enough in the mainframe world, where users of terminals could leave notes for each other in message centers. You usually didn't write to people outside the system, but you could move important information around within it. Then someone figured out how to make the transfer of digital information over phone lines economical by turning the data into sound at the sending end (*modulation*) and back into digital data at the receiving end (*demodulation*—hence, the "mo-dem"). Since it was practical for just about any mainframe to communicate with another mainframe through a simple phone call, systems separated by great distances began to collaborate. Email now moved between systems.

Other things were afoot as well. The Apple computer was born, the IBM PC followed, and the Internet grew. Now there were mainframes, minicomputers, and microcomputers, and it was not long before they all started talking to each other over modems and networks and their users started talking to each other over email. Today email is considered a "mission-critical" application in most businesses and is sorely missed when unavailable to home users. More than 1 trillion email messages were sent in 1995 alone. In contrast, the U.S. Postal Service made about 180 billion deliveries that same year.

So why is email so popular? Because it is a medium ideally suited to mass communication. Its applications are simple to understand, so most people can use it. It doesn't require that the recipient be present upon its arrival, so it can be sent at any time. It costs very little when compared to other forms of communication (especially long-distance telephone), so it can be used frequently. It can be used globally to meet international communications needs inexpensively. It can be made into hard copy for easy reading or be kept digital for easy storage. It can be encrypted for security. Its features can be automated, so it can save time.

Claris Emailer is a logical progression in the evolution of email. There are a variety of ways to move email from one computer to another. Claris Emailer's greatest strength is that it knows how to use several of them, so you need just one application to communicate with many different systems. It was once the case that few people needed to connect to multiple email providers, but as email usage becomes more common this is changing. You might have an account at the office, another at home, and a third at school. Add accounts for family members, and you begin to see the value of a "universal in-box" such as Claris Emailer. It gives you one interface to learn, one place to store all of your email addresses, and one place to keep and manage all your email.

Before we get into the specifics of how Claris Emailer works, let's take a look at what systems Claris Emailer works with.

How Email Gets from Here to There

For simplicity we can lump the email systems most commonly used into three basic types. The first type is systems that are used with office networks, so we call them *Local Area Network (LAN)*-based. The second is systems that rely on a commercial online service provider. The third is systems that rely on the Internet and on *Internet Service Providers (ISPs)*. These are not firm divisions, but they are useful in classifying certain characteristics.

Email on the LAN

If you have an office whose computers speak to each other via a LAN, you might have a proprietary email system such as Claris OfficeMail. Most LAN-based email systems work under a *client–server model*, wherein desktop machines (clients) depend on a specialized machine (server) to route email between a sender and a recipient. Desktop users generally receive an *account* on the server machine, in which their email is stored. They use proprietary software to connect periodically to the server, which then accepts outgoing email from them and forwards incoming email to them. This process is called *store-and-forward*.

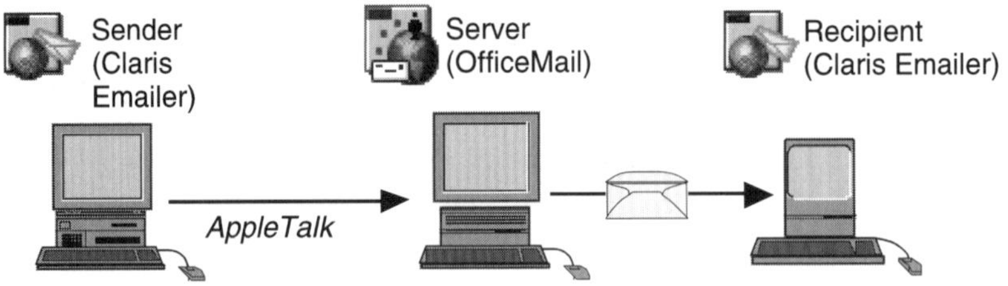

A store-and-forward system requires that the server be always available on the network so that it can collect incoming email. However, client computers can be turned on and off or come and go from the network as they please, and the server holds their email until they return. This is particularly useful for mobile computers. Clients can either log in to their servers periodically to see if email has arrived for them or receive a notification from the server when new email is present.

In addition to providing a place to store incoming and outgoing messages until client machines are ready for them, most LAN-based systems also provide a repository of account addresses. These addresses are kept up to date and accurate by the person designated as the server administrator. When clients log in, the server can pass the latest address information to them so users need not record addresses manually.

Most LAN-based email systems, such as Claris OfficeMail, CE Software's QuickMail, and Quarterdeck's Quarterdeck Mail, are proprietary, closed systems. You cannot gather OfficeMail with QuickMail client software, for instance, because each system must interface with it own components. Despite this, most LAN-based email systems are able to communicate with each other using *gateways*. These are server-based translators that convert data from one system into data that another system's server can understand.

Some gateways work directly between systems. For instance, QuickMail has a gateway that permits its users to communicate with users of Quarterdeck Mail (formerly Microsoft Mail). Other gateways rely on an *open system*—one that uses public standards—to act as an intermediary. Thus, while OfficeMail does not speak directly with QuickMail, it does have an Internet gateway that communicates with an Internet-based mail host via *UNIX-to-UNIX Copy Protocol (UUCP)*. So does QuickMail. An office running OfficeMail might communicate with an office running QuickMail by using the mail hosts of their ISPs as intermediaries.

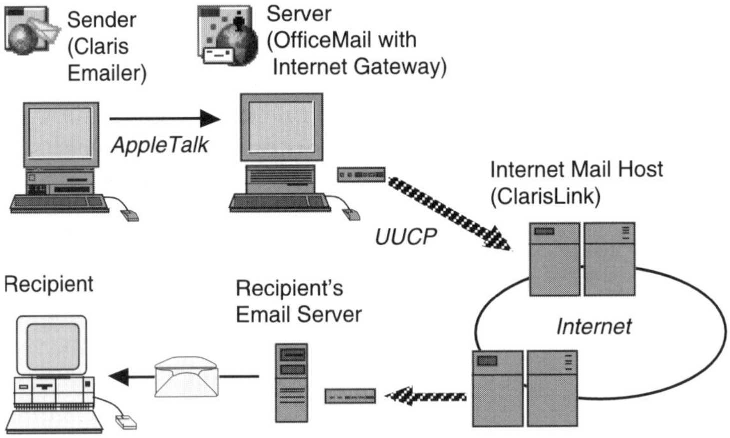

With this method the OfficeMail server does not need to know what type of system the recipient's account resides on. It only has to concern itself with speaking to the mail host, that is, the middleman. The gateways of the destination system will take care of the rest.

When an email system is extended beyond the physical confines of one office through the use of gateways, telecommunications links, and/or the Internet, it is no longer LAN-based. It is now a service on a *Wide Area Network (WAN)*.

Claris Emailer can act as a proprietary client to OfficeMail. It is much smarter than the typical client, however. Most LAN-based clients are wholly dependent on the server and its gateways to communicate with systems beyond the network. As you will see, this is not the case with Claris Emailer. It can use the services of OfficeMail when they are available, but it can just as easily connect with a mail host or a commercial online service on its own.

Email on Commercial Online Services

Many people, particularly those with computers in their homes, depend on commercial online services such as America Online or CompuServe to collect, store, and forward their email through mainframe-based message centers. In these systems, subscribers pay the online service a flat monthly fee or a per-minute connection fee for an account. The online service then provides them with an account name, a password, and dial-up instructions so that they can use modem software to call the mainframe from their home computers and process their email.

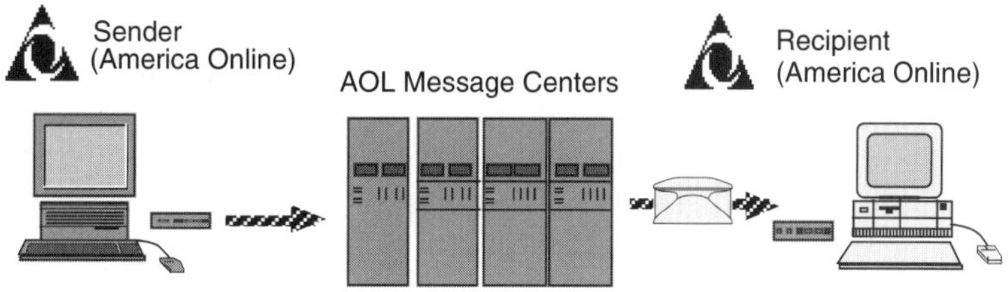

In some cases, particularly when using a bulletin board service, the subscriber composes outgoing email right on the mainframe using terminal emulation software. Unless you are fond of UNIX variations and command line interfaces, however, this is probably not for you. More commonly, as is the case with America Online and CompuServe, the service provider gives subscribers user-friendly client software with which to compose email at their own desktops. This software communicates with the mainframe to transfer email or to look up addresses, just as a LAN-based client does.

There are advantages to this type of service, even for business users who also have LAN-based systems. For one thing, it is reliable. The online services' mainframes are far less likely to go down than your office server is. For another, it is available via a local call from many places throughout the world, which is particularly useful if you travel, since the cost of calling into your office in Chicago from a hotel room in Guam might be prohibitive.

There are a few disadvantages as well. For one, you are often charged for your time online. This makes it advantageous to compose your email offline and then dial up the online service to send only. For another, only a limited number of callers can be accommodated by the system at any one time, so you will sometimes be confronted with a busy signal or an overly sluggish system (for a while people were referring to America Online as "America On-hold").

In this system, Claris Emailer takes over the role of the online service's client software. It is concerned only with email, so you cannot use it to access other areas within the online service. However, because Claris Emailer is concerned only with email, it makes the connection quickly, transfers your email rapidly, and hangs up almost immediately, saving money on your online bill. If you access the online service from multiple cities, Claris Emailer remembers the various phone numbers associated with the different locations for you so you can always place a local call. Finally, Claris Emailer often provides features the online services' software lacks, such as a spelling checker and the scheduling of automatic connections for off-peak hours.

Email on the Internet

By far the most common method of moving email from one place to another is over the Internet. This is because it is an open system, which means that anyone can create applications based on its widely published standards. You have surely heard of these standards and the technologies they define. For example, the network computer language, or *protocol,* of the Internet is *Transmission Control Protocol/Internet Protocol (TCP/IP).* Because it is an open system that is not platform dependent it can be used with mainframes, minicomputers, PCs, Macintoshes, and a wide variety of operating systems (DOS, MacOS, OS/2, Solaris, Windows, etc.). Under TCP/IP, each computer connected to the Internet has a unique number. For instance, the *IP address* for my company's mail host is "38.247.58.2."

An Internet *host* can be defined as any machine that is connected to the Internet with its own IP address. Just as your home has an address that makes it possible for "snail mail" to be delivered to you by the U.S. Postal Service, Internet hosts have addresses that permit data to be delivered to them. Of course, those numbers are not all that easy to work with, so an Internet-based database was created to associate them with more descriptive names. Called the *Domain Name System (DNS),* this database records that the number above is equal to the domain name "smtp.scionnet.com," which is a little easier to remember. To send a message to me, you would address it to trdell@smtp.scionnet.com. Here "trdell" is the name of my account on the mail host "at" (@) "smtp.scionnet.com," which is the domain name of the mail host.

Internet mail hosts work under both client–server and *peer-to-peer* models. Mail hosts provide store-and-forward services to client computers via a special transfer method called the *Post Office Protocol (POP).* Mail hosts exchange email with each other (peer-to-peer) using another method, the *Simple Mail Transfer Protocol (SMTP).* In both cases, communications occur over TCP/IP. One's POP host and SMTP host do not have to be the same machine, but they often are.

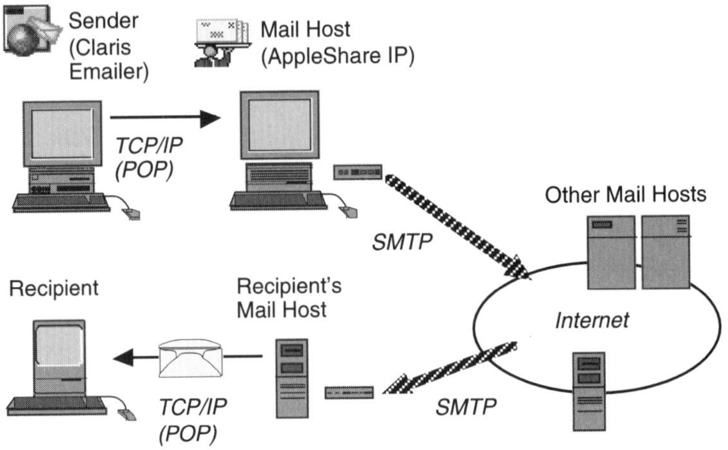

This client–server communication can take place either directly over a LAN or WAN link via TCP/IP or from a remote location over phone lines. In the latter case, the *Point-to-Point Protocol (PPP)* is commonly used to provide a reliable telecommunications bridge over which TCP/IP can run as if it were on a LAN.

Mail hosts can be deployed in many ways and on many types of machines. Most people think of mail hosts as residing only on UNIX-based minicomputers, but Macintosh computers make wonderful SMTP hosts as well. All that is needed is the proper software, such as Apple Internet Mail Server (AIMS) or AppleShare IP.

Claris Emailer is a POP client. It can communicate with a mail host directly over a LAN or WAN link, or it can use PPP to communicate over phones lines. Unlike most other POP clients, Claris Emailer can handle multiple POP accounts, so, for instance, you can communicate with the mail host in your office and the mail host of the ISP you use at home without changing software. Finally, even if you do not have direct email access to the Internet, Claris Emailer still permits you to communicate with Internet email users through the gateways of LAN-based servers or commercial online service accounts.

Types of Email

People usually describe email using the same terms that describe traditional postal services, which makes sense—an email server is much like a post office. The analogy is imperfect when it comes to describing email messages, however. At their simplest, email messages might be described as postcards—you write your message, address it, and send it. But email messages can also contain other files and documents, called *enclosures* or *attachments*. Here you write a message (if you want to), address it, enclose a file, and send it, which makes email more akin to an envelope. Email does not always have to be a communication; sometimes it can be nothing more than a convenient file transfer method.

Email can be both a personal and a mass form of communication. When you send an email message to a friend you expect one person only to read it. But you can also send an email message to a *mailing list* in which case hundreds of people can read it.

Mailing lists are made up of people with similar interests who *subscribe* to a topic provided by a special type of email server called a *list server*. This server does nothing more than collect all email that comes to a certain address and forward it to a list of subscriber addresses. Mailing lists can be a marvelous and timely source of information, although you often have to wade through a lot of messages you do not care about to find those that interest you. To join the list for Claris Emailer users, for example, send email to "Claris Emailer-talk-request@eskimo.com" with the word "subscribe" in the subject field of your message.

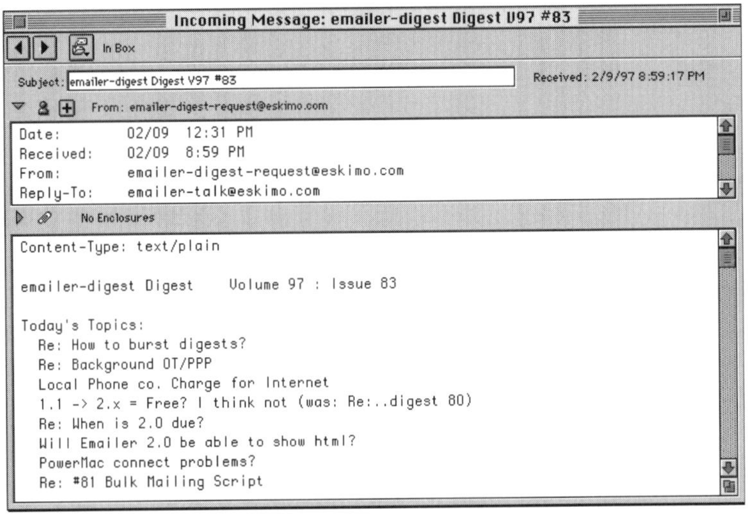

FIGURE 1-1. An example of a mailing list for users of Claris Emailer!

A similar form of email publication is *email-on-demand*. As with fax-on-demand, the idea here is that you send an email message to a particular address and an informational message is returned to you. This is particularly handy in computer technical support, as you can get information day or night and without waiting in long telephone queues.

Of course, it was only a matter of time before people figured out that they could use email to make money. To this end many advertisers now use bulk email, which, just like the unsolicited paper mail you get in your mailbox, comes to your email account. A better term has been coined for it: *Spam*, taken from the Monty Python skit in which the actors are bombarded with the namesake Hormel meat product: "Spam, spam, spam, spam / spam, spam, spam, spam." Remember?

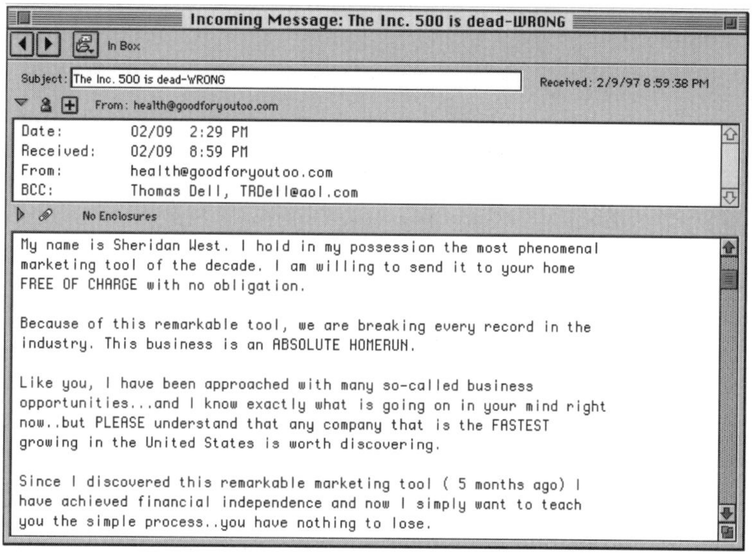

FIGURE 1-2. Typical spam.

After receiving a lot of spam email you may be tempted to reply with a string of profanities. This is called *flaming*. It is considered bad manners to level such an attack against anyone, even bulk mailers. In most cases you can end the deluge of spam by simply *unsubscribing* to the bulk emailer's list.

Summary

Email is a form of text-based communication delivered over a computer network. It gets from one computer to another through a variety of systems and methods, most of which are based on the client–server model. One system makes use of closed proprietary LAN-based applications such as Office-Mail. Another uses the proprietary system of commercial online service providers such as America Online and CompuServe. A third uses the open-standards–based Internet with its SMTP mail hosts and POP clients.

Claris Emailer is a logical progression in the evolution of email. It is a "universal in-box" that can send and receive email from LAN-based OfficeMail, commercial online services, and Internet mail hosts. In so doing, it does away with the need for multiple email clients on a single machine to handle multiple accounts. Instead, it keeps email from multiple sources together in one place, with one database of addresses, under one easy-to-use interface.

In the next chapter, we will configure Claris Emailer to communicate with multiple email service providers and take a brief tour of the application's main features.

2

Getting Started

It is easy to get Claris Emailer up and running. In this chapter I will show you how to use its Installer to copy the software you need to the hard drive of your Macintosh. Then I will tell you what you need before you can use its Easy Setup script to configure Claris Emailer's communications with various email service providers. If you already have Claris Emailer 2.0 installed, you may skip this half of the chapter.

In the second half of the chapter, *Touring Claris Emailer,* I will give you a quick tour of the application's interface so that you will know your way around by the time the email starts pouring in.

Requirements for Your Macintosh

In order to use Claris Emailer, you must have:

- A Macintosh or Mac OS-compatible computer with a 68020 or greater processor. That is any Macintosh, 68K or PowerPC-based, except the Plus, SE, Classic, PowerBook 100—or any other with a 68000 processor. (The Classic II and SE/30 have 68030 processors, so you can use them.)

- About 3 Mbytes (or 3,000 Kbytes) of free memory. You can determine how much free memory your Macintosh has by selecting **About This Macintosh** under the **Apple** menu bar item in the Finder.

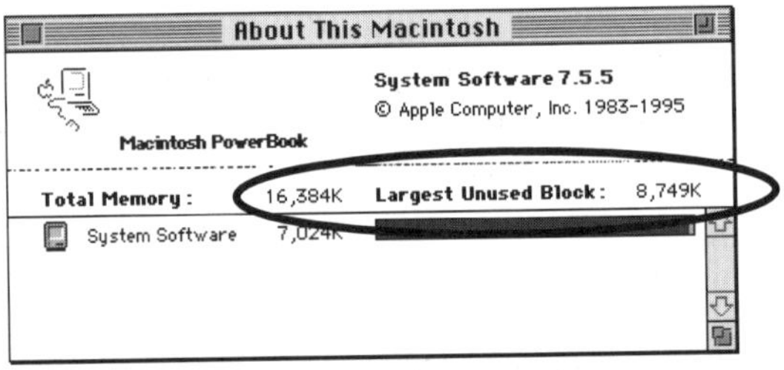

- In addition, you will need another 1 Mbyte of free RAM to run Claris Emailer's online Help. If you have a PowerPC-based Macintosh running Virtual Memory, you can get by with 2 Mbytes of free RAM for Claris Emailer. Virtual Memory can be enabled in the Memory Control Panel as shown in Figure 2-1.

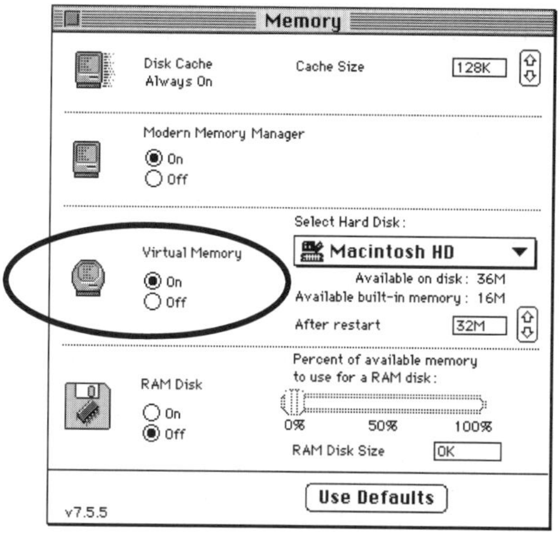

FIGURE 2-1. Enabling virtual memory.

- At least 9 Mbytes of hard disk space for Claris Emailer's files and at least 4 Mbytes for saved messages and other files. You can see how much space you have available in the header of the hard drive title bar.

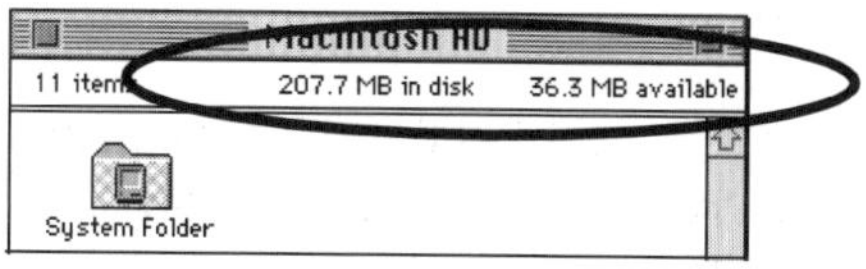

  It is always a good idea to leave an additional 10 Mbytes or so free for print spooling and big file downloads.

- A 1.4 Mbyte Apple SuperDrive or CD-ROM drive to install the software. (A network administrator can also make the software available to you from a shared network volume, assuming enough software licenses have been purchased for your organization.)

- Mac OS System 7.1 or later. You can identify the system version of your Macintosh by selecting **About This Macintosh** under the **Apple** menu bar item in the Finder.

If your Macintosh is running under System 7.1, 7.1.1, or 7.1.2, you would be wise to install Apple's System Update 3.0 as well. You will also need MacTCP 2.0.6 if you wish to connect to the Internet, AppleScript if you wish to automate some of Claris Emailer's functions, and Macintosh Drag and Drop if you wish to be able to drag elements such as email addresses between windows.

If your Macintosh is running under System 7.5 or later, MacTCP, AppleScript, and Macintosh Drag and Drop are built in. If you have System 7.5, 7.5.1, 7.5.2, or 7.5.3, consider upgrading to at least System 7.5.5.

Apple software updates are available on America Online, keyword "Apple," or the World Wide Web (WWW) at http://www.support.apple.com.

You will also need at least one account with an email service provider, whether an office mail host or a commercial system. Claris Emailer does not come with any such accounts. You also need a modem or an Internet feed to connect to them. If you have neither as yet, peruse Chapters 1 and 6 for details.

Installing Your New Software

Before you install your new software disable any anti-virus software that might conflict with the installation. The easiest way to do this is to restart your Macintosh while holding down the **Shift** key to disable extensions.

Next place the first Claris Emailer diskette in the floppy disk drive of your computer (or CD-ROM in your CD-ROM drive) and open "Disk 1."

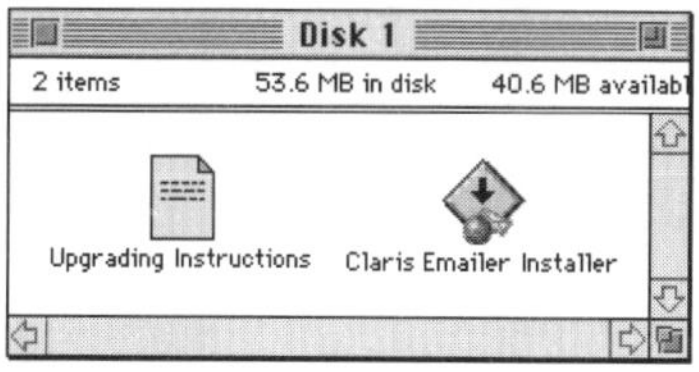

There is an important document here named "Upgrading Instructions." If you are upgrading from an earlier version of Claris Emailer it is vitally important that you read this document before continuing. It will tell you how to preserve your older application's preferences, address list, and email.

If this is the first time you are using Claris Emailer, go ahead and double-click on the "Claris Emailer Installer" application to continue.

At first you will be greeted by Claris Emailer's Installer splash screen as shown in Figure 2-2. Press the **Continue** button to dismiss it.

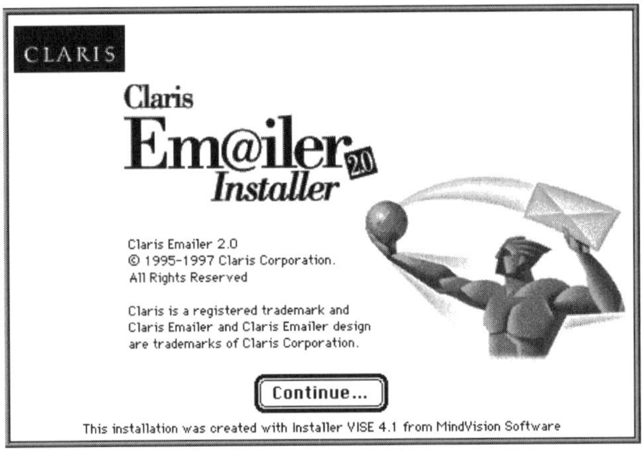

FIGURE 2-2. Installer splash screen.

Next you will be presented with Claris Emailer's license agreement, as shown in Figure 2-3. Read it. Ponder it. Press the **Accept** button if you agree with it. Then get down to the fun stuff.

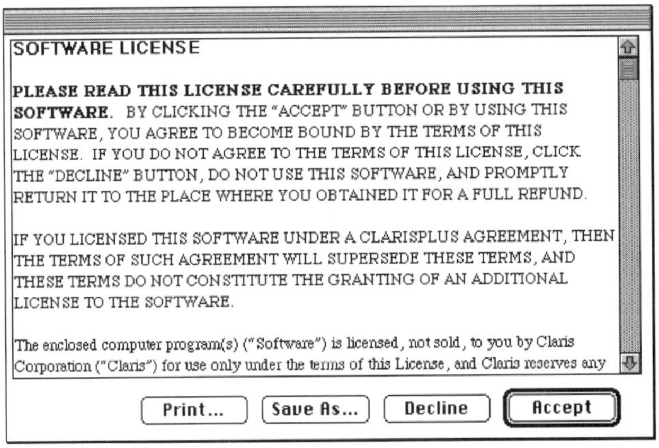

FIGURE 2-3. Claris Emailer licensing agreement.

The Installer window that you are presented with next defaults to the **Easy Install** option, as seen in Figure 2-4. What is included in this installation is shown beneath the pop-up menu.

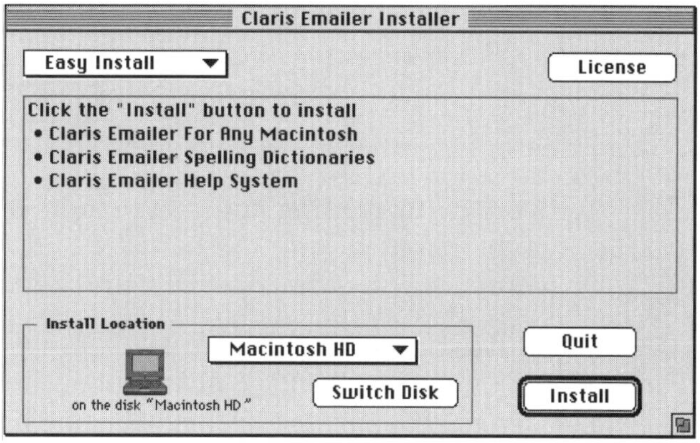

FIGURE 2-4. Claris Emailer Installer window.

This is the best option. It will install a version of Claris Emailer that runs on either a PowerPC-based Macintosh (generally numbered 6100, 7500, 8600, and so on) or an older Motorola 68K-based Macintosh (such as a SE/30, IIci, Classic II, Quadra, or any PowerBook numbered under 5300). It will install a spelling dictionary. Finally, it will install a comprehensive online help system that will be handy in the exceedingly unlikely event that you do not have this book right next to your Macintosh when a question arises.

Assuming you stick with my advice and use the **Easy Install** option, the only decision you need to make here is which hard disk the application should be stored on. The default will always be the startup disk, which is the hard disk that contains the active System Folder, but you can specify any other hard disk that is connected to your Macintosh by pressing the **Switch Disk** button. Press the **Install** button after you have made this decision.

Before you go further, you will be asked if this is the first time you will be using Claris Emailer or if you are upgrading from an earlier release.

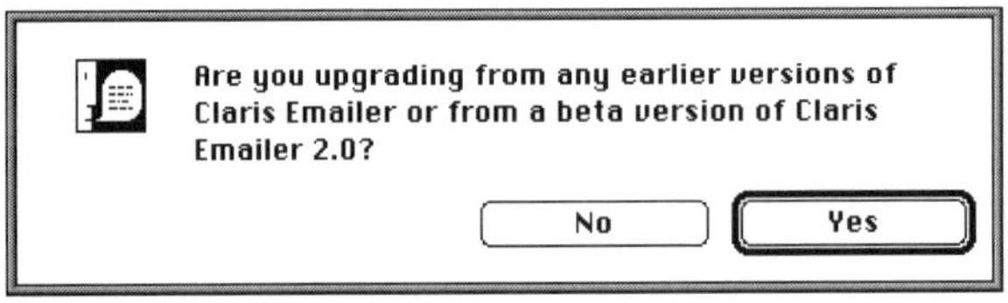

If you are upgrading and you press the **Yes** button here, you will be asked to quit the Installer and read the "Upgrading Instructions" document on the first Installer disk.

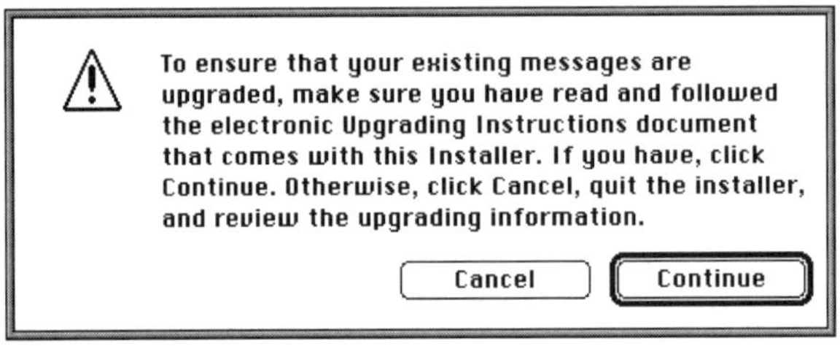

If you press the **No** button, the installation process will continue unchecked.

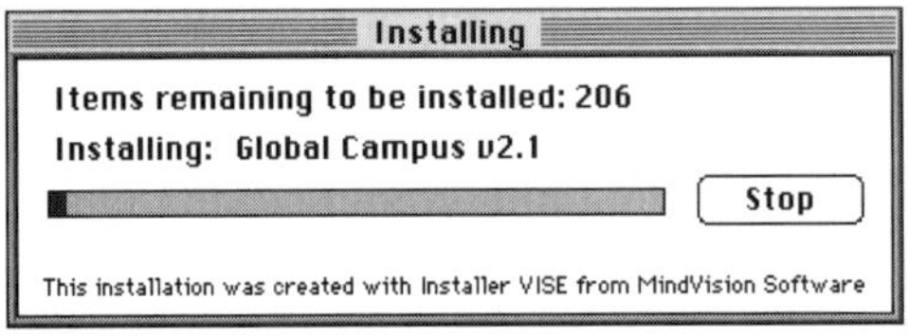

The Installer will copy the files to the proper locations on your Macintosh, prompting you for additional diskettes as it needs them. It will also tell you when its work is done.

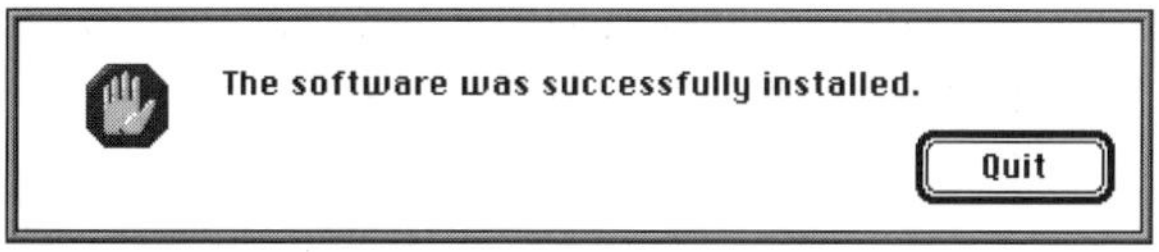

After you acknowledge the good news by pressing the **Quit** button, you will see that the newly installed software has been placed in the "Claris Emailer Folder" on your hard disk.

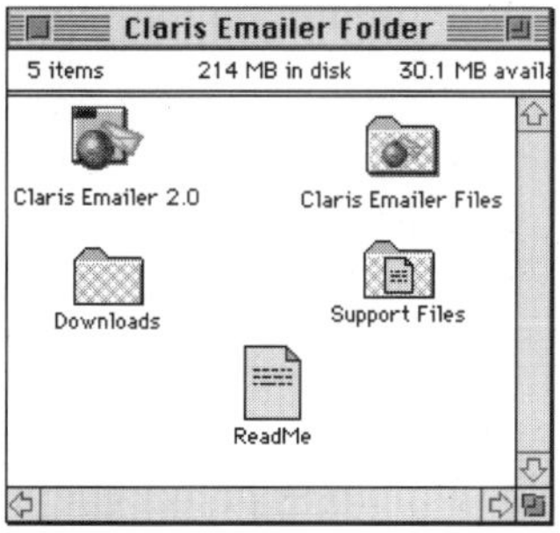

When you launch Claris Emailer for the first time, you will be asked for your name, your organization's name, and the software's serial number.

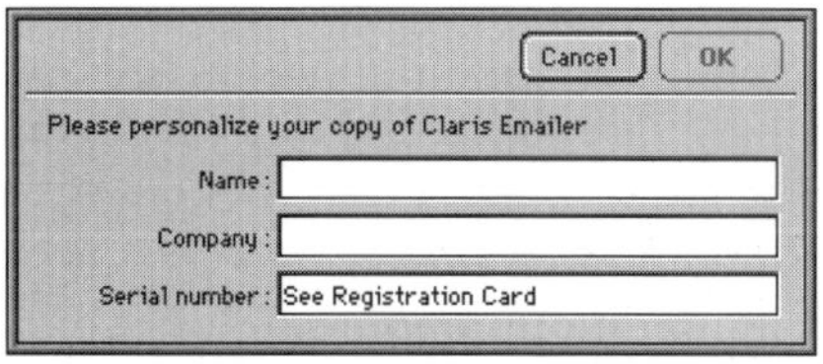

The installation process is then complete.

There are a couple of circumstances in which you might want to exercise a different install option. To do this, pick **Custom Install** in the pop-up menu of the Installer window as shown in Figure 2-5.

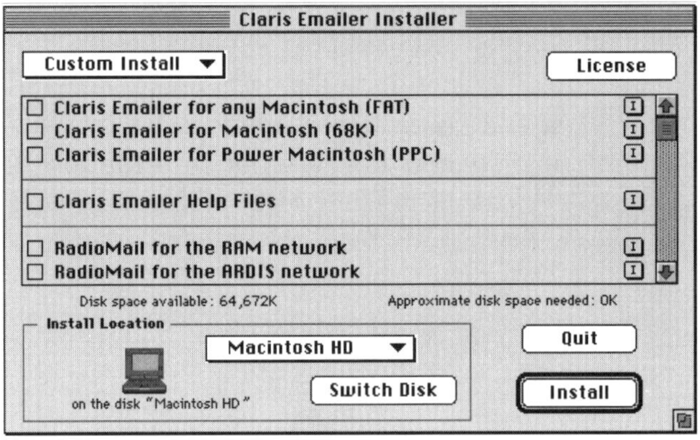

FIGURE 2-5. Custom Install options.

In the first instance you might want to save yourself some hard drive space. To do this select only the check box for the type of Macintosh you have—68K or PowerPC (PPC). FAT is just that—it includes code for both machine types and so it is large. Also select the **Claris Emailer Help Files** and **Apple Modem Tools Prefs** check boxes.

In the second instance you might want to add RadioMail's software to your installation. If so, choose the appropriate check box for either the RAM or the ARDIS radio network.

Setting Up Your Accounts the Easy Way

Before you can receive email you need to tell Claris Emailer which service providers it should contact to gather it. This requires that you establish a list of accounts, which Claris makes simple for you by creating an Easy Setup script that will interview you for the information it needs. All you need to know when you launch Claris Emailer the first time is which services you will connect to, what your account name and password are on those services, and how the connection will be made (i.e., via LAN or modem dial-up).

It is a good idea to read through this section before continuing so you know what information—account names, passwords, and telephone numbers—you will be asked to supply. You can then collect this information from its various sources and have it ready when Claris Emailer asks you for it.

After you have gathered the relevant information you will launch Claris Emailer to use the Easy Setup script. If it does not come up automatically, choose the **Easy Setup** command under the **Setup** menu bar item.

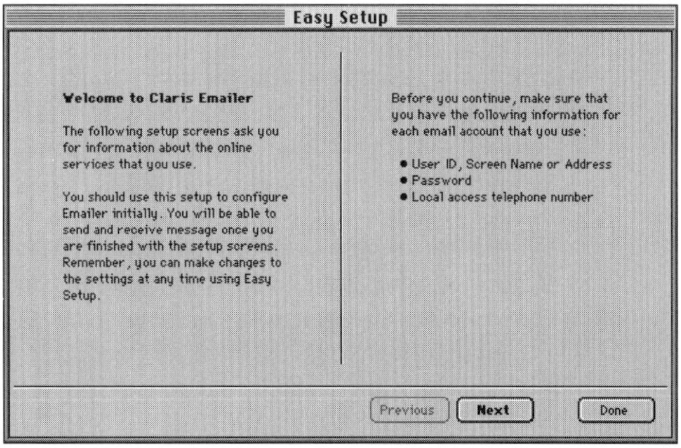

FIGURE 2-6. Easy Setup welcome screen.

When you press that **Next** button (Figure 2-6), Easy Setup will require certain information from you depending on which service providers you wish to connect to. First, it will ask you for your name as you would like the world to know it, as shown in Figure 2-7.

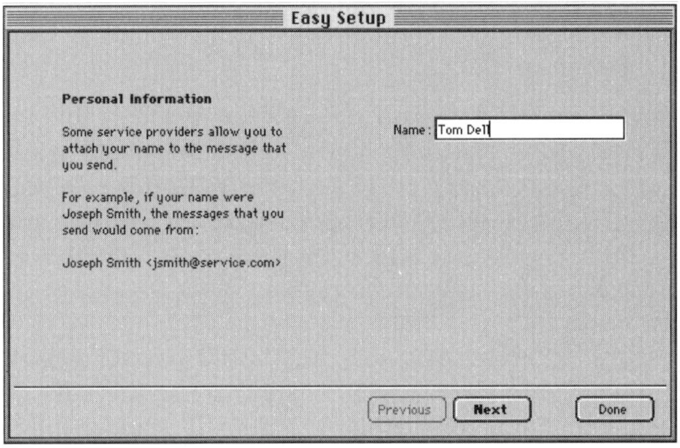

FIGURE 2-7. Your name as it will appear in your Email.

Some services let you tack this name on your email message along with your actual email address. This is handy if your email address is something obscure like "webmaster@trdell.com."

With this setting enabled, recipients will have a better indication of who you are. They will see in the header of their incoming message something like "Tom Dell <webmaster@trdell.com>."

Press the **Next** button to move on.

If you will be using Claris OfficeMail, Easy Setup will want to know that next. Choose the appropriate radio buttons and then press the **Next** button to leave this window.

In the next window select the check boxes to tell Claris Emailer which service providers you have accounts with. If you are connecting over a LAN, you can ignore the **Modem** pop-up menu. If you are connecting over a modem, tell Claris Emailer which port it is connected to, as shown in Figure 2-8.

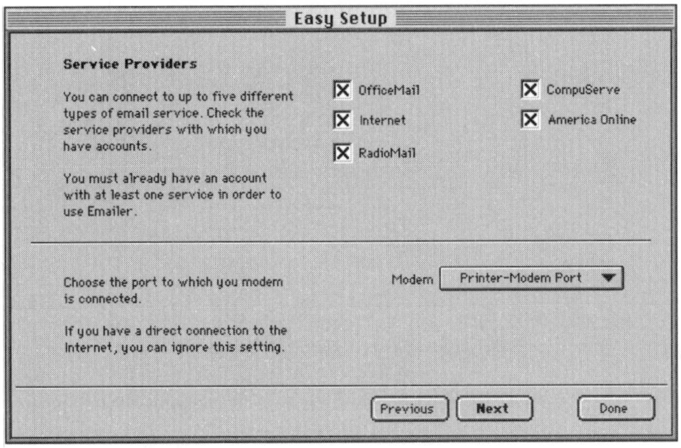

FIGURE 2-8. Checking off your service providers.

I will go through each service provider's setup screen in the order they are presented during Easy Setup.

The Internet

The majority of Internet email is handled by mail hosts using SMTP. Claris Emailer is a POP client that can connect to SMTP servers via TCP/IP in one of two ways: over a LAN link or over a dial-up modem link. I explain the differences between the two and the procedures for configuring TCP/IP on your Macintosh in Chapter 6. For now, here is what you will need to know to get your Internet email through Claris Emailer:

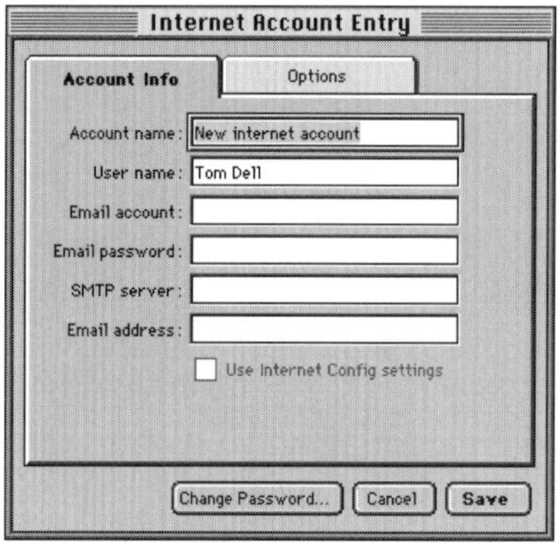

- **Account name**. This is however you want to remember this specific account (i.e., "My Internet account," "Tom's Internet account," "Internet"). If you have multiple Internet accounts, you might want to designate them by their domain names. For instance, the office mail host that I connect to over Ethernet might be under the name "smtp.trdell.com," so I use that name. I also have a dial-up account that I use from home to connect with my ISP's mail host. That one I name "smtp.netcom.com."

- **User name.** This is the name you gave Easy Setup in the beginning.

- **Email account**. This is the name assigned to your account by the postmaster of your office's mail host or by your ISP. It is in two parts: account name and POP server domain name (i.e., "trdell@pop.trdell.com," not just "trdell").

  You can write it down here: ________________________.

- **Email password**. This is the code assigned to your account by the postmaster of your office's mail host or by your ISP. Whether or not you may change it by pressing the **Change Password** button varies from system to system.

You can write it down here: ________________________.

WARNING! *Either change it later or make sure this book does not fall into the wrong hands if privacy is important to you!*

- **SMTP server**. This is the domain name of your mail host (i.e., "smtp.trdell.com"). Sometimes this is the same as your POP server domain name.

  You can write it down here: ________________________.

- **Email address**. In most cases, this will be the same as your Email account (i.e., "trdell@smtp.trdell.com"). Whatever address you put here will be the address recipients reply to, so unless you want their feedback to be sent into oblivion, be careful what you type here!

  You can write it down here: ________________________.

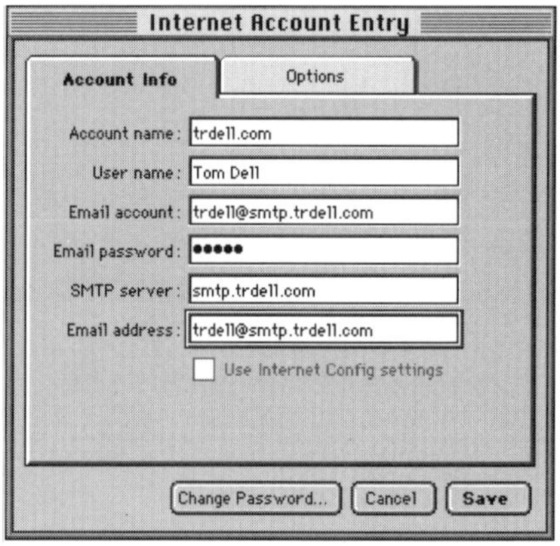

One last thing. Some systems use *Authenticated Post Office Protocol (APOP)* for greater password security, and some do not. If your mail host does, you will need to press the **Options** tab and enable the **Connect using APOP** check box.

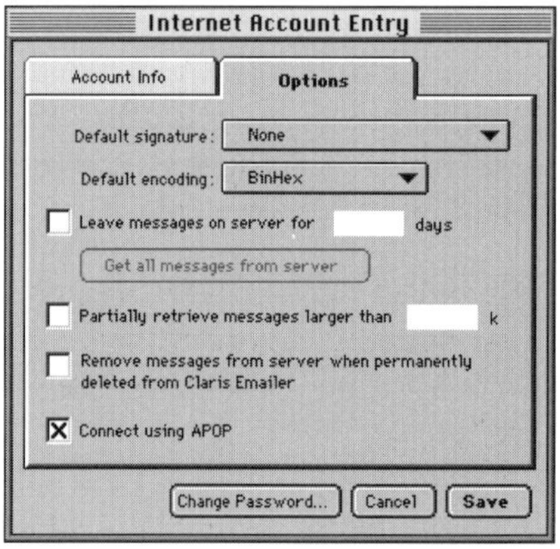

There are other optional settings here as well, which I will explain in Chapter 7.

CompuServe

CompuServe is the older of the two largest commercial online services. It provides direct email communications between its users as well as an Internet gateway under the domain name "compuserve.com." Here is what you will need to connect to it.

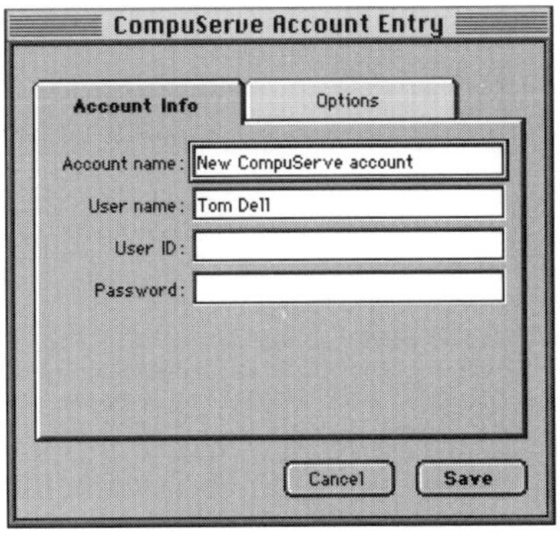

- **Account name**. This is however you want to remember this specific account (i.e., "My CompuServe account," "Tom's CompuServe account," "CompuServe").

- **User name**. This is the name from Easy Setup's second window.

- **User ID**. This is the number assigned to you by CompuServe (i.e., 75104,2333).

  You can write it down here: ______________________.

- **Password**. This is your private access code.

You can write it down here: ________________________.

WARNING! *Either change it later or keep this book in a safe place!*

CompuServe is generally accessible by dialing up a local access exchange with a modem. This requires that you tell Claris Emailer what the local telephone number is as well as what kind of modem is in your Macintosh, as shown in Figure 2-9.

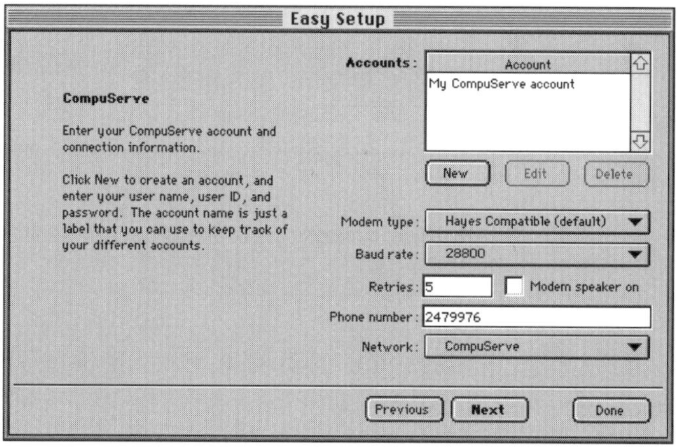

FIGURE 2-9. Configuring your CompuServe connection.

- **Modem type**. This is your make and model of modem, as listed in the pop-up menu.

- **Baud rate**. This is the speed of your modem, measured in *bits per second (Bps)*.

- **Phone number**. This is the local access number for CompuServe, which you can get from your CompuServe Information Manager software by choosing the **Connection** command in the **Settings** fly-out menu under the **Special** menu bar item.

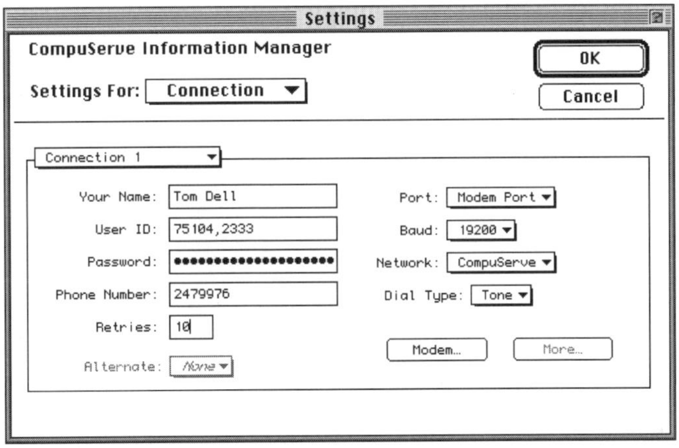

FIGURE 2-10. Settings window from MacCIM.

You can write it down here: ________________________.

You may also call CompuServe at 1 (800) 769-6747 (U.S. and Canada) or 1 (303) 894-7336.

- **Network**. This is the telecommunications network associated with the local access number, as listed in the pop-up menu.

It is also possible to access CompuServe via the Internet. That is quite a bit more complex, however, so I will show you that in Chapter 6.

America Online

America Online (AOL) is the biggest commercial online service. It provides direct email communications between its users as well as an Internet gateway under the domain name "aol.com." Here is what you will need to connect to it.

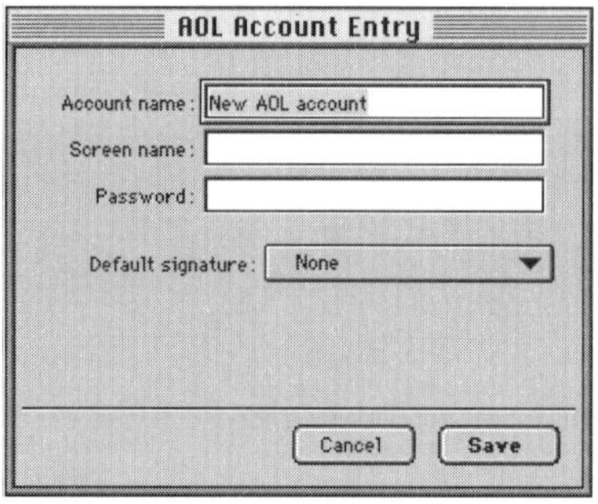

- **Account name**. This is however you want to remember this specific account. A good idea is to name it by the *screen name* that you want to check email for. Each AOL account can have up to four different screen names, and you can check email coming in to all four with Claris Emailer.

- **Screen name.** This is AOL's account identifier. Each AOL account has a primary screen name (associated with the user who gets the bill) and up to three more that can be used to share with family members or to hide your true identity!

  You can write screen name 1 here: ____________________.

  You can write screen name 2 here: ____________________.

You can write screen name 3 here: ____________________.

You can write screen name 4 here: ____________________.

- **Password**. This is your private access code.

  You can write password 1 here: ______________________.

  You can write password 2 here: ______________________.

  You can write password 3 here: ______________________.

  You can write password 4 here: ______________________.

WARNING!

Make sure you either change them later or keep this book under lock and key!

AOL is accessible by dialing up a local telephone number with a modem. This requires that you tell Claris Emailer what the local number is as well as what kind of modem is in your Macintosh, as shown in Figure 2-11. AOL is also accessible through the Internet.

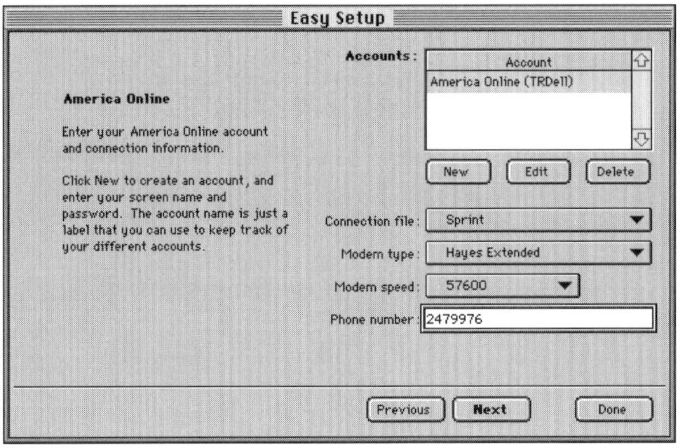

FIGURE 2-11. Configuring your AOL account.

- **Connection file**. This is either the telecommunications network associated with that local access number, as listed in the pop-up menu, or **TCP/IP** for direct (LAN) Internet access.

- **Modem type**. This is your make and model of modem, as listed in the pop-up menu. If you are accessing the Internet via an ISP or AOL with a dial-up account, you can choose **TCP Connection**.

- **Baud rate**. This is the speed of your modem, measured in Bps.

- **Phone number**. This is the local access number for AOL. You can get it from your AOL software by pressing the **Setup** button in the startup screen, as shown in Figure 2-12.

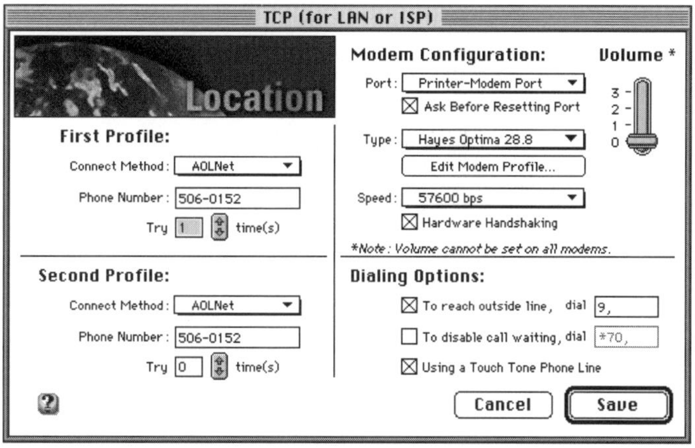

FIGURE 2-12. Settings window in America Online.

You can write it down here: __________________________.

You may also call AOL at 1 (800) 827-6364.

RadioMail

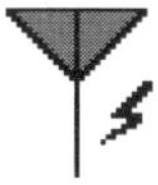

RadioMail provides an Internet email gateway to mobile users who have RF modems. To get your Internet mail through Claris Emailer via radio, you must first use the **Custom Install** option as shown at the beginning of this chapter to install RadioMail's client software. If you have a Mobidem modem, you will usually select the **RadioMail for the RAM network** check box here (Figure 2-13). If you have a Motorola modem, you will usually select the **RadioMail for the ARDIS network** check box.

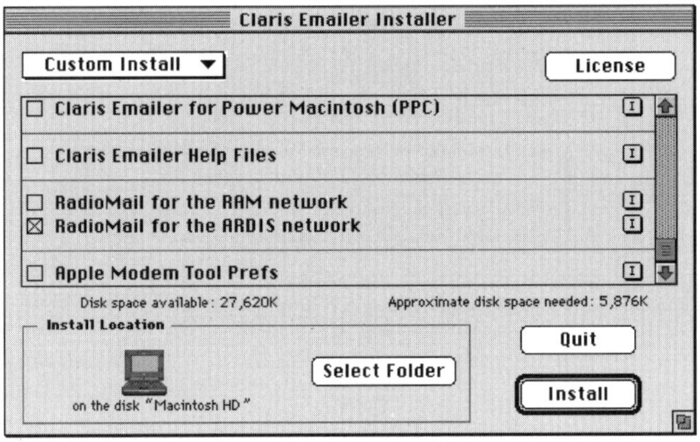

FIGURE 2-13. Installing RadioMail software.

The Installer will put the new software in the "RadioMail Folder" inside the Claris Emailer Files folder, as shown in Figure 2-14. You will need to use the RadioMail program to configure your RF modem.

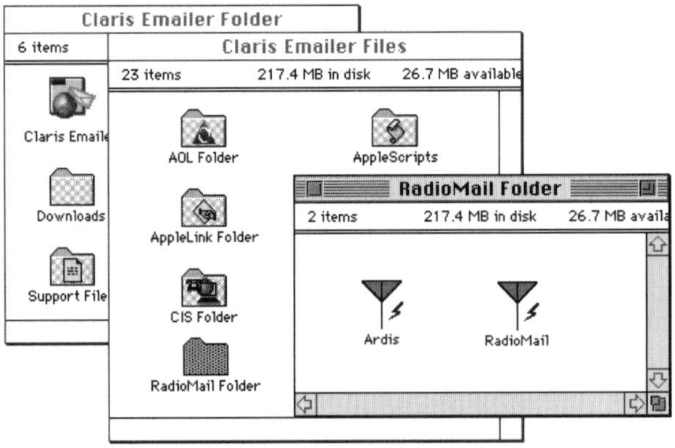

FIGURE 2-14. Location of RadioMail software.

To do this, launch the RadioMail application and choose the **Configure** command under the **File** menu bar item. The default settings shown in Figure 2-15 should work, but you might need to change the port setting if the modem is not connected to the modem port.

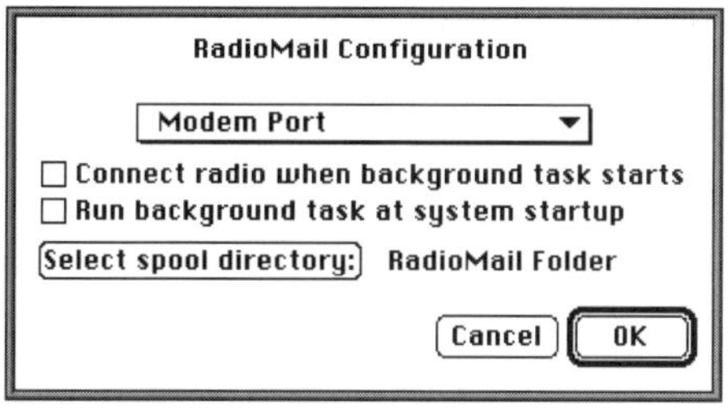

FIGURE 2-15. RadioMail's default settings.

Claris Emailer's Easy Setup will ask you to enter the information shown in Figure 2-16.

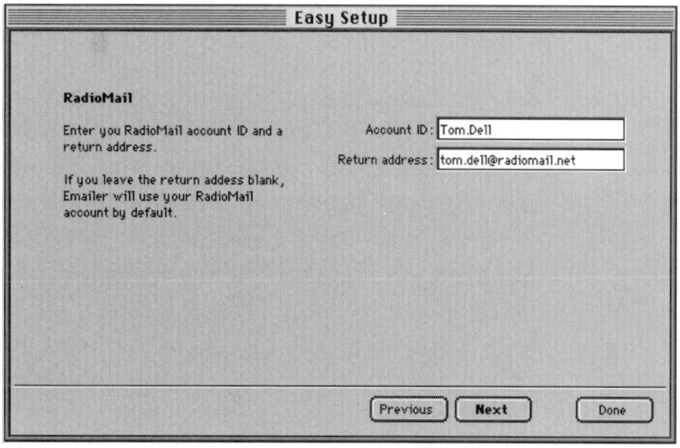

FIGURE 2-16. Configure your RadioMail account.

- **Account ID**. This is your short RadioMail account name and not your full Internet address (i.e., "Tom.Dell," not "tom.dell@radiomail.net).

You can write it down here: ________________________.

- **Email address.** In most cases this will be the same as your full RadioMail Internet address (i.e., "tom.dell@ radiomail.net"). This could be a different Internet email address than that of your RadioMail account. Whatever address you type will be the address that recipients reply to, so make sure there is a real address here.

  You can write it down here: ________________________.

Claris OfficeMail

Claris OfficeMail is a Macintosh server-based email system that uses a store-and-forward methodology. It supports both AppleTalk and TCP/IP users and has an Internet email gateway. If your computer is connected to a LAN and your organization has Claris OfficeMail, you will need to supply Claris Emailer with the following information:

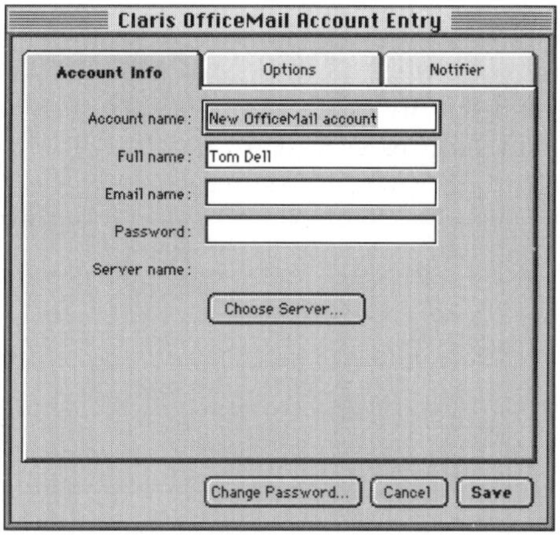

- **Account name**. This is however you want to remember this specific account (i.e., "My OfficeMail account," "Tom's OfficeMail account," "OfficeMail").

- **Full name**. This is the name entered in Easy Setup's second window.

- **Email name**. This is the name assigned to your account by the OfficeMail administrator. It might be the same as your first name (OfficeMail's default), or it might differ (e.g., "Tom Dell" "TRDell," "Webmaster"). It all depends on what naming convention your organization has adopted, so ask your administrator about this.

  You can write it down here: ______________________.

- **Password**. You will need to get this security code from your administrator. OfficeMail uses your first name initially, but as soon as Claris Emailer communicates with the server for the first time you will be asked to choose a new password known only to you.

  You can write it down here: ______________________.

- **Server**. If you have a big network, you might have more than one OfficeMail server. Your administrator can tell you which one to select when you press the **Choose Server** button.

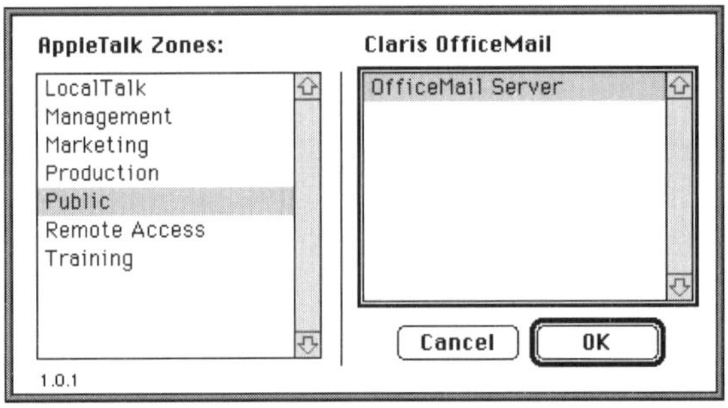

You can write it down here:

AppleTalk zone (if any): ______________________________.

OfficeMail server name: ______________________________.

Run Easy Setup

Now that you know what Claris Emailer is going to ask you for, go ahead and run through the Easy Setup script. If you have any problems, consult your *Claris Emailer Getting Started* guide or skip ahead to Chapter 6.

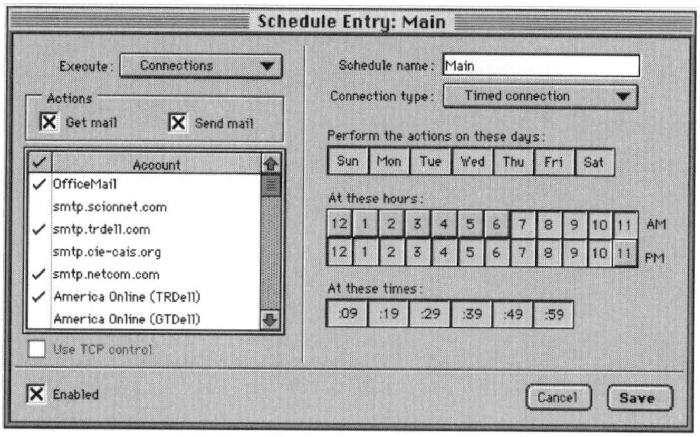

FIGURE 2-17. Setting up your schedule.

One of the last things Easy Setup will ask you to do is to tell Claris Emailer if and when it should gather your email automatically. In the Schedule Entry window you can leave the default setting of **Connections** in the Execute pop-up window. Next, select the accounts you want it to check automatically in the left pane of the Schedule Entry window, and then choose the exact times at which connections should occur in the pane at the right under Connection type **Timed Connection**, as in Figure 2-17.

Alternately, you can accept less precise time settings by just choosing **Repeating Connection** from the Connection type pop-up menu and selecting an interval in the resulting Frequency pop-up menu, as shown in Figure 2-18.

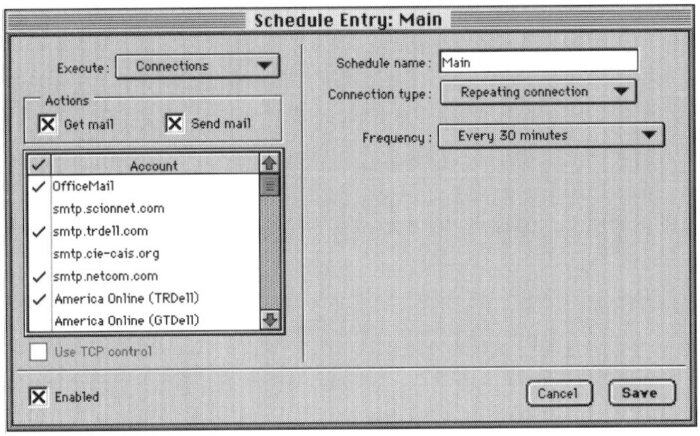

FIGURE 2-18. Configuring schedule for repeating connection.

You can always return to the Schedule Entry later. Claris Emailer permits you to maintain multiple schedules for different purposes. These are stored in the Schedules List, which can be opened by choosing the **Schedules** command under the **Setup** menu bar item.

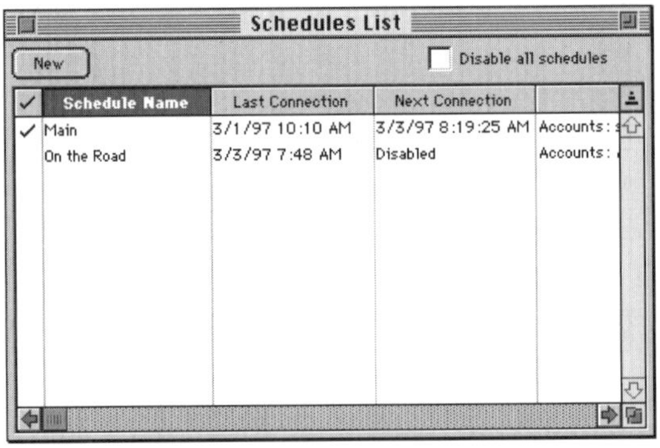

When you want to create a new schedule, perhaps one for checking accounts at longer intervals from your hotel room while you are on the road, choose the **Schedule** command from the **New** fly-out menu under the **Edit** menu bar item. Multiple schedules can be selected from the fly-out menu of the **Execute Schedule** command under the **Mail** menu bar item. You can remove a schedule from the Schedules List by selecting it and choosing the **Delete Schedule** command from under the **Edit** menu bar item (or by pressing **Command-D**).

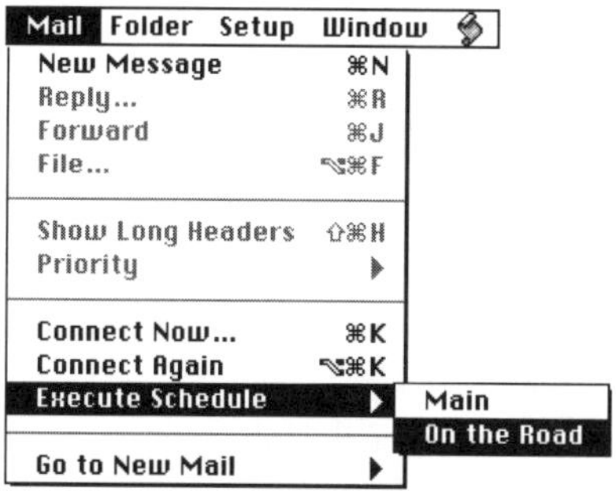

Press **Save** when you are done working with the Schedule Entry window.

Are you starting to realize what a time saver Claris Emailer is? Imagine how long it would take to boot up a POP client such as Eudora to get your Internet email, CompuServe Information Manager to get your CompuServe email, America Online software to get your AOL email, and a LAN-based email client to get your office mail. I used to have to do that. Trust me, it takes a lot of time, RAM, and patience. With Claris Emailer you get all your email in one place, at one time, automatically.

Touring Claris Emailer

Now that you have some accounts set up, let's take a look at the interface that will be your window onto a whole new world of communications. It contains four primary elements.

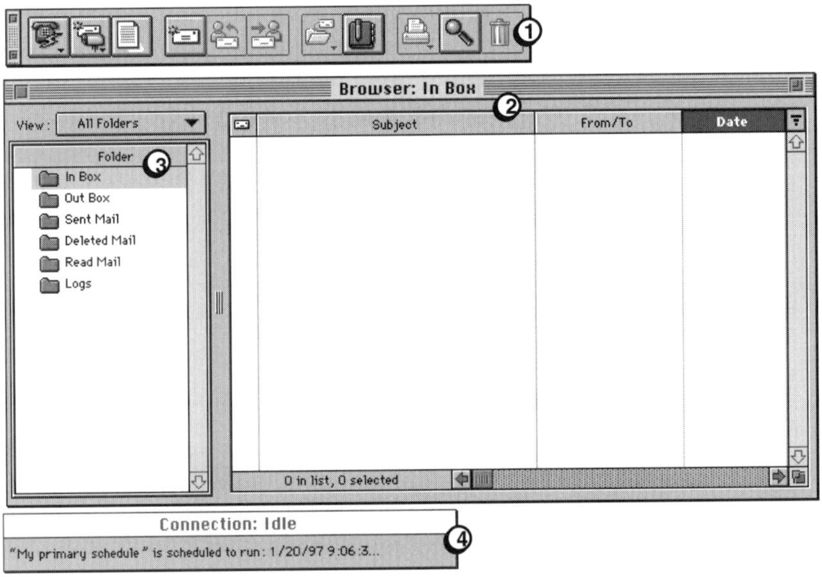

FIGURE 2-19. The Claris Emailer interface: (1) Toolbar (2) Browser (3) Folder List (4) Connection Status.

Toolbar

The Toolbar (1 in Figure 2-19) gives you quick access to Claris Emailer's major functions. You can drag it around on the screen. You can make it appear or disappear by choosing the **Toolbar** command under the **Window** menu bar item. You can resize it using the minimize box in the lower left corner.

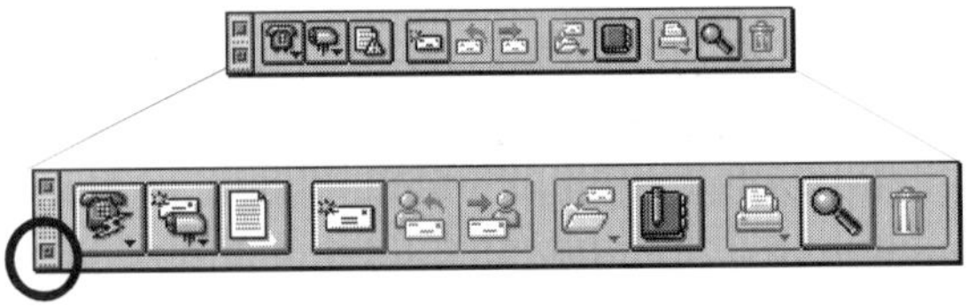

The Toolbar's components are:

Connect Now/Connect Again

Pressing this button directs Claris Emailer to send and collect your email immediately.

If you choose **Connect Now** in the pop-up menu, this feature overrides the schedule you set up in Easy Setup, giving you immediate access to any of your accounts without forcing you to reconfigure Claris Emailer. You need only check off the account you want to use and press the **Connect** button in the Connect Now Setup dialog box.

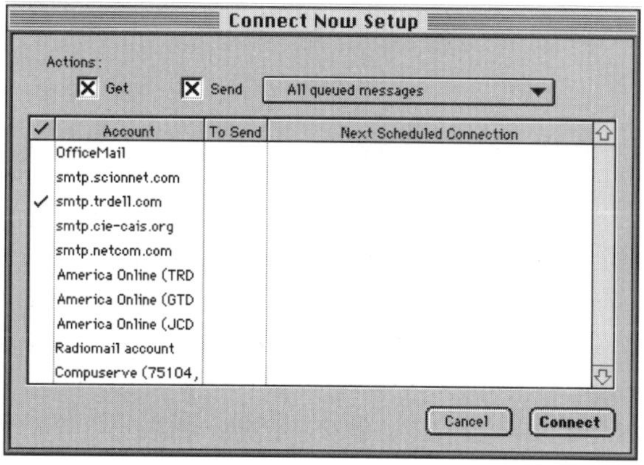

If you choose **Connect Again** in this button's pop-up menu, Claris Emailer will check the accounts you specified in your schedule immediately.

Unprocessed Mail

Claris Emailer has a very complete filing system and powerful, rules-based automated email handling features. You can, for instance, create a folder like those seen in Figure 2-19 and have all email from a given source dropped into it automatically. I know that certain email addresses are associated with garbage I would never want to read about or buy. I have these annoying little notes chucked into a "spam" folder so I do not have to look at them. Because I have not opened and dragged my eyes across these messages, they are considered *unprocessed*. Should I suddenly feel the need to "earn big bucks by watching TV" or need "1001 places to show my Web site," I can press this button and select from a list of folders that have unread mail in them.

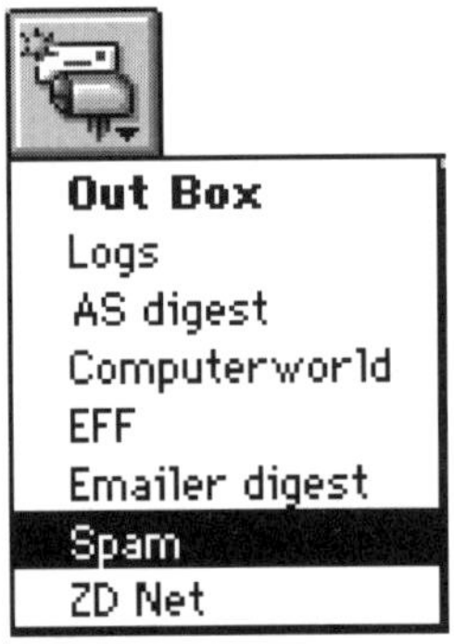

This is a useful feature because it ensures that you will always know which messages you have not yet read even if you move them around in Claris Emailer.

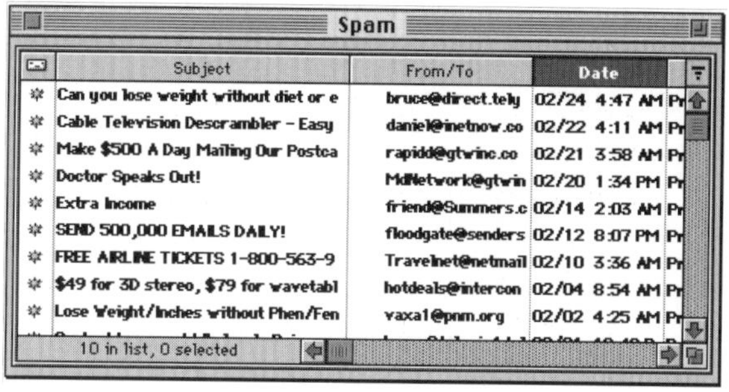

Connection Log

When all is well with Claris Emailer, this button will appear as a simple page icon. But if Claris Emailer has trouble getting into one of your accounts, it will alert you by flashing this button with an exclamation point (!) icon. You can then press it to see what is the matter.

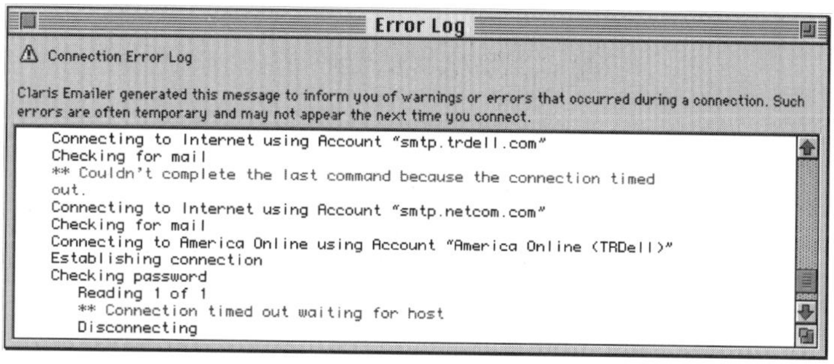

Connection problems, especially over phone lines, are pretty common, so do not freak out the first time you see one. They will often clear themselves the second time around. This Error Log helps you determine which problems are a fluke and which are chronic. For the latter, the log supplies information valuable to tech support people when they help you fix the problem.

New Message

Pressing this button generates a new email form in which you may write a message, as shown in Figure 2-20.

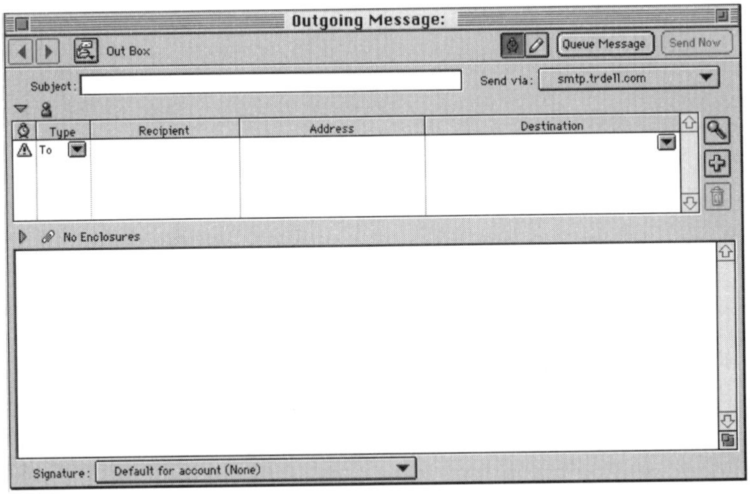

FIGURE 2-20. A new message form.

I will tell you all about this in Chapter 3.

Reply

Pressing the button with the curved blue arrow on it directs Claris Emailer to take a message you have just read, make its sender the recipient, and let you type in a response, as shown in Figure 2-21.

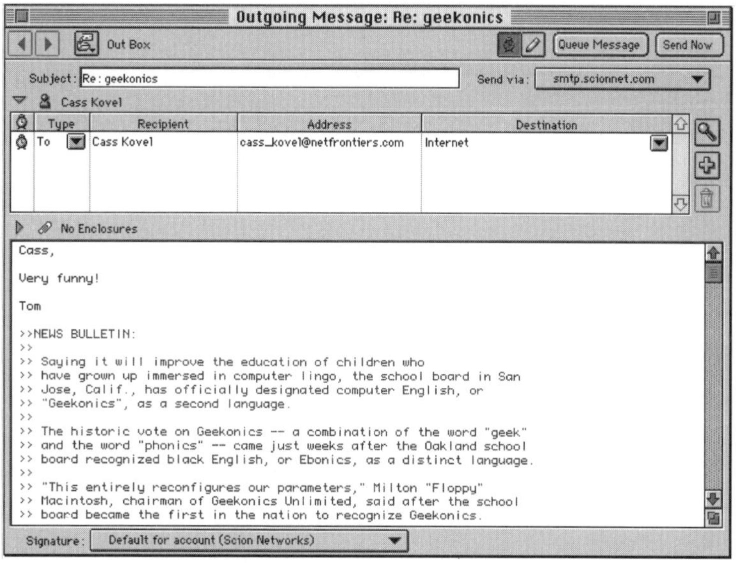

FIGURE 2-21. A new reply.

Forward

Pressing this button with the straight green arrow on it directs Claris Emailer to pass a message on to someone else you have an email address for, with or without your own comments added.

File Message

Pressing this button directs Claris Emailer to take a message and drop it into the folder of your choice. Remember my description of the **Unprocessed Mail** button? Here is how I would manually file junk mail:

Out of sight, out of mind . . . at least until I press the **Unprocessed Mail** button.

If you do not want a folder to appear in this pop-up menu, you must de-select the **Appears in folder pop-up menu** check box when you create it.

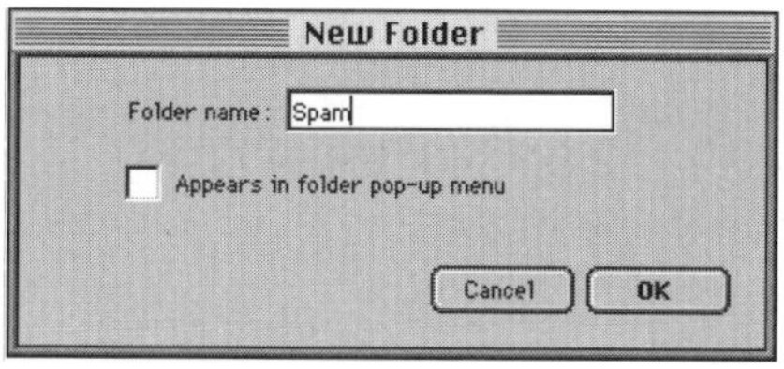

Address Book

Pressing this button will open a digital Address Book in which you can store the email addresses of everyone you want to communicate with.

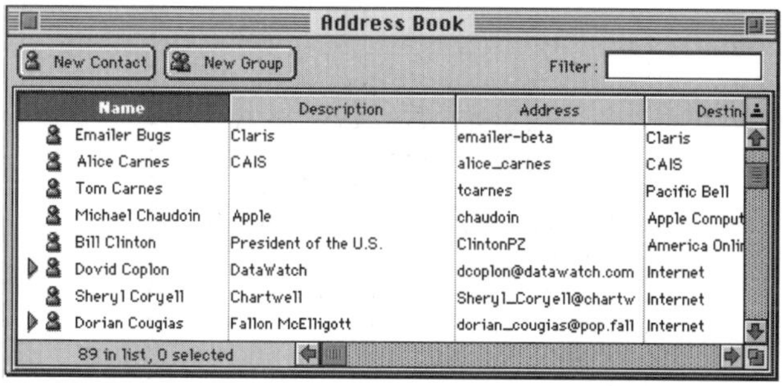

I will tell you all about this in Chapter 4.

Print

I will hazard a guess that you have a fairly good idea what this button does. It will enable you to print your email. It is a little handier than most such buttons because it lets you operate the printer without making you go to the Chooser.

When printed, your email looks like this:

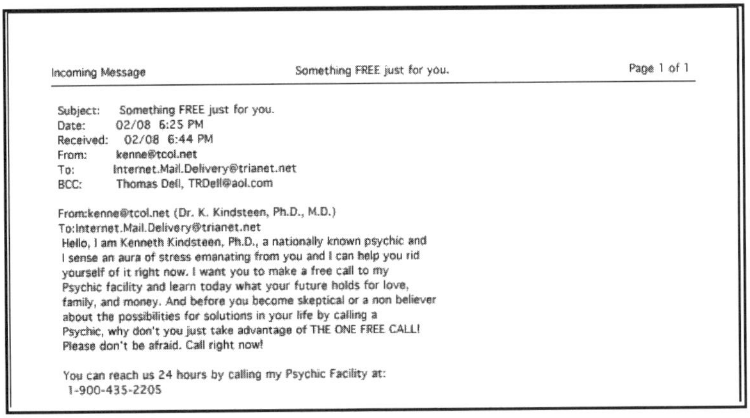
Incoming Message   Something FREE just for you.   Page 1 of 1

Subject: Something FREE just for you.
Date: 02/08 6:25 PM
Received: 02/08 6:44 PM
From: kenne@tcol.net
To: Internet.Mail.Delivery@trianet.net
BCC: Thomas Dell, TRDell@aol.com

From:kenne@tcol.net (Dr. K. Kindsteen, Ph.D., M.D.)
To:Internet.Mail.Delivery@trianet.net
Hello, I am Kenneth Kindsteen, Ph.D., a nationally known psychic and I sense an aura of stress emanating from you and I can help you rid yourself of it right now. I want you to make a free call to my Psychic facility and learn today what your future holds for love, family, and money. And before you become skeptical or a non believer about the possibilities for solutions in your life by calling a Psychic, why don't you just take advantage of THE ONE FREE CALL! Please don't be afraid. Call right now!

You can reach us 24 hours by calling my Psychic Facility at:
1-900-435-2205

Find

The button with the magnifying glass on it is my favorite. With it you can find an email message anywhere in Claris Emailer simply by typing in a word that is anywhere in the message's subject, body, or address. Need to find that message that was titled something like "where is the Claris Emailer book?" Type "Claris Emailer" or "book" or "Claris Emailer book" into the Find field.

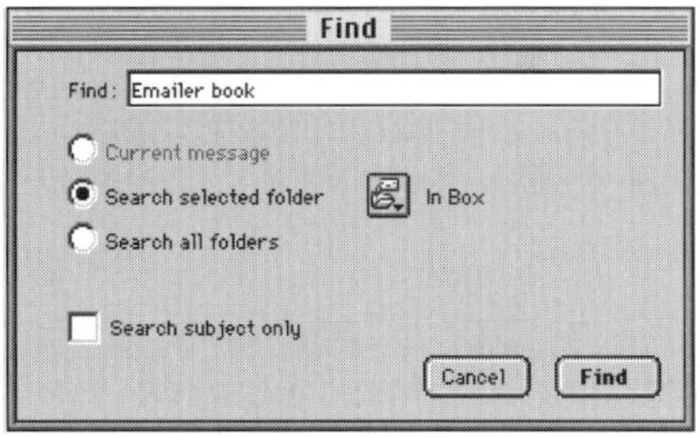

Need to find the message that describes some ultra secret project? Type "project x" into the Find field. You cannot remember what Michael's last name is? Type "Michael" into the Find field. Handy, no?

Delete

Pressing the trash can button tosses the email you do not want. Sorry junk emailers! Of course, you could make a mistake or change your mind. To protect you from this, Claris Emailer does not really throw the email away, but moves it to a "Deleted Mail" folder. You can empty this manually, or automatically after a specified time has elapsed.

I do not expect you to remember all of these buttons at first. Fortunately, you do not have to. If you forget what one of the buttons does, just point at it. Claris Emailer will remind you!

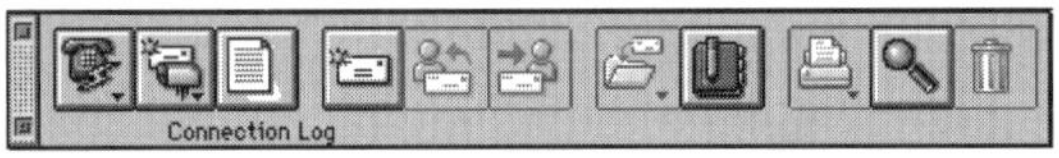

Maybe you would rather execute these commands from the keyboard. Always eager to give you choices, Claris Emailer will tell you what keyboard equivalents you can use if you point at the buttons while holding down the **Command** key.

As nifty as it is, you do not have to use the Toolbar at all if you do not want to. Deselect the **Toolbar** item under the **Window** menu bar item to make it go away. You can use the keyboard equivalents to perform all these functions or choose their commands from the menu bar.

Browser

The Browser window (2 in Figure 2-19) is where you can view a listing of all the email in any given folder (3 in Figure 2-19).

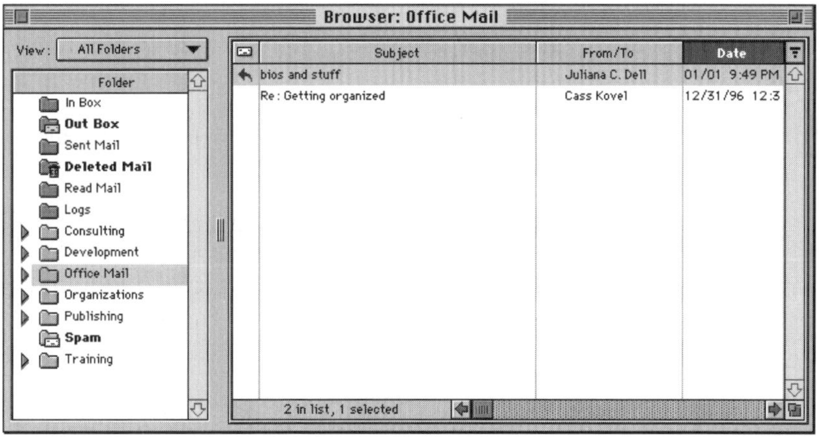

FIGURE 2-22. The Browser window.

Double-clicking on one of these list items will open the email message.

This scrollable window is divided into four columns, each one topped with a button. Pressing any of these buttons directs Claris Emailer to sort all messages by the ascending or descending order of that column's contents. For instance, press the **Date** header button, and the most recent email will be listed first, the oldest last.

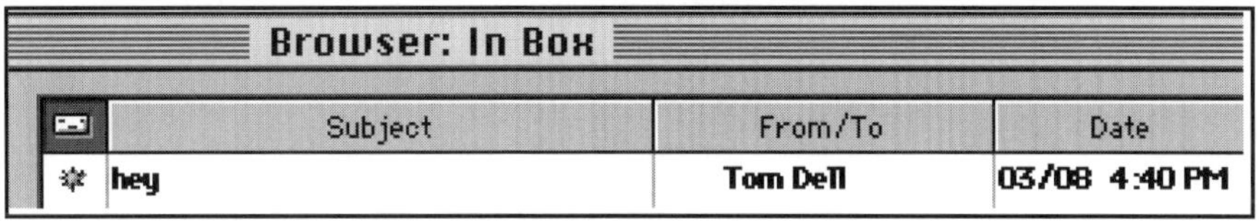

These buttons are:

Status

The first column, indicated by an envelope icon, gives you a visual cue as to the status of an email message.

 This symbol denotes a message that has been replied to.

 This symbol denotes a message that has not been read.

 This symbol denotes a message that is waiting to be sent.

 This symbol denotes a message that you are still writing but have saved to work on later.

If there is nothing in the column, then you have read these messages.

Subject

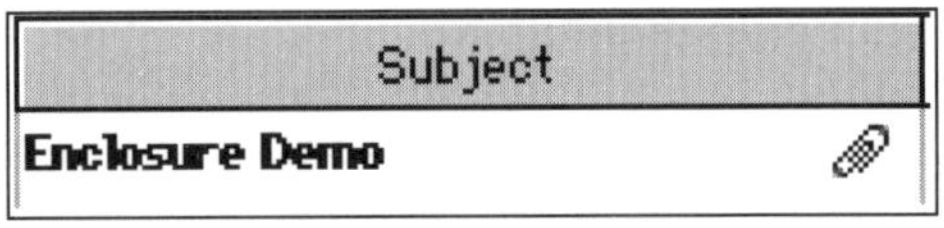

This is the short description you type into the Subject field of all email messages to give the recipient some idea of what you are about to say in the body. If the message you see in your Browser is a reply to a message of yours, you will see "Re>:" amended to your Subject. If the message has been forwarded to you, "FWD>" will be amended to it. If you see

"Earn Big Bucks By Watching TV," you have a prime candidate for the **Delete** button.

From/To

Depending on the folder whose contents you are viewing, this will be the name of either the message's recipient or its sender. If a sender has amended his or her full name to the email address, you will see a real name here (i.e., "Tom Dell"). If the sender did not or does not have the capability, you will see only an actual email address (i.e., "trdell@trdell.com").

Date

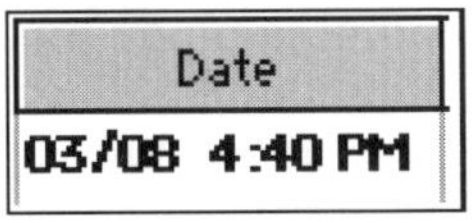

This is the date and time at which the message left the sender's computer.

If the time you see in your outgoing messages is inaccurate, check to make sure your Macintosh has the correct settings in the Date & Time control panel.

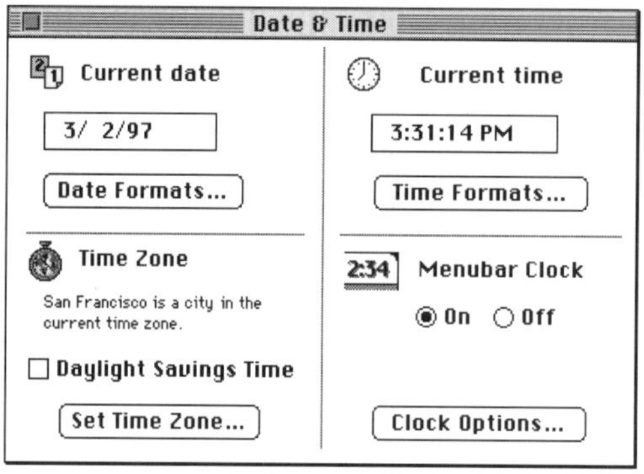

Priority

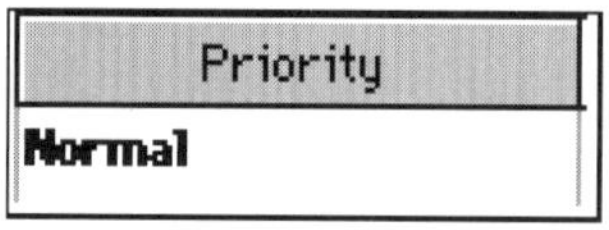

The idea behind this column is to give you a color code for ranking the relative urgency of your email messages. You program these headings yourself in Claris Emailer's Preferences window, which can be opened by choosing the **Preferences** command under the **Setup** menu bar item. This makes it easy to create your own grading system. You can then sort your messages from high to low priority.

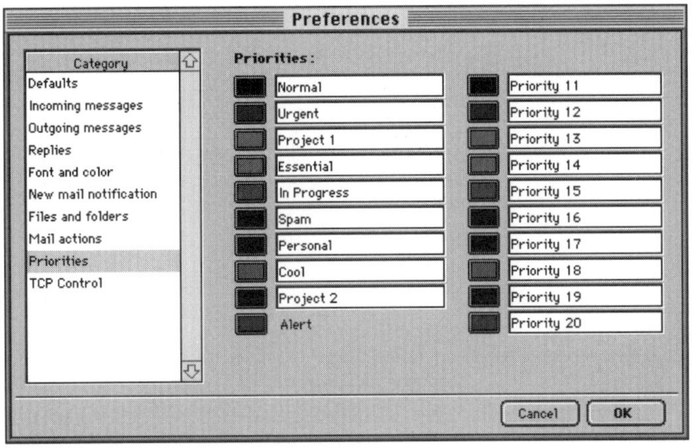

FIGURE 2-23. Establishing priorities.

Unfortunately, since your grading system may differ from that used by another email system or Claris Emailer user, it does not necessarily mean anything to anyone but you. An exception is where a whole organization has OfficeMail. There you can standardize on certain priorities throughout the organization.

To give a message a priority, select it in the Browser and choose an item from the **Priority** command under the **Mail** menu bar item.

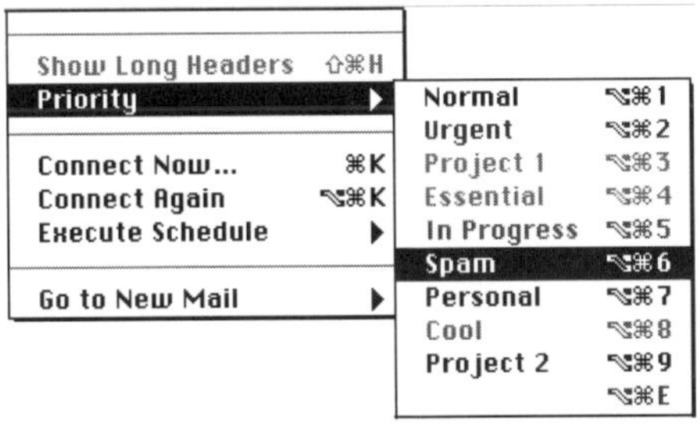

Priorities can also be assigned by Mail Actions, as I will show you in Chapter 5. Claris Emailer reserves one priority for itself: the red "alert." By default, all incoming messages assume the first priority.

Account

This column shows you where the message came from. This is the name you assigned to each account, not just the name of the service provider.

Sort

The last heading lets you toggle between ascending and descending order.

Folder List

Since all email is stored in Claris Emailer folders, just as all documents are stored in folders in the Mac OS, you can think of the pane in the left side of the Browser window as a filing cabinet (3 in Figure 2-19). When you first start using Claris

Emailer you will see that several folders have been created by default.

In Box

All email is stored in this folder when it first arrives. You can move it into other folders, either manually or automatically, thereafter.

Out Box

All email you create and send is stored in this folder until a connection is made. After the message is sent, it is moved to the Sent Mail folder.

Sent Mail

One neat thing about having the email moved to this folder and not just thrown away after it is sent is that you can always go back and see what you said. Then you will know how many flowers you need to buy your secretary for having been so rude. You can tell Claris Emailer to keep the email for a certain amount of time and then delete it in the application's preferences.

Deleted Mail

This folder is the message equivalent of the **Undo** command. It is here that you get one last chance to decide whether or not you want to keep a message. You can tell Claris Emailer to keep the email for certain amount of time, then *really* delete it. After that, it is gone for good.

Read Mail

This folder is an option. If you want to keep your Browser nice and clean, you can direct Claris Emailer to move the messages you have read to this folder when you close them. You can also tell Claris Emailer to leave messages you have read in the In Box folder until you manually delete them. Different strokes for different folks.

Logs

Here Claris Emailer stores its logs so you can retrieve them when you are troubleshooting or when you just want to see what email has been moving through your accounts at a given time.

As with your messages, Claris Emailer uses a few icons to indicate what is going on within your folders.

 This icon is used by the Deleted Mail folder.

 This icon is used for folders that have read email in them.

 This icon is used for folders that have unread email in them. If a folder's name is in italics, it contains subfolders that contain unread email.

It is worth noting also that folders created by Claris Emailer appear in dark blue while the folders you create appear in light blue. Also be aware of the fact that you can only create subfolders within the folders you create.

When you start getting email you may want to create your own folders for filing it. You can do this by choosing the **New Folder** command under the **Folder** menu bar item. For instance, I might create a folder for email received from my readers as shown:

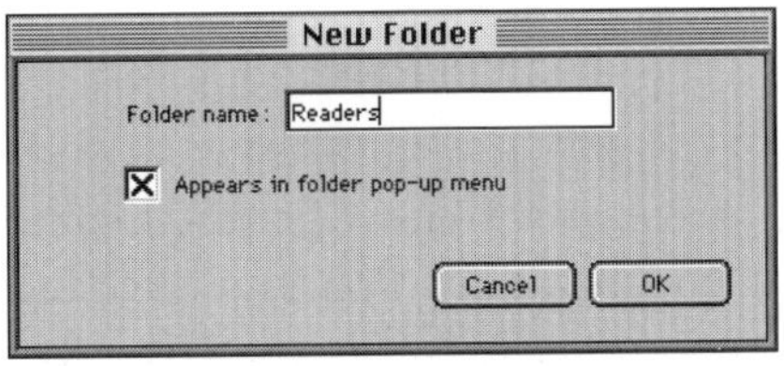

Now, that is neat! This is even more neat: I can also create a subfolder within that folder just for readers of this book by highlighting the **Readers** folder and choosing the **Create Subfolder** command under the **Folder** menu bar item. Claris Emailer has a hierarchical folder structure just like the Mac OS itself.

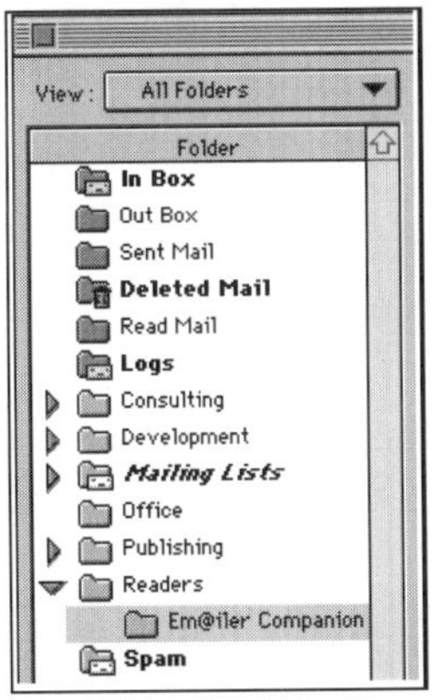

You can file your messages either by dragging and dropping them into the folders or by selecting a message and then choosing the destination folder in the pop-up menu generated by the **File** button in the Toolbar.

Folders that appear in the **File** button's pop-up menu are considered *marked.* Another way to see them, without using the Toolbar, is to choose **Marked Folders** in the Folder List's **View** pop-up menu.

Connection Status

Claris Emailer does not keep its workings to itself. It will tell you everything it is doing every step of the way in the Connection Status window (4 in Figure 2-19). You can make this window visible or invisible by selecting the **Connection Status** command under the **Window** menu bar item. Among the details you will see here are what accounts Claris Emailer is connecting to, whether or not it finds email there, and how fast the transfer of email is occurring.

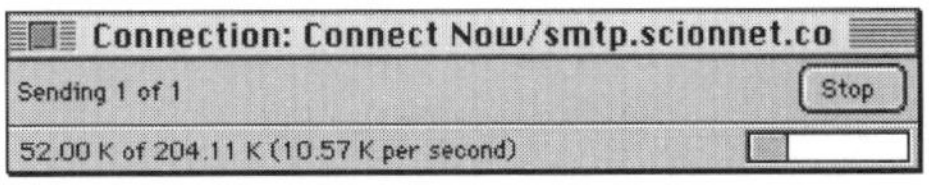

Getting Help

Afraid you will forget all this? Fear not. Help is never very far away. You can always get more information from Claris Emailer's **Help** menu bar item.

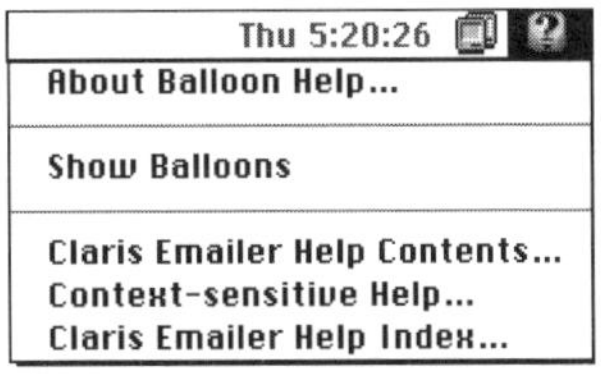

Here you will find fully indexed documentation that is comprehensive and easy to understand.

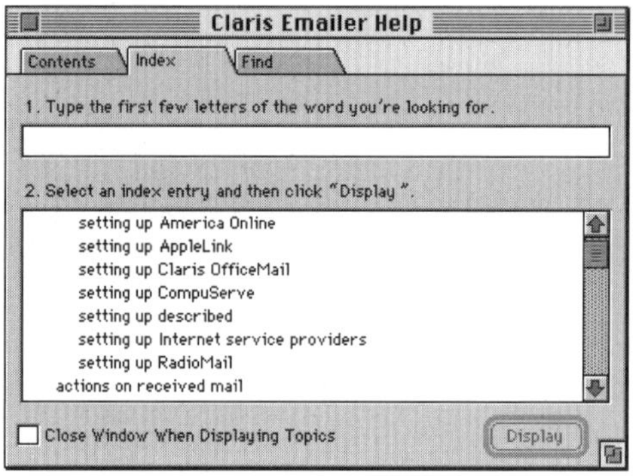

Summary

Claris Emailer is simple to install. First you run the Installer application to copy it to the hard drive of your computer; then you use the Easy Setup script to establish Claris Emailer's communications with your email service providers. After that, Claris Emailer will gather your email from multiple accounts automatically in accordance with a schedule you create.

Claris Emailer's interface contains four basic elements. The first is a Toolbar in which all of the major functions can be accessed with a click of the mouse. The second is a Browser in which all email messages can be read and sorted. The third is a filing-cabinet–like folder list in the Browser that permits the storage of messages in a hierarchical folder structure. The last is a Connection Status window that displays the progress of Claris Emailer's communications with various service providers.

Ready to start sending email? We will do that next.

3

Sending and Receiving Email

Enough with the preparation already! In this chapter we will use Claris Emailer's *message form* to send email messages. In this way you will learn what each part of the message form does and when each should be used. You will also learn how to reply to and forward incoming messages, and how to enclose other documents with your email.

Creating and Sending Messages

To begin, press the **New Message** button in the Toolbar (or press **Command-N**).

This will generate Claris Emailer's message form, which you can think of as the email equivalent of a blank sheet of paper.

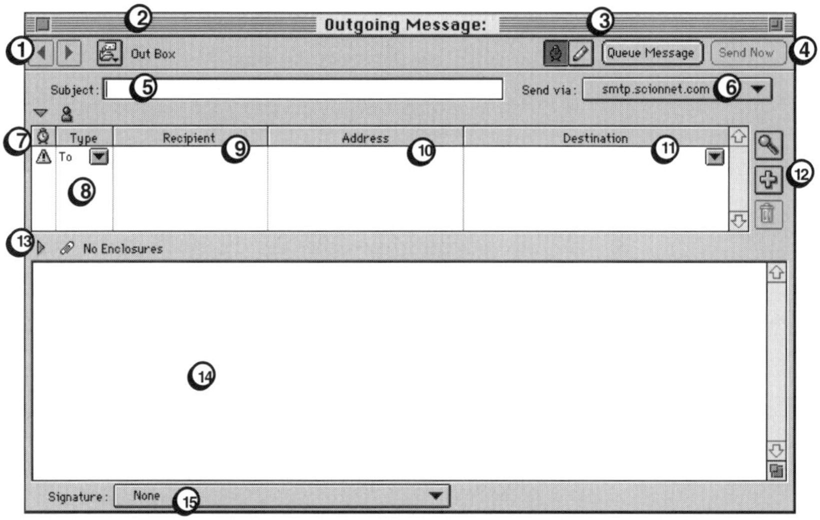

FIGURE 3-1. (1) Previous/Next (2) File (3) Queue Message/Save As Draft (4) Send Now (5) Subject (6) Send via (7) Send status icons (8) Addressing type (9) Recipient (10) Address (11) Destination (12) Address look-up buttons (13) Enclosures (14) Body (15) Signature.

As you can see in Figure 3-1, the message form has quite a few parts. I will tell you about all of them in time, but for now let's just get on with the business of sending a message.

To do this you are required to fill out just three of the fields: *Subject, Address,* and *Body*.

To illustrate how the process works let's begin by sending a message to the most important person in your life: Yourself! This will have the benefit of verifying that your account is set up properly.

Subject

The Subject field (5 in Figure 3-1) is used to identify the contents of your message in a single line. Subjects can be as short as "Hi" or as long as "Here is that report you requested on ROI." Whatever you type here will be the line that identifies the message to the recipients in whatever email system they are using.

By way of example, type "Testing, testing" in the Subject field of the message form you have open.

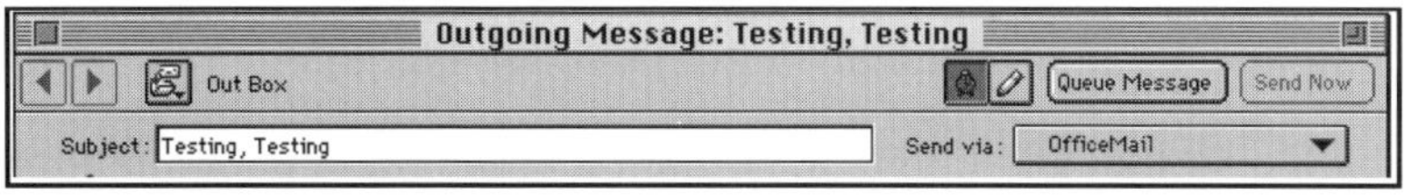

Note that the title bar of the message changes from just "Outgoing Message" to "Outgoing Message: Testing, testing." Note also that the **Send Now** button is not available (grayed out). Claris Emailer knows you have not finished writing yet and does not want you sending out half-written email by accident.

Address

The Address field (10 in Figure 3-1) is where the valid email address of the recipient needs to go. There are other fields as well, but this is the only one Claris Emailer must have filled in to send your message.

By way of example, type your own email address that is valid for whatever system is listed in the Send via pop-up menu (6 in Figure 3-1); then press the **tab** key twice to move to the Body field.

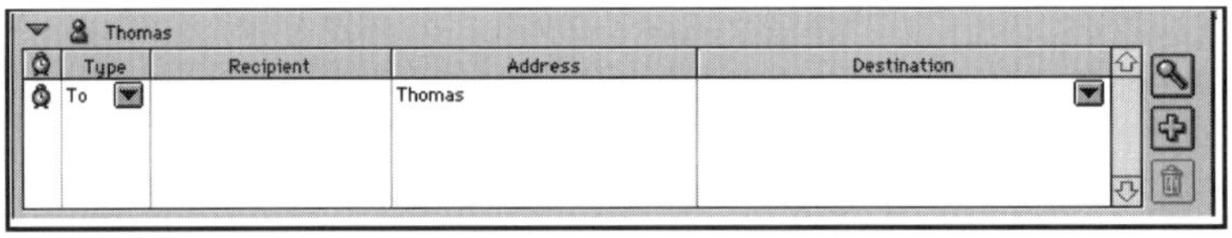

Note that the **Send Now** button becomes active. Claris Emailer has all the data it needs to send a message, although you will almost always add more to your message than just what is in the Subject field. An exception is when you subscribe or unsubscribe to a mailing list or request data from an email-on-demand system.

Body

The Body field (14 in Figure 3-1) is where you type your actual message. You may pour forth your words of wisdom with reckless abandon here, but do not try to format them. Most email systems are designed to accommodate just plain old boring text—no fancy fonts, no pretty indents, no nifty styles, no pictures.

By way of example, type a quick note to yourself.

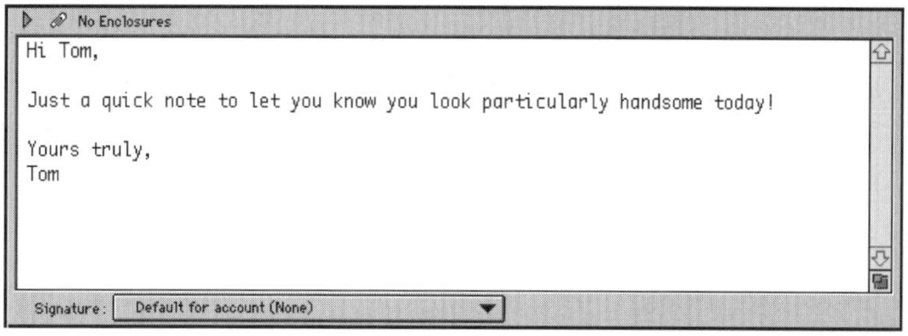

That, gentle reader, is the gist of it. Go ahead and press that **Send Now** button. Are we having fun or what?

If all is well, your first message will pass through the email system that was designated in the Send via pop-up menu and then come back to you; you will see it in the Browser's In Box.

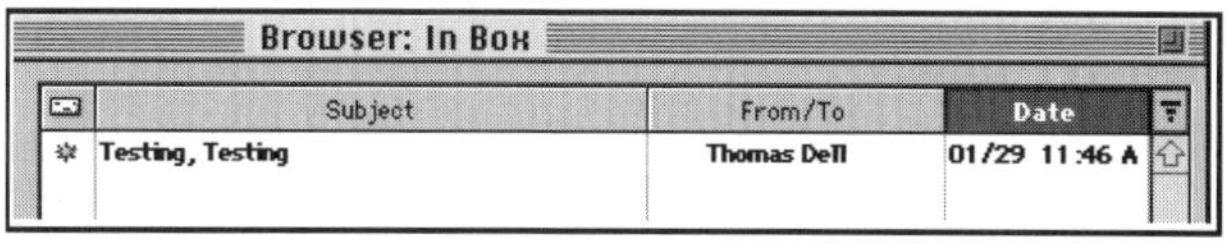

If all is not well, you will probably see an alert flashing over the **Connection Log** button. Click on it to see what the problem is.

Remember, new messages appear in boldface and are accompanied by a sunburst icon.

Reading Messages

To read a message simply double-click on its listing in the Browser. Go ahead and try this with the message you just received from yourself.

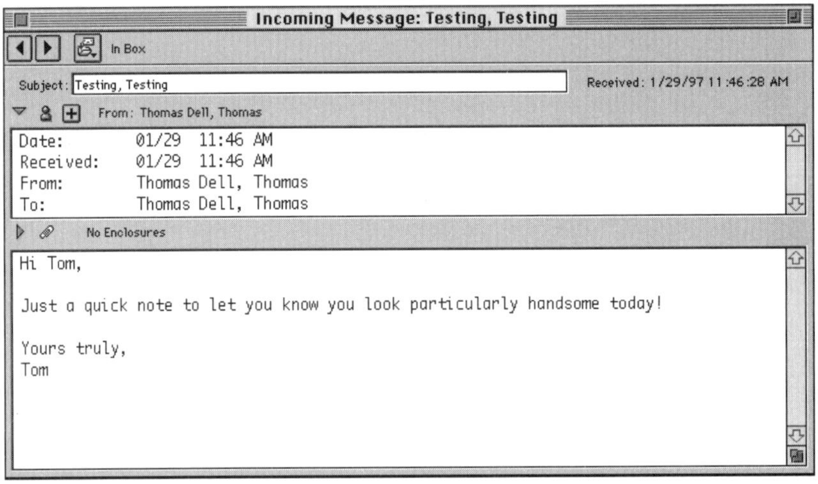

FIGURE 3-2. Incoming message.

Once you have read the message, click on the box in the upper left on the title bar to close it. What happens to it next will depend on your preferences. You can permit the message to remain in your In Box, in which case its boldface title will become plain and the sunburst icon will disappear so that you will know it has been read. Alternately, you can move it automatically to the Read Mail or the Deleted Mail folder (as I will show you in Chapter 7).

Replying to Messages

Much of the time you will want to send a reply to the message you have read. Rather than go through the whole process of retyping the subject, address, and body data, it is easiest to respond by choosing the incoming message in the Browser window and then pressing the **Reply** button in the Toolbar (or press **Command-R**).

This will open the same message form with some important differences in content.

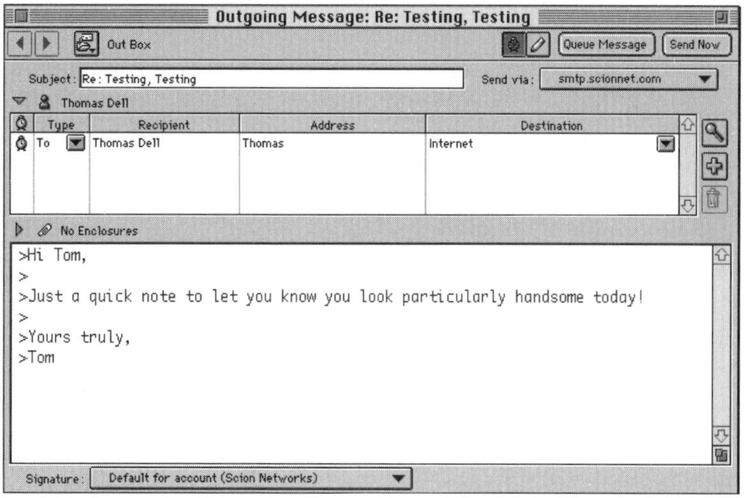

FIGURE 3-3. Reply message.

First, notice that "Re:" has been appended to the Subject of the message. This signals the recipient that you are continuing the conversation previously begun and not starting a new communication. Second, what was the sender's address in the previous message now becomes the recipient's address. Finally, you can have the body of the previous message appended to the body of the new message by setting one of Claris Emailer's default preferences (as I will show you in Chapter 7). The text will be a different color, however, and each line will be preceded by ">." By appending the previous message's text to the reply, you recall for the recipient parts of the conversation he or she might have forgotten. The person will know which lines are new and which are old by whether or not the ">" precedes them.

For practice, type a reply into the Body field. Sometimes you will type complete paragraphs at the top of the body, expecting the reader to scroll down to refer to the older message if necessary. At other times, you will type your new comments between the lines of the older message, particularly if the older message contains a list of questions. Press the **Send Now** button when you are done.

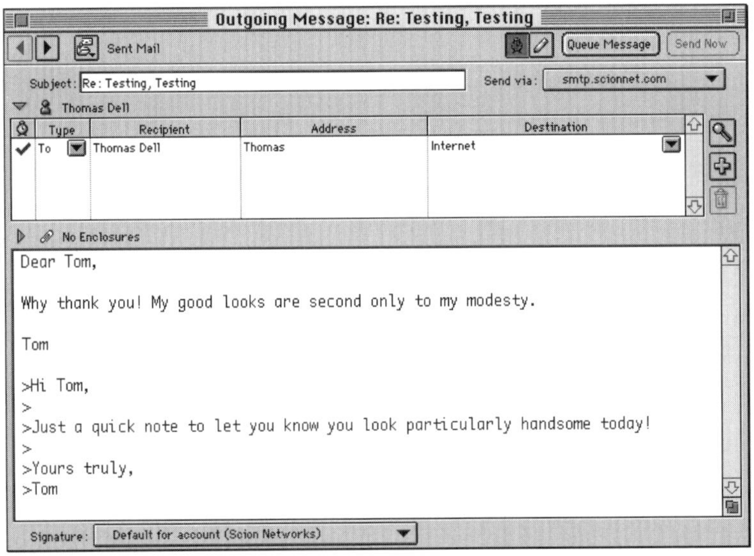

FIGURE 3-4. Old message appended to reply message.

There will be no visible changes to the body of the message in your In Box, although it will now be listed with the blue curved arrow next to it. Your reply message will be moved to the Sent Mail folder after it is sent.

Forwarding Messages

At other times you will want to pass on a message you have read to a new recipient, either with or without your own comments added. It is easiest to do this by choosing the incoming message in the In Box and then pressing the **Forward** button in the Toolbar (or press **Command-J**).

As with the reply message form, the contents of the forward message form are essentially the same as that of the original message form with a few additions.

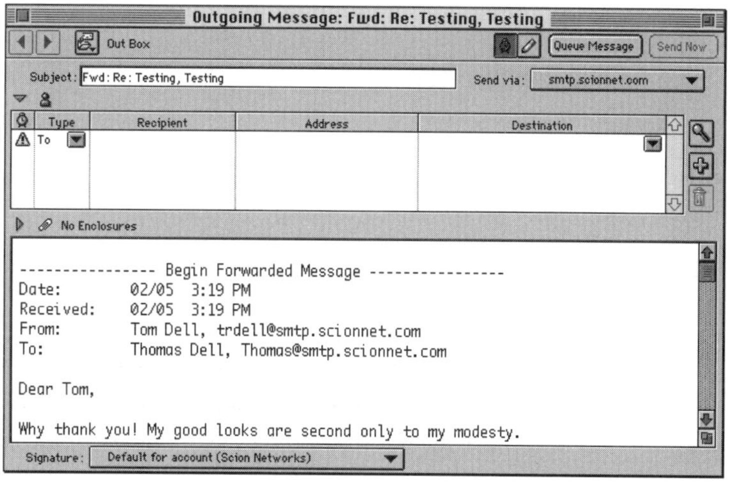

FIGURE 3-5. Forward message.

First, you will notice that "Fwd:" has been appended to the subject of the message. This signals the recipient that you are sending him a message that was originally addressed to you. Second, there will no longer be a recipient's address. You will need to add that. Finally—if this is your preference—the body of the previous message will be appended to the body of the new message. Above it will be a divider:

```
----------- Begin Forwarded Message -----------
```

This separates your comments at the top from the original message at the bottom. Type your comments into the body, if you want to, and then press the **Send Now** button. Your forwarded message will be moved to the Sent Mail folder after it is sent.

Working within the Message Form

Now that you know how to send, receive, reply to, and forward your messages, let's take a look at what else you can do within the message form.

Previous and Next Buttons

These buttons (1 in Figure 3-1) provide you with an alternative to opening and closing all messages in the Browser window when you want to read them. Instead, simply double-click on the first message to open it, then press the right arrow to move on to the next one when you are ready.

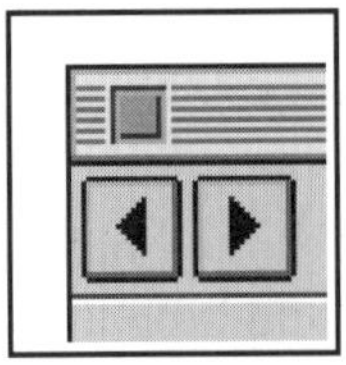

Press the left arrow if you want to go back again. Press the box in the upper left of the title bar to close the message form.

File Button

This button (2 in Figure 3-1) is functionally identical to the **File Message** button in the Toolbar. To the right of the button, you will see the name of the folder from which the message you are reading has been pulled (i.e., "In Box"). Pressing the button will generate a list of folders to which you may move the message.

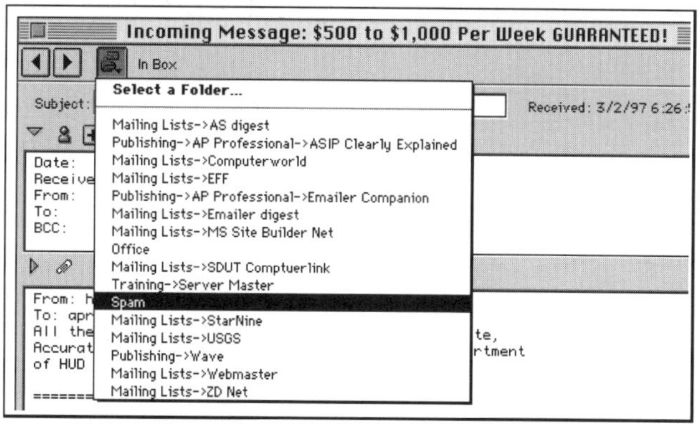

Simply select a folder's name in this pop-up menu to file the message in it.

Queue Message/Save As Draft Button

These buttons (3 in Figure 3-21) are used when you are not yet ready to send a message. For instance, when you have written your message but are not yet ready to have it delivered—perhaps because you do not want your work interrupted by Claris Emailer triggering your modem—you can press the clock icon to generate the **Queue Message** button. When you press the **Queue Message** button, the message will be moved to the Out Box folder. Here it will remain either until you select it again and send it manually or until your schedule triggers a connection.

When you have only partially written a message and are not yet ready to have it delivered, but you need to close Claris Emailer for some reason, you can press the pencil icon to generate the **Save As Draft** button. When you press this button, the message will also be moved to the Out Box folder. Here it will remain until you get around to finishing it. It will not be sent when your schedule triggers a connection.

 You can tell the two types of messages apart by their accompanying icons.

Send Now Button

This button (4 in Figure 3-1), with which you have some experience, will send your message on its way as soon as you press it. That means that if the destination is reached via modem, a new phone call will be placed each time you press this button.

If a message is urgent, go ahead and use this button. Otherwise, it is a good idea to write all your messages and save them in the Out Box, using the previously described **Queue Message** button. Then you can wait until your schedule dictates that it is time to connect, at which time all the saved mail will go out at once.

Send via Button

This button (6 in Figure 3-1) dictates which account will be used in sending out a message.

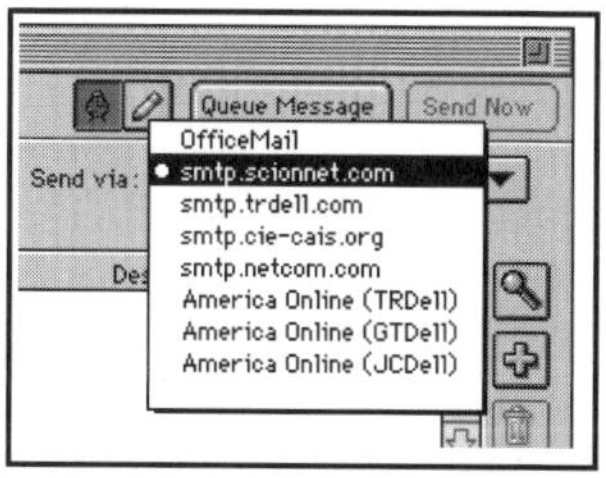

The account through which you receive email does not need to be the account through which you send email. For instance, I often receive email from my America Online account, but I usually send email—even that destined for America Online subscribers—through my company's mail host. For me, this makes for faster delivery.

You designated the account that is selected by default here when you ran Easy Setup. To change it select the **Accounts** command under the **Setup** menu bar item and choose a different service in the pop-up menu in the upper right of the Account List:

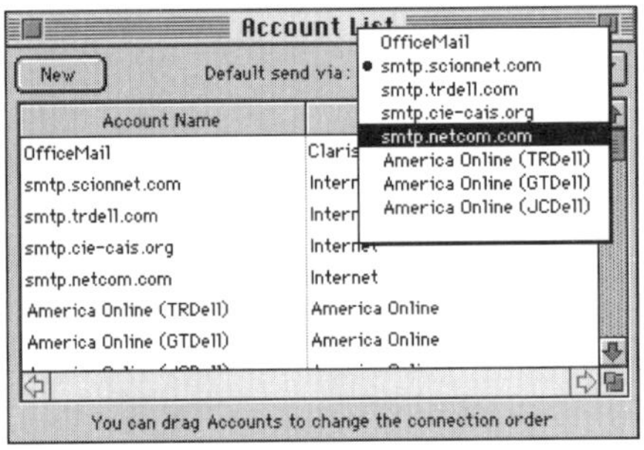

Send Status Icons

This icon (7 in Figure 3-1) changes depending on whether or not you have typed a valid address in the Address field.

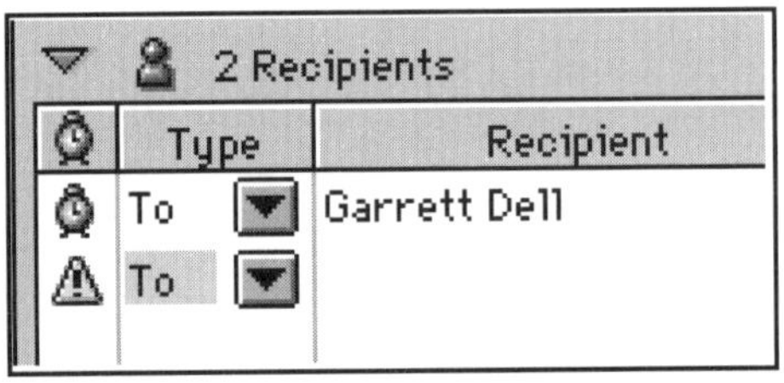

An incomplete address is denoted by the alert icon. When you type in a full address and press the **return** key, the alert icon changes to a clock icon to show that Claris Emailer is waiting for you to finish the message and send it.

Addressing Type Pop-Up

This pop-up menu (8 in Figure 3-1) provides you with three choices for how each recipient will be listed in the header of each message.

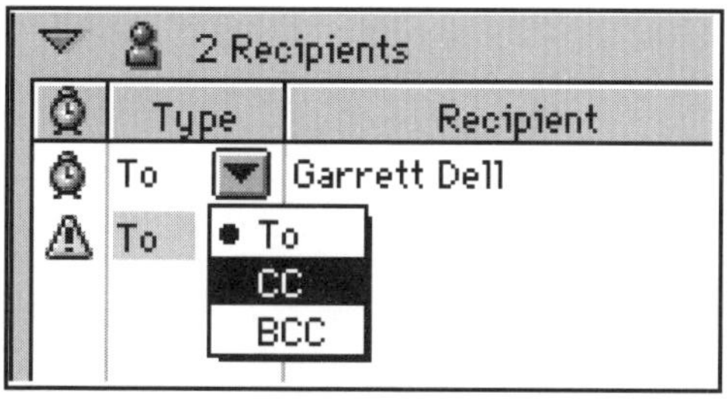

When you want multiple recipients to attach equal importance to your message, designate each address with **To**. When you address your message to a primary recipient but also want others to be aware of the communication, designate the secondary recipients with **CC** (for "carbon copy"). When the recipients receive the message they will be listed in the header as illustrated:

Received:	02/05 12:32 PM
From:	Tom Dell, trdell@smtp.scionnet.com
To:	Garrett Dell, Garrett@smtp.scionnet.com
CC:	Michael Hytopoulos, Michael@smtp.scionnet.com

This header will be visible to all who receive the message, so all recipients will be aware of who else has received the same information. What if you do not want the primary recipient to know you have sent the message to others as well? Use **BCC** ("blind carbon copy") instead of **CC**. This will leave the names of these secret recipients out of the message headers of other recipients.

WARNING!

*The **BCC** recipients will be secret so long as your ISP has configured the SMTP mail host to permit this. To be on the safe side, send a different message to recipients you want to be sure are kept a secret.*

Recipient Field

Until you have your Address Book set up (as I will show you in the next chapter), this field is only significant to you personally and can even be left blank (9 in Figure 3-1).

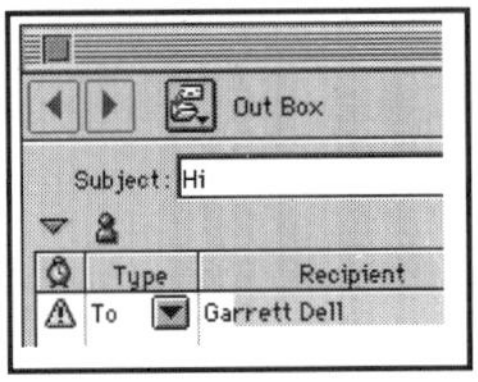

After you have your Address Book configured you will find that this field provides one of Claris Emailer's greatest time-saving features. Claris Emailer treats the field as look-up input to the Address Book's database. Simply type the name of the intended recipients as you have listed them in your Address Book, and Claris Emailer will look up the rest of the necessary addressing information for you! You do not even need to type in the entire name. For instance, I needed to type just "Ga" before Claris Emailer looked up the possible entries in my Address Book and provided me with the correct address for "Garrett Dell" (as illustrated).

Address Field

As I noted before, this field must contain a valid address in order for any message to be sent (10 in Figure 3-1).

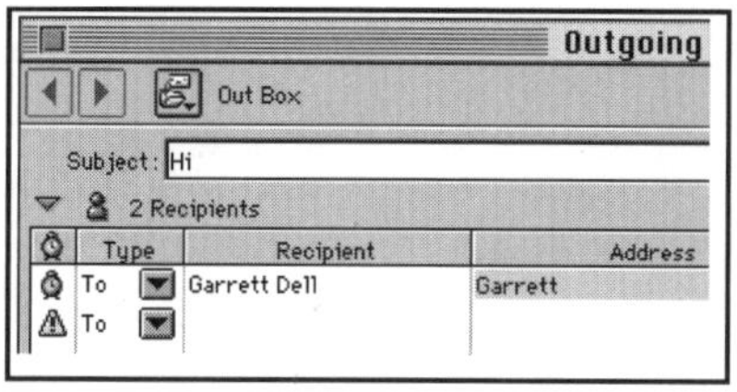

This address can come from one of two places. Either you can type it in manually, as we did at the beginning of this chapter, or it can be placed there by Claris Emailer after it looks up the name you type in the Recipient field and takes the address from your Address Book.

Destination Pop-Up

In this pop-up menu are listed service providers under which your recipients' email accounts may be held (11 in Figure 3-1).

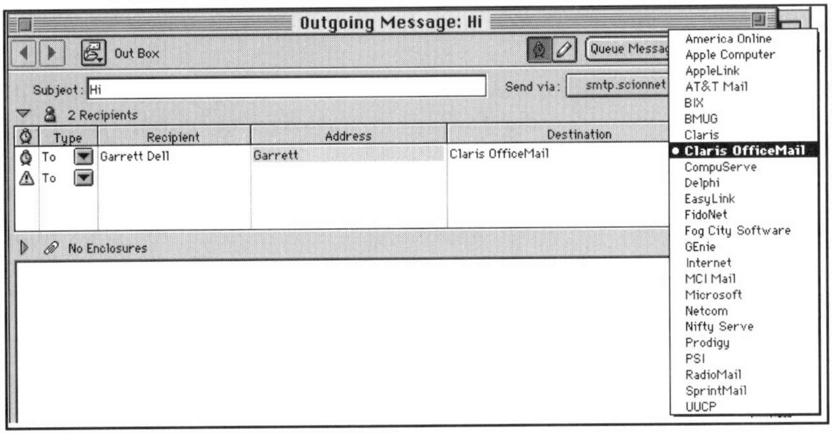

Here you can tell Claris Emailer which of the several accounts a recipient might have that you want the message to be routed through. As with the Address field, this address can come from one of two places. Either you can choose it manually or it can be chosen automatically by Claris Emailer after it looks up the name you type in the Recipient field and pulls it from your Address Book.

This can be a very handy feature. Let's say that I have an urgent message that I want to get to "Garrett." He has a Claris OfficeMail account, so I use that destination first. After I send the message, however, I realize that I am not sure he will be in the office this week. Fortunately, I know he has an America Online account that he uses at home as well. It is also listed under his name in my Address Book. I reopen the message I just sent and choose **America Online** in the Destination pop-up menu instead of Claris OfficeMail (all of the possible destinations listed in my Address Book for this recipient appear in boldface). Claris Emailer is smart enough to change the Address field from "Garrett," the OfficeMail account name, to "GTDell," the America Online screen name. Now when I press the **Send Now** button, Claris Emailer will connect with America Online's servers and upload the message.

In this scenario I have my own America Online account, but it is not necessary. If I had only an Internet email account, I could choose **Internet** in the Destination pop-up menu and send the same message to an America Online user via its Internet gateway. In this case Garrett's address would change from just "GTDell," the America Online screen name, to "gtdell@aol.com," a valid Internet email address.

Address Look-up Buttons

Although you will usually find it easier to let Claris Emailer execute these functions automatically, you can also use these buttons to perform addressing commands manually (12 in Figure 3-1). They are, from top to bottom, **Find**, **Add**, and **Delete**.

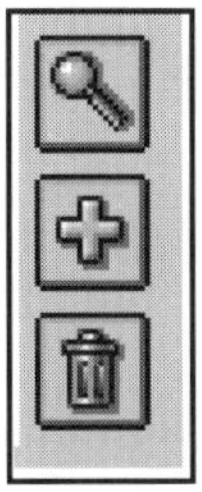

When you type the first few letters of a recipient's name in the Recipient field, Claris Emailer will attempt to match the letters to a name in your Address Book. Failing that, you can press the **Find** button to open the Find Address dialog box.

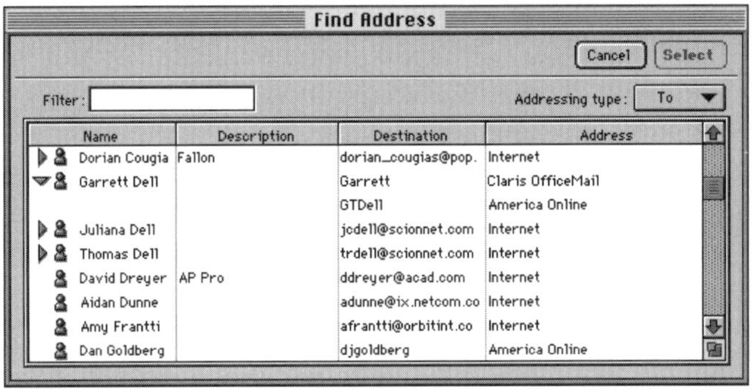

Highlight the address you want to use, and then press the **Select** button to add it to your message. Recipient names that are associated with multiple accounts will have a triangle next to them. Click on this triangle to expand the entry and see all the possible account destinations.

After you click on the first line in the addressing pane and enter one address, simply press the return key to begin a new line. Alternately, you can press the **Add** (+) button to add a new address line.

Finally, to get rid of an address that you previously typed in, select its line and press the **Delete** button.

Enclosures Window

When you want to attach another file to your email message, begin by clicking on this triangle (13 in Figure 3-1). It will open the Enclosures window.

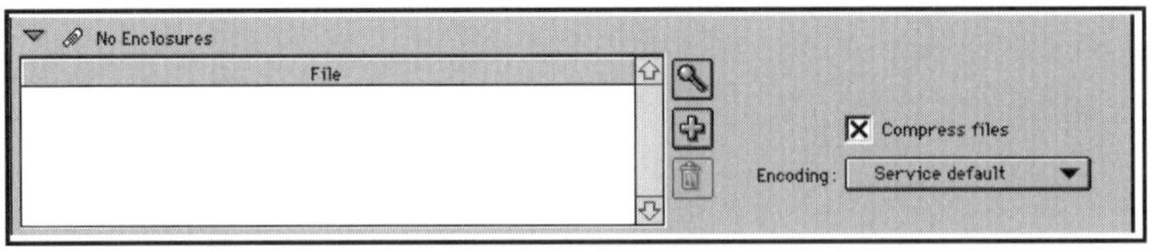

Here you will find the same buttons that perform addressing look-up commands (12 in Figure 3-1). These have a different purpose, however. The **Find** button is used to generate a Find Files dialog box.

Instead of opening and closing numerous folders to find the files you need, simply type the name of the files you want here and Claris Emailer will locate them for you. You do not even need to know the full name of the files you seek. For instance, I might want to include an address database file with my message, as illustrated, but have forgotten the name of the file and where I have it stored. I direct Claris Emailer to look for all files whose name includes "book." All possibilities are returned to me, and I choose the correct file from the list when I recognize its name or icon. I then just press the **Select** button (or double-click) to add it to the Enclosures window.

The **Add** (+) button is used to generate the standard Macintosh Select File dialog box.

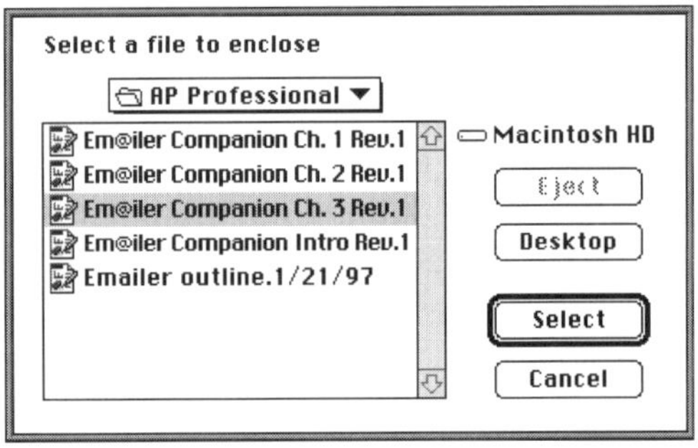

Use this button when you know where the file you want to attach is stored. There is an even easier way. Depending on the version of the Mac OS you are running, you can just drag-and-drop a file into the Enclosures window to enclose a copy of it. You can even just drop a file onto the paperclip icon without opening the Enclosure window.

The **Delete** button is used to delete files from the Enclosures window. It will not delete the file from your hard drive.

Once you have chosen the files you wish to attach to your message, you can compress them and encode them before they are sent.

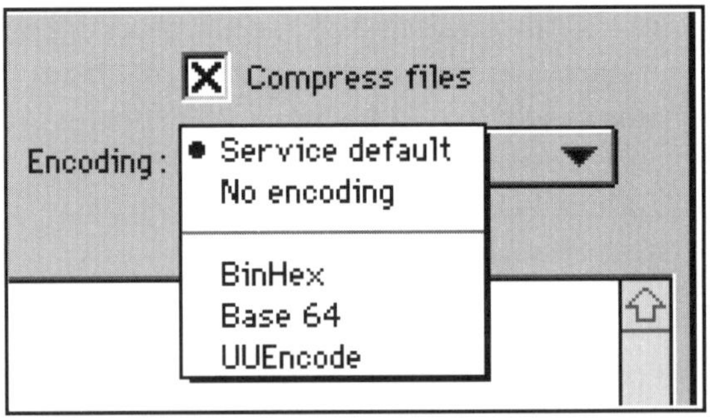

If you compress your enclosed files, you have but one choice for the method. If you select the **Compress files** check box, Aladdin's StuffIt will be used. In most cases you will want to enable this option. Since it will reduce the size of the files being transferred, it will also reduce the time it takes to transfer them.

If you choose to encode your enclosed files, you have several choices for the method that depend on the destination system's requirements. Essentially, your choices are Internet email or not Internet email. If you select **No encoding**, that is just what you will get. This works fine for OfficeMail and most service providers, but Internet email usually uses SMTP, which requires that all messages be comprised solely of ASCII text. When you send a note to someone, this is no big deal. But when you send a document, picture, or application to someone, you need to translate the binary file into the ASCII character set. The recipient will then reverse the process to make your ASCII enclosure a binary file again. The **BinHex**, **Base 64,** and **UUencode** commands refer to three methods for performing this translation. The one you choose will depend on what your recipient uses. **BinHex** is the most common for Macintosh users, **Base 64** for Windows users, **UUencode** for UNIX users.

Once you know which encoding type a given service requires, you can make this the service default. This is set in each account entry that can be accessed by choosing the **Accounts** command under the **Setup** menu bar item. For instance, since I know most recipients will use BinHex when they receive files from my company's mail host, I make that the default for "smtp.scionnet.com."

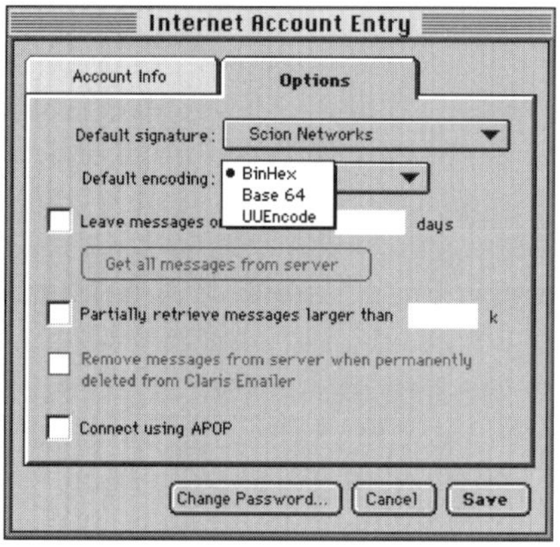

Once you have attached a file to your email message, its name will be listed next to the paperclip symbol after you close the Enclosures window (by clicking on the triangle).

There is nothing more you need to do. Files are compressed and encoded automatically as soon as you press the **Send Now** button. Messages that contain enclosures have the paperclip icon attached to them in the Browser.

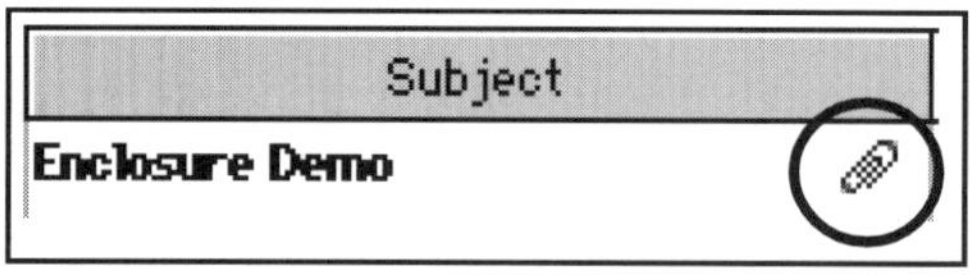

Body Field

As you learned at the beginning of this chapter, the Body field (14 in Figure 3-1) is where you type the contents of your messages. Enough said about that. You will notice when you receive messages over the Internet, however, that there is more than just what the sender typed in the body. This is because Internet email standards dictate that other delivery information be included here as well. You can break Internet email messages into two parts: *header* and *body*.

For instance, here is the header of one Internet email message:

```
From trdell@smtp.scionnet.com Sat Jan 25 09:56:18 1997
Received: from relay1.smtp.psi.net
(relay1.smtp.psi.net [38.8.14.2]) by mx1.eskimo.com
(8.7.6/8.6.12) with ESMTP id JAA32214 for <Claris
Emailer-digest-request@eskimo.com>; Sat, 25 Jan 1997
09:56:15 -0800
Received: from smtp.scionnet.com by
relay1.smtp.psi.net (8.8.3/SMI-5.4-PSI)
id MAA05502; Sat, 25 Jan 1997 12:45:54 -0500 (EST)
Received: from [38.247.58.8] by smtp.scionnet.com
with SMTP (Apple Internet Mail Server 1.1); Sat, 25 Jan
1997 09:44:15 -0800
Subject: subscribe
Date: Sat, 25 Jan 97 09:44:18 -0800
x-mailer: Striper x37, December 23, 1996
From: Tom Dell <trdell@smtp.scionnet.com>
To: <Claris Emailer-digest-request@eskimo.com>
Mime-Version: 1.0
Content-Type: text/plain; charset="US-ASCII"
Message-ID: <1357937041-140021532@smtp.scionnet.com>
```

The header can be interesting. It shows you which systems the message traveled through on its way to you, at what times, and how it was transferred. In the case of forwarded email, this header can grow quite long. You can toggle between long and short headers by choosing the **Show Long Headers** command under the **Mail** menu bar item (or by using the **Shift-Command-H** key combination).

Checking Your Spelling

Once you have typed something in the Body field of the message form, you can check its spelling. To use this feature, highlight the word or paragraph(s) you want Claris Emailer to check and then choose **Check Spelling** in the fly-out menu accessed from the **Spelling** command under the **Edit** menu bar item.

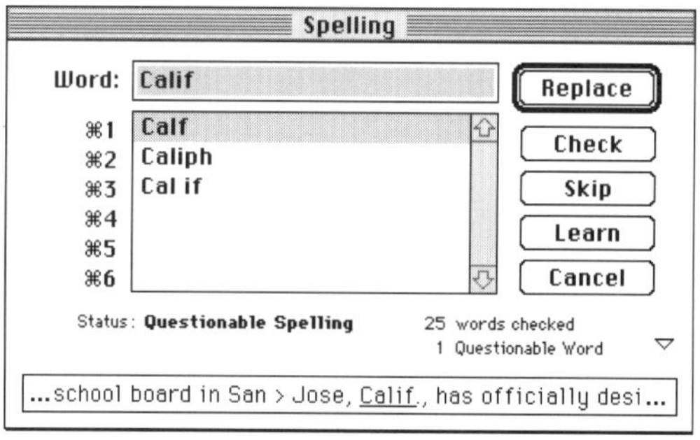

Signatures

This pop-up menu permits you to select which signature information file you want appended to your messages automatically (15 in Figure 3-1). This is a convenient way to append the information that you commonly use in signing your email, such as name, title, office address, phone number, and URL. It is also commonly used to add a quotation or humorous remark to make the email lighter in tone, or to add instructions for the reader.

To create a Signature file choose the **Signature** command under the **Setup** menu bar item. This will open the Signature List window. Here press the **New** button.

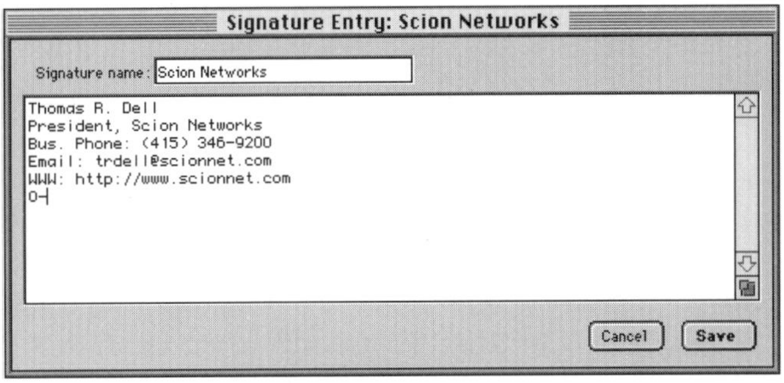

This will present you with a window in which you can type information you would like to have automatically appended to each of your messages.

You can have multiple signatures to perform different functions or to reflect different locations. For instance, you might have one signature file with your work contact information, and another containing your home address. You might create others that contain short jokes to brighten the recipient's day.

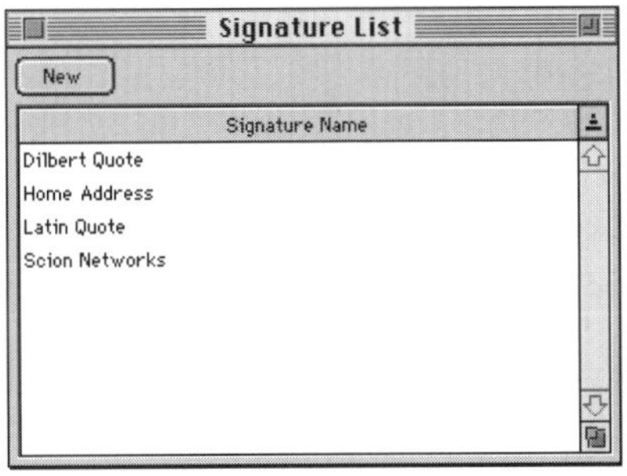

To invoke them, choose the name of the signature file that you want appended to your message in the pop-up menu.

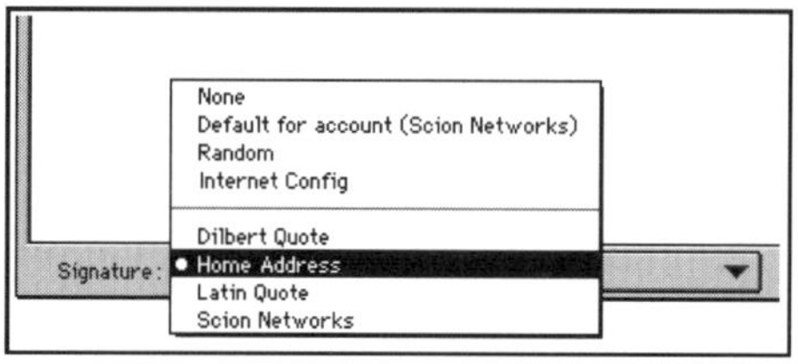

You can also choose a different default signature to be associated with each of your accounts in the Accounts preferences, which I will show you in Chapter 7.

Summary

Email is composed in the message form, which contains three basic parts: address, subject, and body. The address must be a valid email address for the system to which the message is being sent. This information can be called up automatically from an Address Book database simply by typing in a few characters of a recipient's name. The subject contains a short line that describes the contents of the message. The body contains the actual message, which can be entered in the way it is with a word processor, except that formatting and pictures cannot be embedded in the text.

In addition to text messages, email can also contain file enclosures. Claris Emailer messages can be checked for spelling before they are sent. Informative signatures can be automatically appended before they are sent as well. Incoming mail can be replied to, in which case the body of the incoming message can be appended to the body of a new message. Incoming mail can also be forwarded to another recipient, with or without additional comments.

Next we will set up and use the powerful Claris Emailer Address Book.

NOTE *Email is a great way to ask questions of people you might not ordinarily be able to contact. I could never possibly afford to spend time on the phone with my readers, but I usually have time to answer their email. Sometimes I am able to help them out. Here is one of my favorite examples:*

```
To: Thomas Dell
From: Dr. Ken ...
I bought your book Designing AppleTalk Network Archi-
tectures earlier today. It looks like a comprehensive
work.
I am a dentist. I have two PowerPC Macs in different
rooms. One for me and one for my hygienist. I use them
primarily for patient education purposes, e.g. captur-
ing images, scanning xrays and displaying them to pa-
tients, simple "Astound" presentations, etc. I want to
be able to network the two together. (The administra-
tive functions of the office run on a PC based network,
which I would like to link to the Macs eventually, but
one step at a time).
What is the simplest way to accomplish this task? Can
you direct me to a section of your book or another pub-
lication? I don't need to become a networking expert,
just able to make the connection.
Thank you for whatever help you are willing to give,
Dr. Ken
```

That's an easy one!

```
To: Dr. Ken
From: Thomas Dell
Short answer? PhoneNet. Go to the nearest computer
store and buy two Farallon PhoneNet "transceivers."
Should be no more than $25 each. Attach these to the
Printer ports on the backs of the PowerMacs. Between
them string a cable of ordinary telephone wire from the
hardware store. Dig out your Mac manual and follow the
instructions for "Personal File Sharing." That's it.
You have a LocalTalk daisy chain network. Aren't Macs
great?
Check out Page 17 in our book for the details,
Tom
```

It works!

```
To: Thomas Dell
From: Dr. Ken
I went down to Computer City over lunch. They had a 3
for the price of 2 special on the PhoneNet connections.
I hooked them all up, including the printer, and it
works!
Thanks again.
Somehow, it seemed more complex when they were setting
up our PC network.
```

I'm sure it was.

4

Your Address Book

The Address Book is one of Claris Emailer's greatest time-saving features. Without it you would have to enter a recipient's address information manually each time you sent a message. With it, most address information is entered automatically at the touch of just a few keys. The Address Book is a convenient database in which to store all the email addresses of your friends and colleagues. Here you will learn about the email addressing conventions used by different email systems, how to create addresses for individuals and groups, and how to import addresses from databases and other email applications.

Email Addressing Conventions

You can send email to users of many email systems using either of two types of addresses. One type is used by the system internally and the other is associated with the system's Internet gateway. For example, while on a LAN you might be an OfficeMail user communicating with another user who has the address "Garrett." If you were not on the LAN, you could still send messages to this user over the Internet by adding the domain name used by OfficeMail's gateway, such as "garrett@trdell.clrs.com."

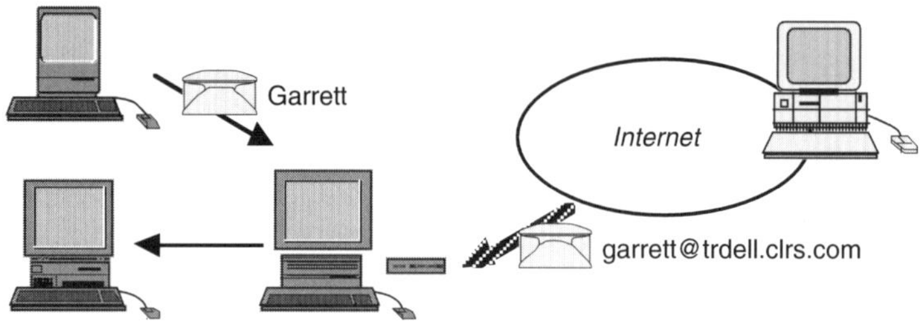

FIGURE 4-1. Email can take two different paths to the same recipient.

Addresses pertaining to proprietary systems of which you are an account holder do not contain domain names. An OfficeMail account can be as simple as "Thomas" or "Thomas Dell." An America Online screen name is a single combination of upper- and lowercase alphanumerics, such as "TRDell" or "NLau101741." CompuServe accounts usually use numbers, such as "75104,2333."

Addresses pertaining to systems of which you are not an account holder can often be reached via the Internet. Internet addresses must contain a valid domain name (e.g., "thomas@trdell.clrs.com"). The domain name part of the address comes after the "@."

Program	**What is the internal address?**	**What is the Internet address?**
America Online	TRDell	trdell@aol.com
CompuServe	75104,2333	75104,2333@compuserve.com
OfficeMail	Thomas	Thomas@trdell.clrs.com
Internet	Not applicable	trdell@trdell.com
RadioMail	Not applicable	tom_dell@radiomail.net

Internet email is based on public standards that prevent the system from becoming a Tower of Babel. Valid domain names are no longer than 26 characters and contain letters, numbers, and dashes. They are divided with periods only, no other punctuation marks, and are in lowercase (although there is no harm in uppercase letters). The addresses will usually end with one of these suffixes: .net, .com, .org, .edu, or .gov. If you have an email address for someone that does not meet these criteria, you might have taken it down incorrectly. Double-check it.

The rules are not so strict for the user name portion of the address, which comes before the "@." For instance, some punctuation, such as the underscore, can be used. It is not uncommon to see user names in a format such as "tom_dell@radiomail.net."

So, what's in a name?

(1) (3)

tom_dell@smtp.trdell.com

(2) (4)

The user name portion of the address (1) is usually a person's name or a generic account designation such as "sales" or "tech_support."

The first part of the domain address (2) is usually the name of the mail host, such as "smtp" or "pop." Most email will still be delivered if you drop this part.

The second-level domain (3) usually designates the name of the site, such as a company, school, agency, or other organization.

The top-level domain (4) usually designates the type of site. In the United States the type is most often .net (network), .com (commercial), .org (organization), .edu (education), or .gov (government). Foreign countries have additional top-level domains, such as .uk (United Kingdom).

Take Me to My Destination

A short domain name such as "aol.com" is pretty easy to work with, but not all Internet addresses are so concise. A domain name such as "smtp.cie-cais.k12.ca.edu" is more of a headache to type and offers more opportunity for making mistakes while doing so. To save you from such hassles, Claris Emailer provides a *Destinations List,* which associates shorter and more comprehensible names with Internet domain names. To see this list, choose the **Destinations** command under the **Setup** menu bar item.

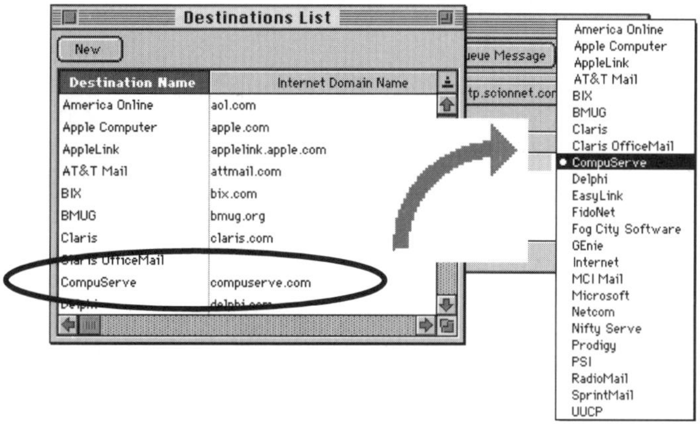

FIGURE 4-2. The Destinations List and the message form's corresponding Destination pop-up menu.

The Destinations List corresponds to the Destination field's pop-up menu that you see in the message form. Claris has thoughtfully entered many common addresses here for you, which saves you time. You need only select the **Compuserve** item in the pop-up menu, for example, to properly address a message to a CompuServe account holder, even if you do not have a CompuServe account. Claris Emailer will look up the valid domain name, "compuserve.com," in the Destinations List and automatically append it to the recipient's internal CompuServe address. It can then reach the CompuServe account holder by way of CompuServe's Internet gateway.

If you are a CompuServe account holder, there is no need to send the message over the Internet, because you can upload it to the online service directly. You do not have to use your CompuServe account to send the message, however. If you are sending most of your email over a LAN, it may be faster and more convenient to send out all of your messages through a POP account rather sending some directly to CompuServe through a slower modem connection. Make your choice by selecting either an Internet POP account or your

CompuServe account in the message form's **Send via** pop-up menu. If you choose to send via the POP account, Emailer will modify the CompuServe address to work over the Internet (i.e., "75104,2333@compuserve.com"). If you choose the **Compuserve** item, the address will not be modified (i.e., "75104,2333") and you will route the message internally.

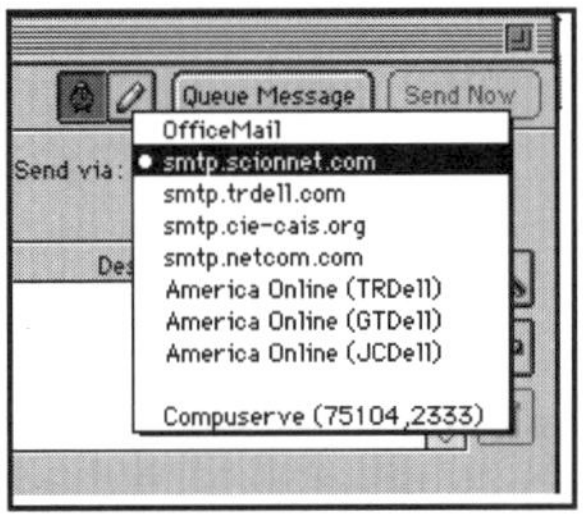

A nice thing about the Destinations List is that you can create your destinations. For instance, rather than type "smtp.cie-cais.k12.ca.edu" over and over again, I can create a destination by pressing the **New** button in the Destinations List window and typing in the appropriate information once in the resulting dialog box. I can also open this dialog box by selecting the **Destinations** item in the fly-out menu of the **New** item under the **Edit** menu bar item.

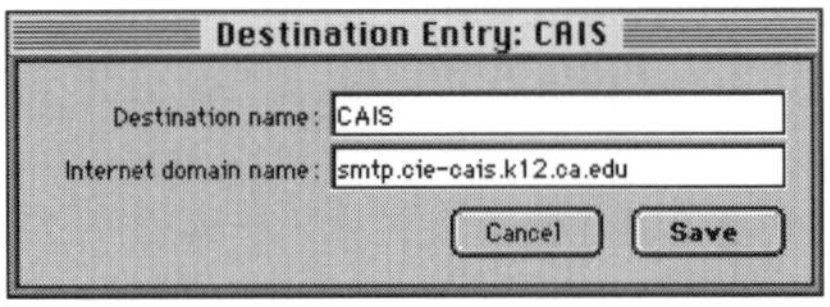

The correct domain name must be typed into the Internet domain name field of the dialog box. You can type whatever you want in the Destination name field. For instance, I chose just the acronym "CAIS," which stands for "Chinese American International School," which this domain name represents. I could just as easily have made it "Our School." Type whatever means something to you here. Now when I wish to send a message to a recipient at this site, I need only choose the new **CAIS** item in the Destination field pop-up menu of the message form.

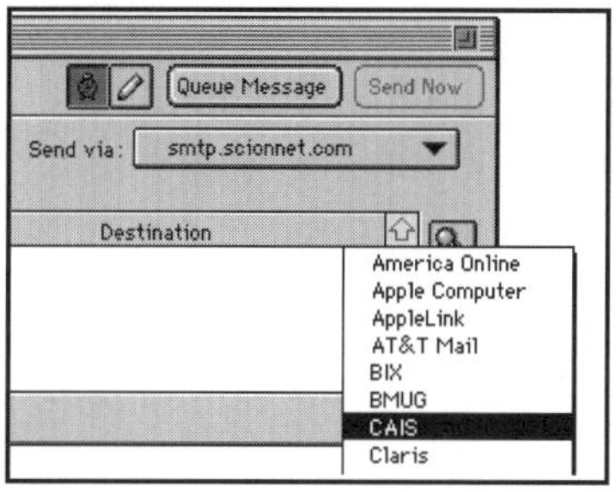

The Destinations List is particularly helpful when you work with your Address Book, as you will soon see.

Filling Your Address Book

Open your Address Book by clicking on the **Address Book** button in the Toolbar or by choosing the **Address Book** command under the **Window** menu bar item. You can also use the key combination **Command-4**.

There are several ways in which you can include an address in your Address Book. You may find that you use all of them at one time or another.

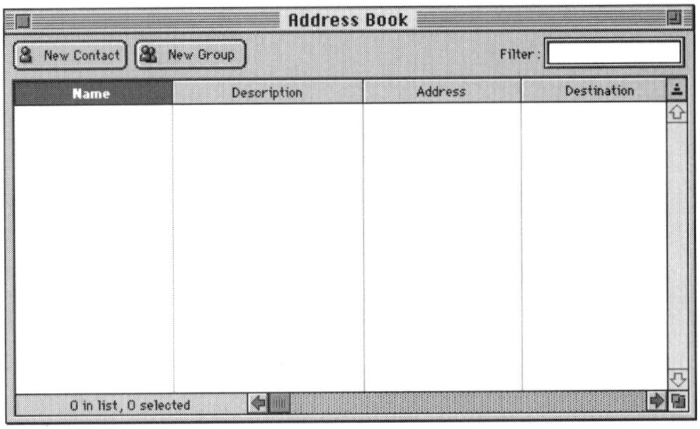

FIGURE 4-3. An empty Address Book window.

Entering Addresses Manually

To record an email address for an individual, press the **New Contact** button in the Address Book window. Alternately, select the **Contact** item in the **New** fly-out menu under the **Edit** menu bar item, or use the key combination **shift-command-N**. This will open a Contact Entry dialog box.

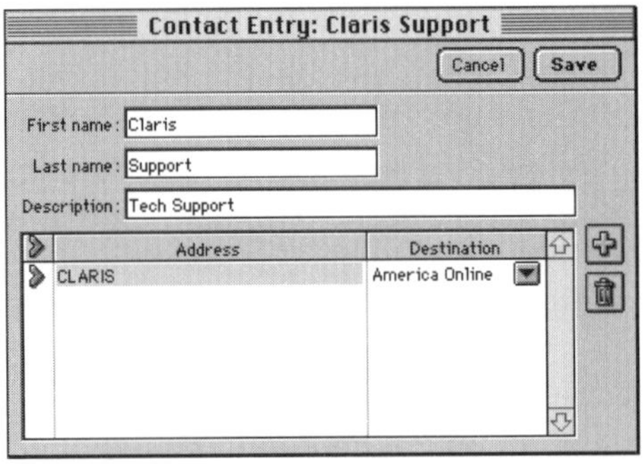

In this dialog box there are fields for email recipients' first and last names and for a short description of who they are or where they work. By way of example, here is how you might enter a technical support address for Claris Corp. Type the actual address after the arrow in the Address field. Then in the pop-up menu in the Destination field, choose the system the address belongs to. When you press the **Save** button, the new contact will appear in the Address Book window.

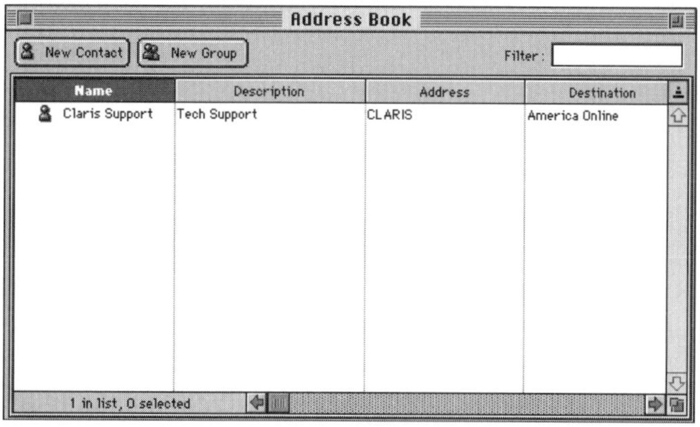

FIGURE 4-4. A new contact in the Address Book.

What if someone has more than one address? Do you want to create multiple Address Book records like this (Figure 4-5)?

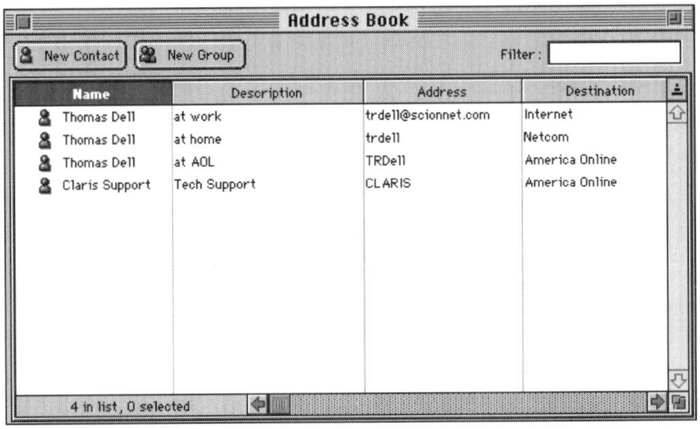

FIGURE 4-5. Multiple recipient addresses are unnecessary.

Don't be silly; that's too much work! Claris Emailer permits you to record multiple addresses with each contact, so you should only have to type the first name, last name, and description once.

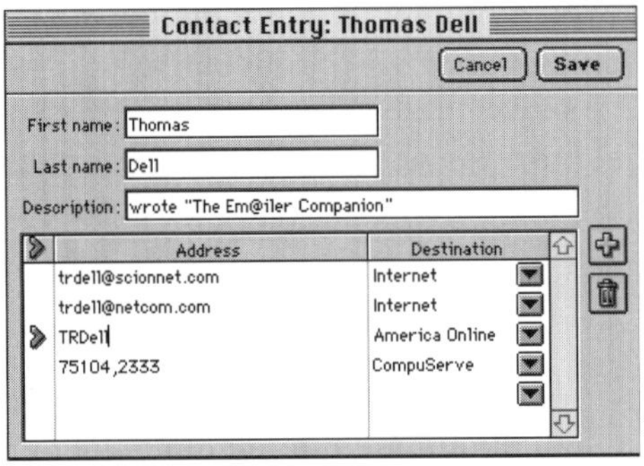

Click in the column to the left of the Address field to designate which default address Claris Emailer should use for this recipient when you type his name in the Address field of the message form. This default address is marked with the arrow.

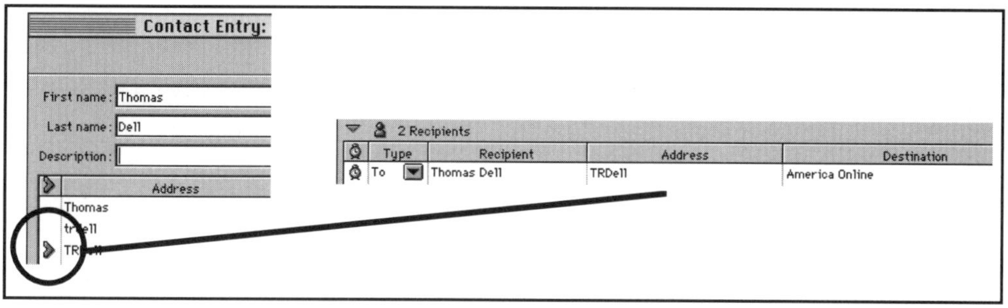

Contacts that contain multiple addresses appear in the Address Book window with triangles next to them. Clicking on the triangles expands them and reveals the additional addresses.

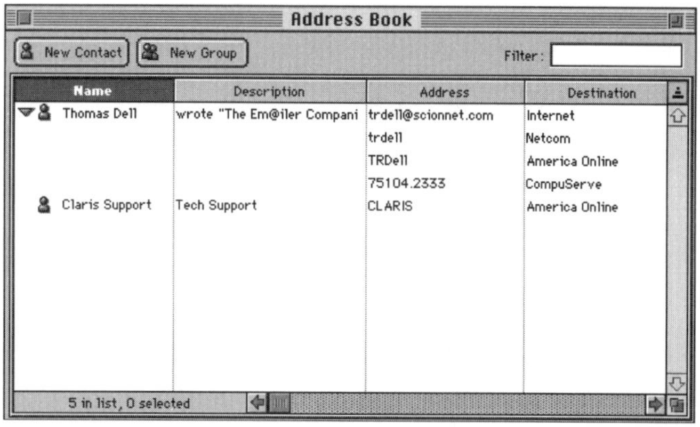

FIGURE 4-6. Contact with multiple addresses in the Address Book window.

Remember the Destinations List? The services associated with a given recipient all appear in boldface in the pop-up menu of the Destination field in the message form. You can switch between recipients' various accounts here regardless of what address was originally entered for them. Claris Emailer will make sure the correct address convention is used.

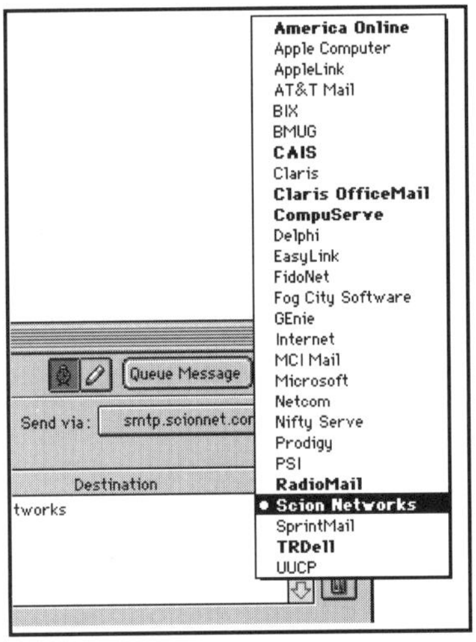

This is the most cumbersome method for entering addresses into the Address Book, but when you get an address from a business card or over the phone, you will have to use it. Once the contact is entered, updating it is a simple matter of double-clicking on it in the Address Book window and typing in the new information.

Importing Addresses from Other Email Applications

Before you make extra work for yourself by rekeying all the addresses from your old email application, let me point out that you can easily import the addresses from many applications directly into Claris Emailer.

Program	What is the Address Book?	Where is the Address Book?
America Online	Address Book	In the AOL folder, in the Online Tools folder
CompuServe Information Manager	CompuServe Addresses	In the System Folder, in the Preferences folder, in the CompuServe folder
CompuServe Navigator	CompuServe Addresses	In the Navigator folder
Eudora	Eudora Nicknames	In the System Folder, in the Eudora folder
eWorld	Address Book	In the eWorld folder, in the Online Tools folder

To do this, first choose the **Import Addresses** command under the **File** menu bar item. This will generate the standard Macintosh Select File dialog box.

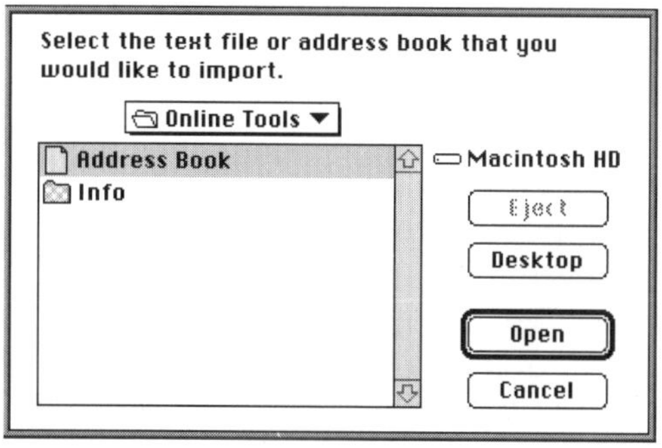

Use this dialog box to locate the address file containing the data you wish to import (e.g., America Online's "Address Book").

In a flash, Claris Emailer will pull the addresses into its Address Book. You can then manually edit the First name, Last name, and Description fields in the Contact Entry dialog boxes.

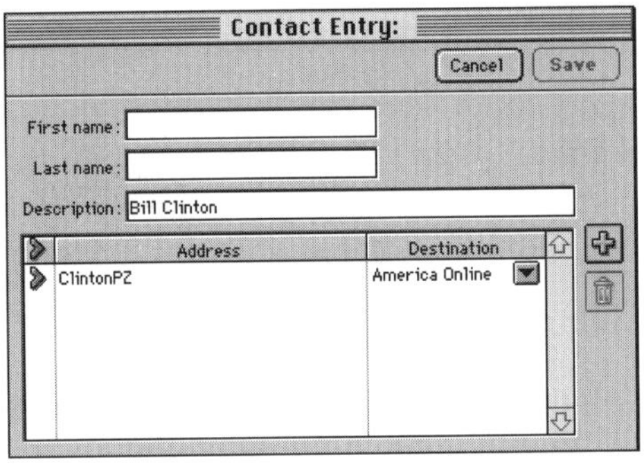

Claris Emailer can also accept addresses from other email systems such as QuickMail and Quarterdeck Mail, although this requires a few extra steps and the help of your email administrator. That is part of the next topic.

Importing Addresses from Databases

Your Claris Emailer Address Book is a database. Like other databases, it contains *records*, that is, each Contact Entry. In these records are *fields*, in this case the First name, Last name, Description, Address, and Destination fields in the Contact Entry. Because the Address Book is a database, it is easy to take the information it needs from other databases such as those used by personal information managers and other email systems. All that is needed is a format both databases can agree on. Such a format is *tab-delimited text*.

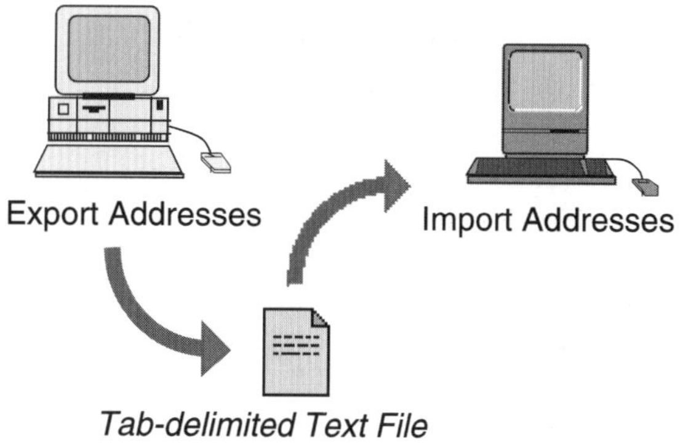

A tab-delimited text file contains database records, one on each line. Within each line of text are fields separated from each other by a *delimiter*, or tab. It looks like this:

```
Thomas♦ Dell♦TRDell♦    trdell@trdell.com↵
Garrett♦Dell♦♦     GTDell@aol.com↵
Michael♦Hytopoulos♦Ariz·U♦   ·hytopoum@u.arizona.edu↵
```

Claris Emailer can accept records from any database that can export a tab-delimited text file, which is most of them. Let's take a look at how this works with Claris FileMaker Pro.

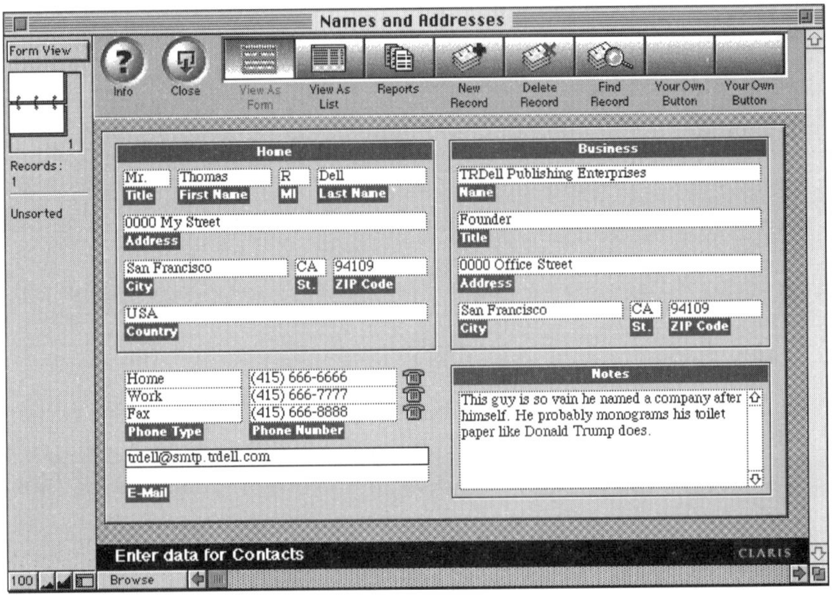

FIGURE 4-7. A Claris FileMaker Pro database record.

Figure 4-7 shows a contact database whose records contain several fields, only some of which are useful to Claris Emailer. First we tell FileMaker Pro that we want to save a tab-delimited text file by choosing the **Export Records** command under the **Import/Export** item of the **File** menu bar item.

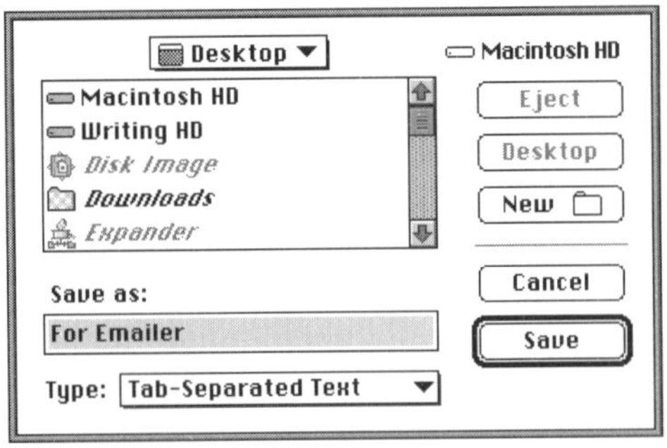

In the Macintosh Select File dialog box we choose **Tab-Separated Text** in the Type pop-up menu, name the file, and press the **Save** button.

Next we tell FileMaker Pro which fields we want in the records that will be saved in the file destined for Claris Emailer.

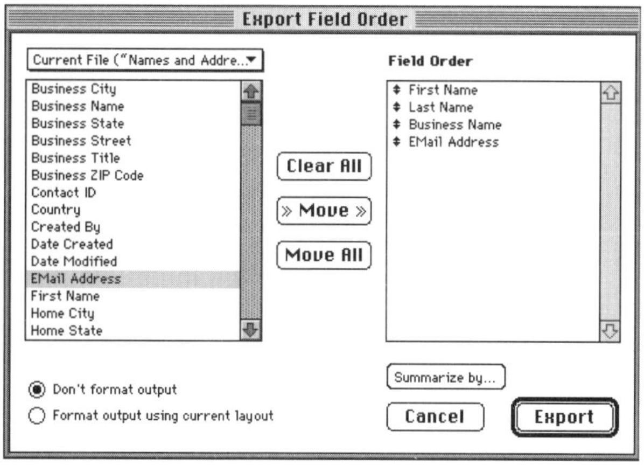

FIGURE 4-8. Choosing Email fields In FileMaker Pro.

These fields will correspond to the Contact Entry dialog box's Last name, First name, Description, and Address fields. It is easiest to press the **Clear All** button first to empty the Field Order pane on right side and then add the necessary Address fields using the **Move** button, as shown in Figure 4-8. The order counts!

Once we have saved the file, we reverse the process to bring the new records into our Address Book by choosing the **Import Addresses** command under Claris Emailer's **File** menu bar item.

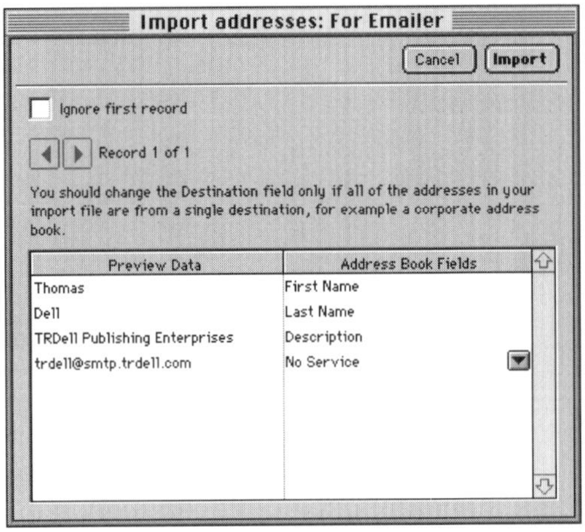

FIGURE 4-9. An imported database record.

Claris Emailer will generate a record dialog box in which we can verify that the right data will go in the right fields and add data as needed, such as the Destination (via the pop-up menu shown in Figure 4-9). When we are satisfied that all is accurate, we can press the **Import** button.

tip

This technique also works nicely for the addresses stored by email systems. Imagine that a department in your company uses CE Software's Quick-Mail. This server has an Internet gateway containing all the email addresses of your important clients, and you would like to have those addresses with you in Claris Emailer. Contact the QuickMail server's administrator and ask him to export a tab-delimited text file containing the First name, Last name, and Address fields from QuickMail's Internet gateway "MailCenter." Then simply use the import procedure.

Exporting Addresses

This is a two-way street, by the way. If you want to make your Address Book available to other email users, choose the **Export Addresses** command under the **File** menu bar item, and Claris Emailer will create a tab-delimited text file that you can give them.

Downloading Addresses from Claris OfficeMail

If you are an OfficeMail user on an AppleTalk LAN, you might have noticed the email addresses already in your Address Book when you opened it. The OfficeMail server automatically downloads the addresses of its users to Claris Emailer when you first log in to it. These addresses are established by the email administrator through the OfficeMail application, as shown in Figure 4-10.

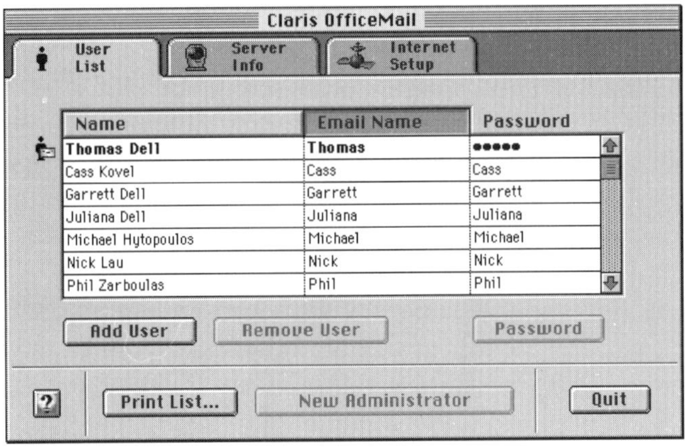

FIGURE 4-10. The OfficeMail server's User List.

This only works if you are connecting to the OfficeMail server over AppleTalk. If you are connecting over TCP/IP, the email administrator can give you a user list from which you can enter addresses manually.

NOTE

*The list you see here was generated by Claris OfficeMail's **Print List** command.*

CLARIS OfficeMail User List **Saturday, February 15, 1997**
Server Name: OfficeMail Server

Name	Email Name	Password*
Thomas Dell	**Thomas**	●●●●●
Juliana Dell	Juliana	Juliana
Garrett Dell	Garrett	Garrett
Michael Hytopoulos	Michael	Michael
Cass Kovel	Cass	Cass
Nick Lau	Nick	Nick
Phil Zarboulas	Phil	Phil

Note that "Thomas" appears in boldface and his password is replaced by bullets. All others are in a plain typeface and their passwords are visible. Because these users have not yet logged in to the server for the first time and have therefore not established new passwords, as we discussed in Chapter 2.

Copying Addresses from Messages

A more impromptu way to get data into your Address Book is to grab addresses from your incoming messages, which you can do in several ways. One way is to use the **Add** button (+) that appears next to the sender's name in the message form.

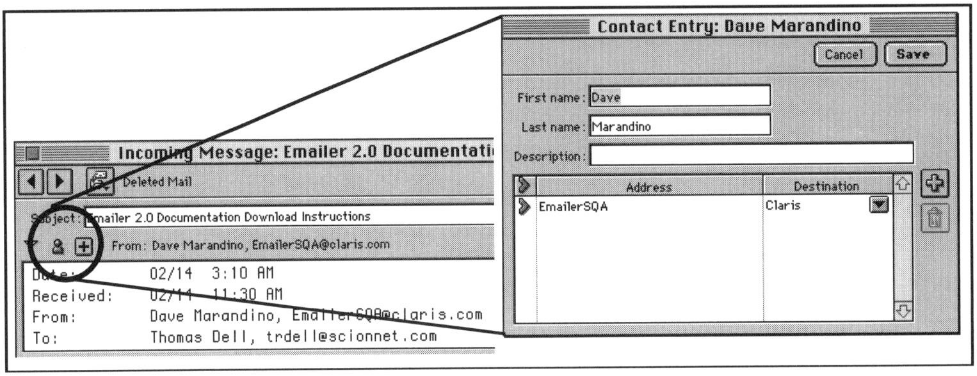

This will open a Contact Entry dialog box and paste the address into it. Add something to the Description field if you want to; then press the **Save** button.

The address you want will not always be the sender's address, however. In that case, you can add the address from anywhere in a message's text by highlighting it and then selecting the **Copy to Address Book** command under the **Edit** menu bar item.

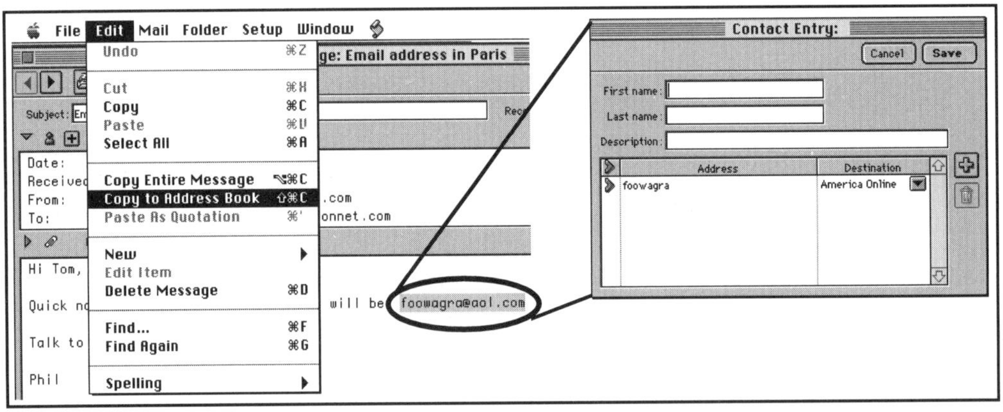

This will open a Contact Entry dialog box and paste the address into it.

You can also use Macintosh Drag-and-Drop to collect addresses. This feature is built in to System 7.5 and is available as an extension on older Mac OS's such as System 7.1. To use Drag-and-Drop, highlight the address you want in the message form and drag it into the Address Book window.

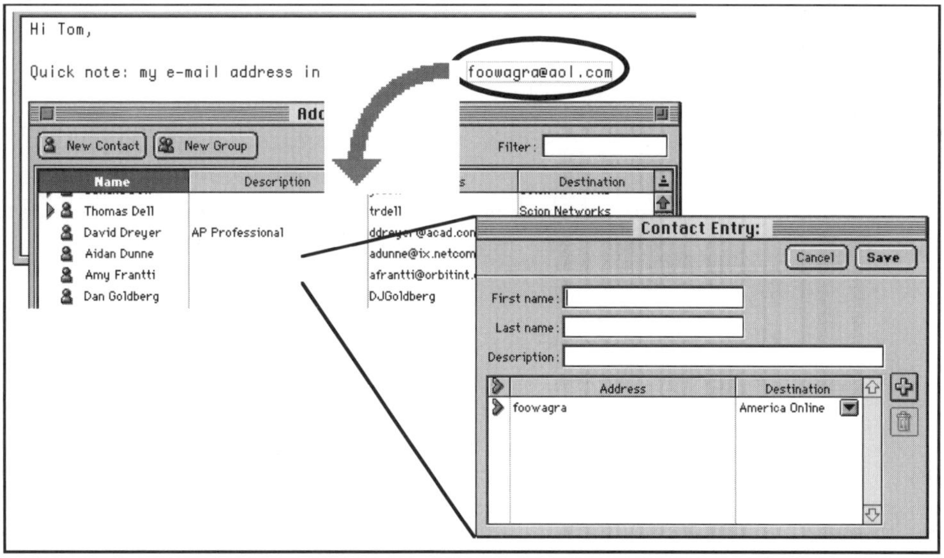

Like the previous command, this will open a Contact Entry dialog box and paste the address into it.

Macintosh Drag-and-Drop is handy for moving data between applications as well. For instance, you might drag an address from the Address Book into a ClarisWorks or Claris HomePage document. It will appear within a Hypertext Markup Language (HTML) Universal Resource Locator (URL), making it handy for use in World Wide Web (WWW) publishing.

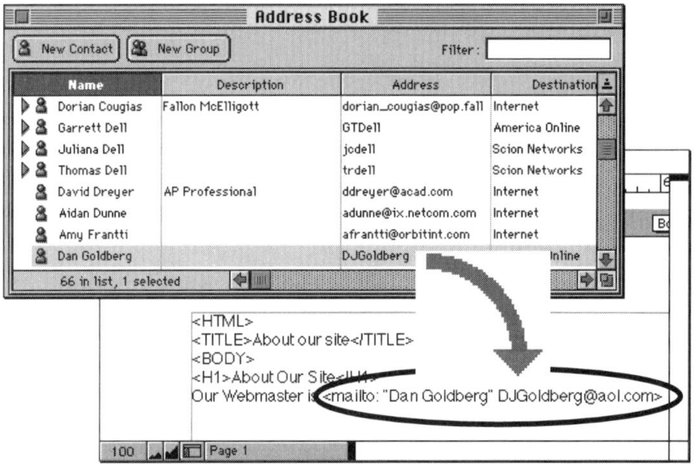

tip *The HTML tag for an address link is "<mailto:"address@domain.name">Email me</A>."*

If you have the Clipping extension that is part of System 7.5 and newer systems, you can also drag addresses from the Address Book onto the Desktop and vice versa. Doing this creates *desktop clippings,* which can be dragged into other applications or exchanged with other users for inclusion in their Address Books.

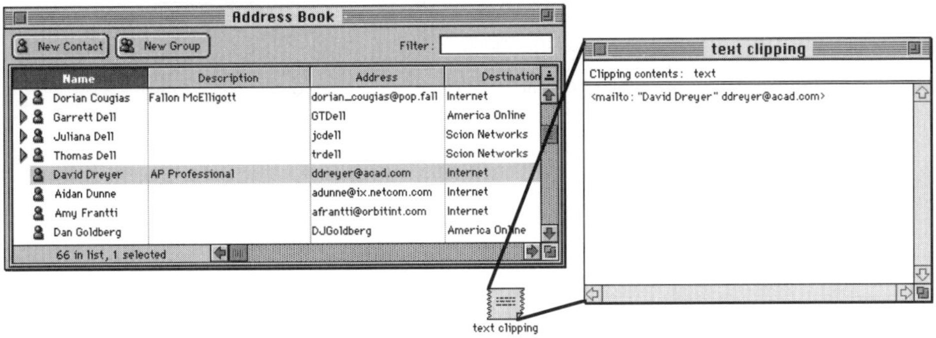

Finally, you can use this feature to drag addresses from the Address Book into the Address field of your Claris Emailer message forms.

Creating Address Groups

When you want to send email to many recipients, even Claris Emailer's quick controls become cumbersome. To overcome this, the Address Book allows you to make group entries permitting you to use just one address to contact multiple recipients.

First, press the **New Group** button in the Address Book window. You can also select the **Group** item in the fly-out menu of the **New** command under the **Edit** menu bar item, or use the key combination **shift-command-G**. This will open a Group Entry dialog box, in which you give the group a name and a description.

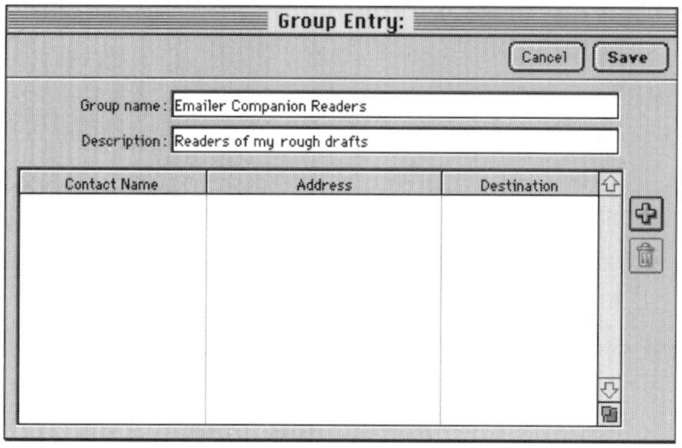

Next, enter addresses for all the members of the group by pressing the **Add** button (+) to create each new line. You can type in the information manually, or drag-and-drop the addresses from the Address Book window. You can also select all the addresses that are to be added while holding down the **Command** key, and then press the **New Group** button. All of the selected addresses will be added to the group.

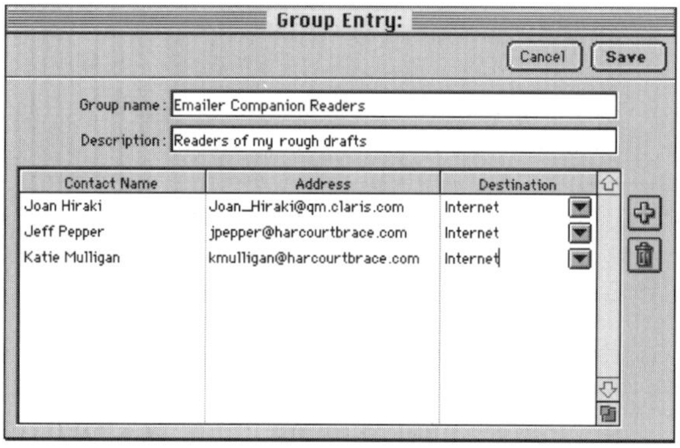

Group addresses and contact addresses are not linked, which means, on the downside, that if an individual is a member of several groups and his address changes, you will have to update it manually in both his contact record and in all the group records of which he is a part. On the upside, when you delete a recipient from a group, you do not also delete the user from the Address Book.

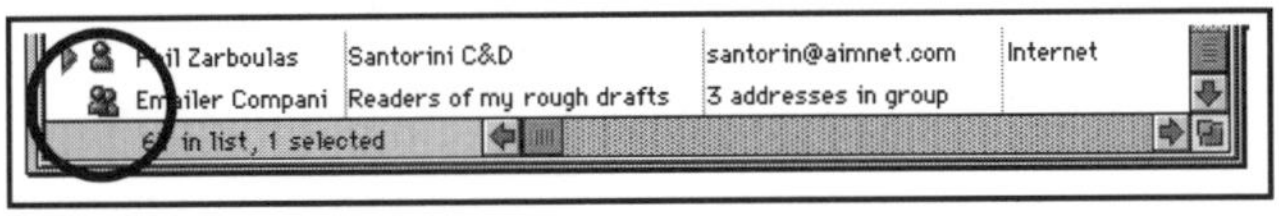

You can distinguish a group entry from a contact entry in the Address Book by their different icons.

Viewing Your Address Book

Now you should know how to set up your Address Book the way you want it. You also have a few options for how you view its contents.

The **Name** and **Description** headings in the Address Book window are also buttons.

If you press the **Name** button, the contents of the Address Book will be sorted in alphabetical order by recipients' last names. If you press the **Description** button, the contents are sorted in alphabetical order by description. You can designate the sort in ascending or descending order by clicking on the **Sort** button located at the far right of the Address Book's heading row.

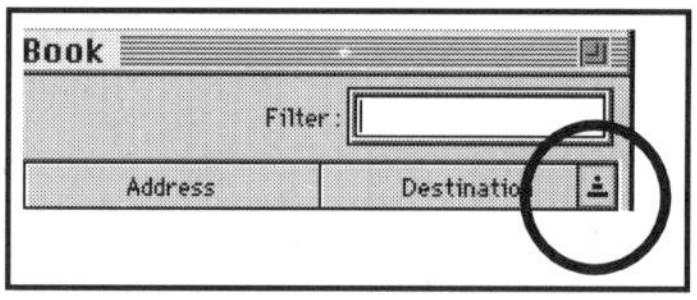

Finally, you can use the Filter field to gather together all the addresses associated with a given name. For instance, if I want to see the addresses I have for recipients at AP PROFESSIONAL, I sort by Description and type "AP" into the Filter field.

Only addresses associated with the letters "A-P" are now shown in the Address Book window.

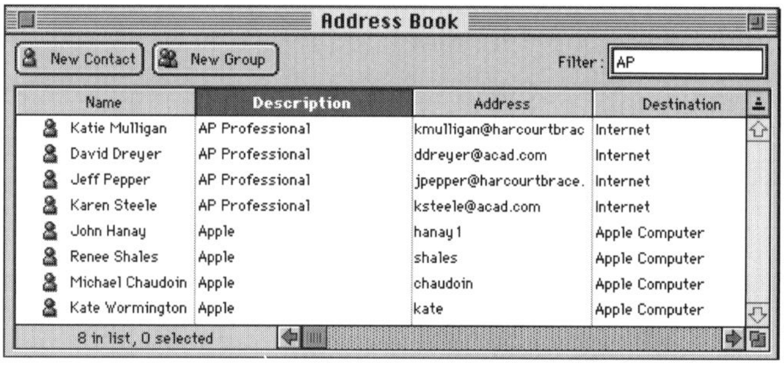

In the illustration, note that this includes addresses for "Apple." To narrow my sort to just AP PROFESSIONAL employees, I should type "AP (space)."

Summary

The *Address Book* is a database of addresses for the people to whom you regularly send email, whether via America Online, CompuServe, or OfficeMail, or the Internet. The service providers and their particular addressing requirements can be stored in a *Destinations List*. You can add email addresses manually, copy sender's addresses from incoming messages, or drag-and-drop them from text. You can also import addresses from other email applications or any database that can export its records into a *tab-delimited text file*. Multiple recipients can be arranged in *groups*. All addresses can be viewed and sorted in various ways.

5

Working with Mail Actions

I have a new motto for you: "Anything that is worth doing is worth getting Claris Emailer to do for you!" Here I will show you how to use Claris Emailer's handy *Mail Actions* feature to automate repetitive tasks and filter incoming messages for your convenience.

Creating Mail Actions

At its simplest, creating a mail action is a two-step process that involves writing a basic "if-then" statement: "if" this *cri-*

terion is met, "then" perform this *action*. In the abstract, the idea can be expressed as:

```
If X is true, then do Y.
```

To create an automated routine, choose the **Mail Actions** command under the **Setup** menu bar item. This will open the Mail Actions List window.

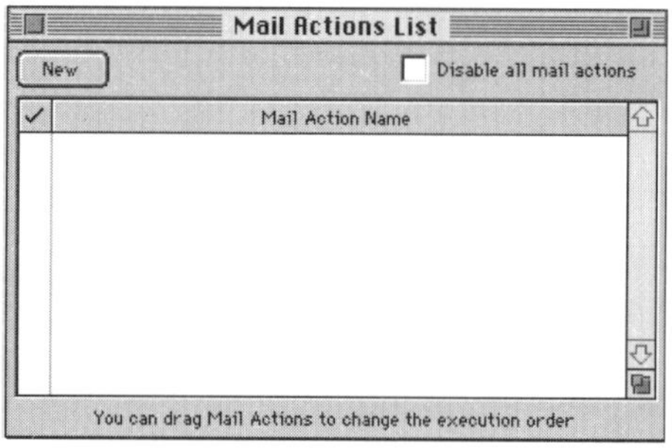

Here press the **New** button or choose **Mail Action** in the fly-out menu of the **New** command under the **Edit** menu bar item. This will open the Mail Action Entry dialog box.

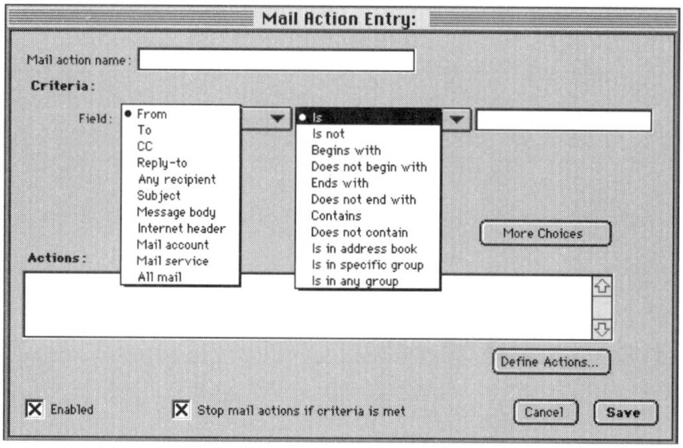

FIGURE 5-1. The Mail Action Entry dialog box.

In the Mail Action Entry dialog box is a field for naming the routine along with several fields for defining criteria, as shown in Figure 5-1. Once you have established the "if" part of the statement, press the **Define Actions** button to establish the "then" part.

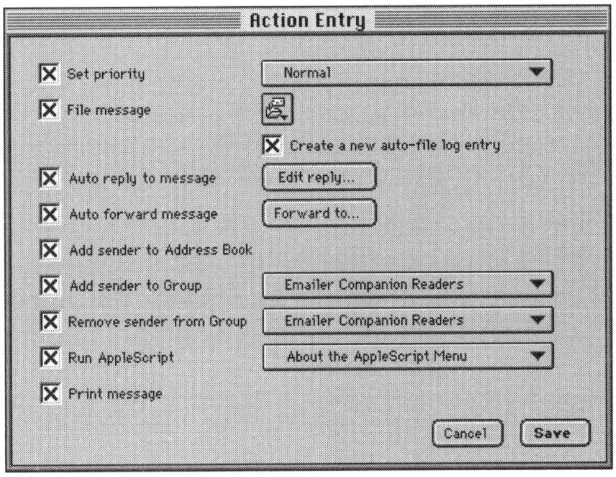

FIGURE 5-2. The Action Entry dialog box.

This will open the Action Entry dialog box, in which there are many things you can direct Claris Emailer to do with your messages. You can prioritize them, file them, reply to them, forward them, print them, or process them further using AppleScript. Mail actions are performed after all email has been downloaded during a connection.

A Mail Actions Sampler

To apply this concept, let's create a few simple mail actions that you can put to use right away. I came up with my own names for these. You can call them whatever you like.

File-O-Matic

This is an "I'll get to it later" mail action. I use it mostly with the email I get from mailing lists. Although I receive many messages from these sources daily, I only get around to reading them on weekends. Rather than have them fill up my Browser window in the meantime, I file them as they come in.

I have created a mail action for handling the email I get from Raven System Ltd.'s great Emailer-Talk mailing list. Since these digests always come from the same sender, I can set my criterion as shown in Figure 5-3 to begin the statement "if the **From** field in the incoming message **is emailer-digest-request@eskimo.com . . .**"

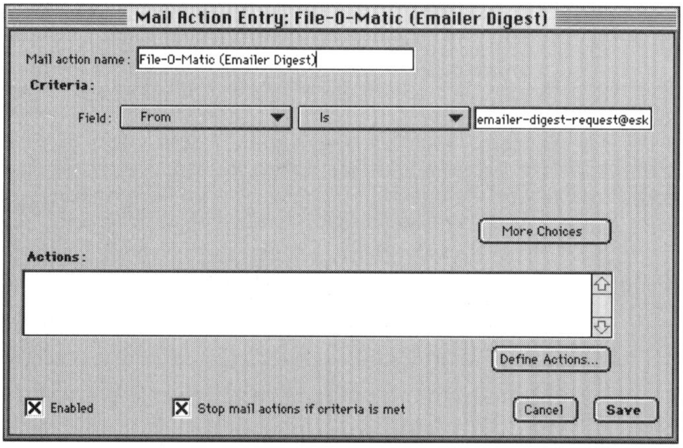

FIGURE 5-3. File-O-Matic criteria.

Now I press the **Define Actions** button to finish the statement, as shown in Figure 5-4. In the Actions Entry dialog box I click on the **File Messages** check box to enable the **Select a folder** pop-up menu. In the pop-up menu I choose the folder I previously created for this purpose: "Emailer digest."

The **Create an entry in the Logs folder** check box is selected by default. It directs Claris Emailer to create a log file in which I can see when and where it filed my messages.

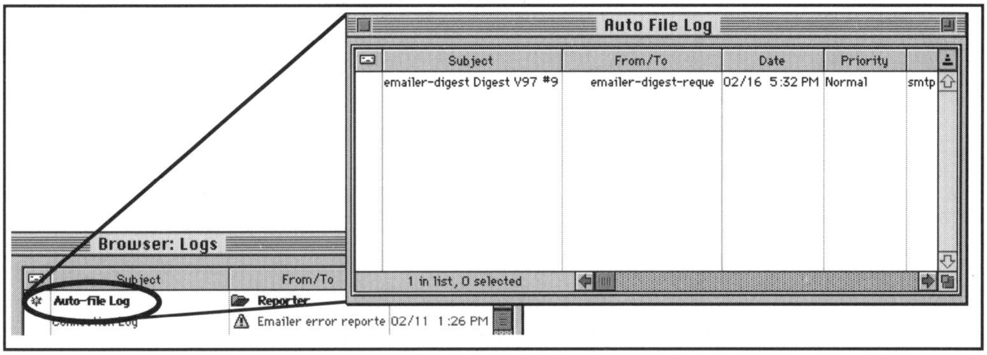

When I press the **Save** button, my statement is complete: " . . . then **File message** in the folder **Emailer digest**."

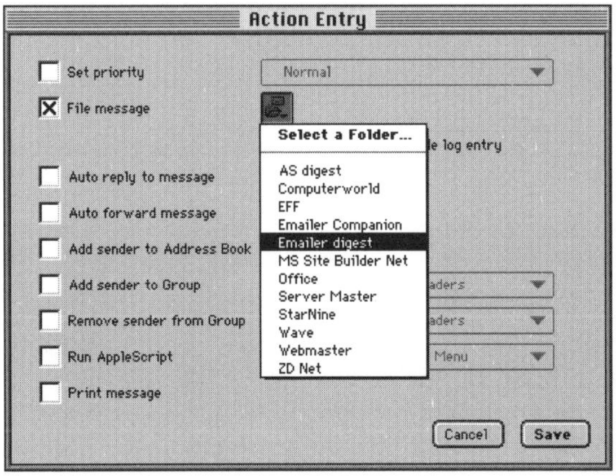

FIGURE 5-4. File-O-Matic Action Entry.

I can now review both the criteria and the action in the Mail Action Entry dialog box.

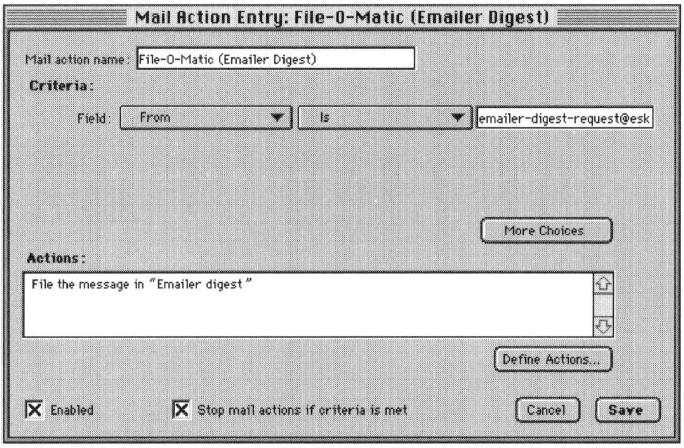

FIGURE 5-5. Complete File-O-Matic.

When I press the **Save** button, the routine is added to the Mail Actions List and is ready to run.

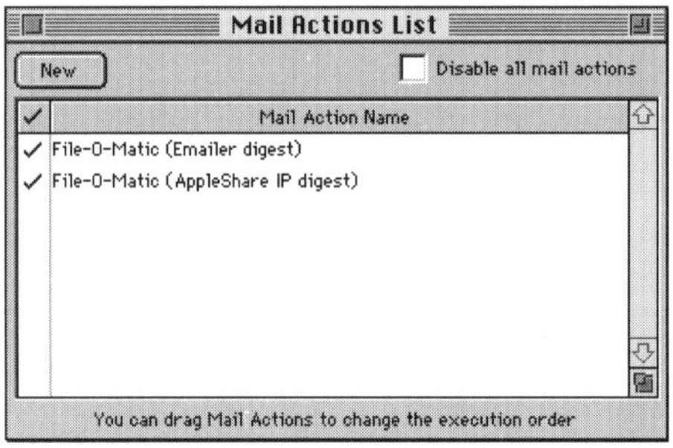

tip *Would you like to join the Emailer-Talk mailing list? You can sign up for it by visiting Raven System Ltd.'s WWW page. The URL is: "http://www.eskimo.com/~ravensys/emailer-talk.html."*

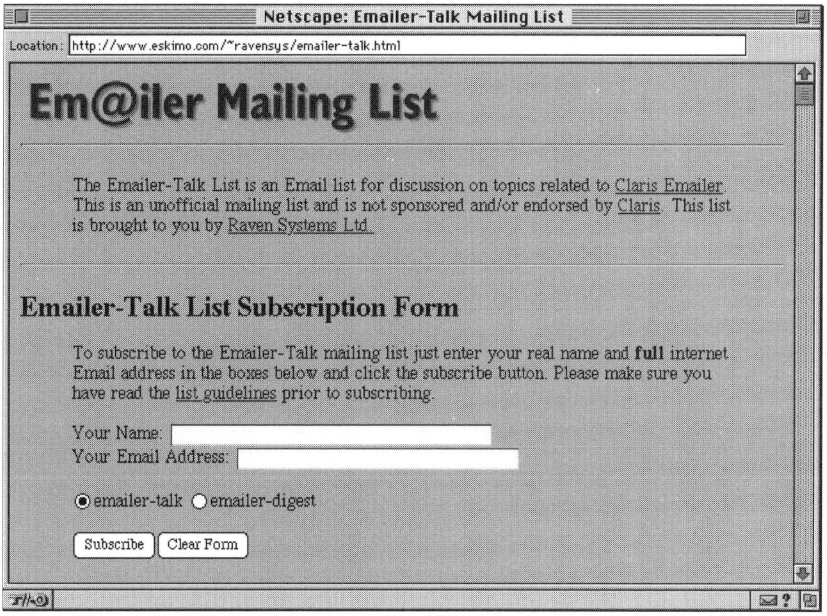

This mailing list is independent of Claris Corp. It is owned by Erik C. Thauvin, "ravensys@eskimo.com. "

Gone Fishing

Next let me show you a mail action I use when I am not around to answer my email but want its senders to know I received it. First, I set the criterion in the Mail Actions Entry dialog box, as shown in Figure 5-6 to begin the statement with "when **All Mail** is received . . ."

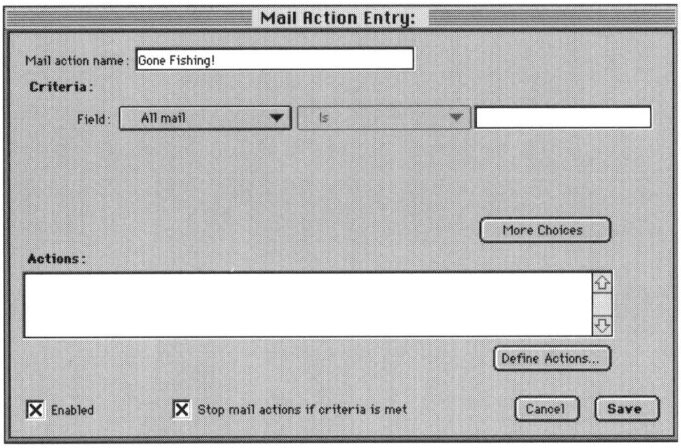

FIGURE 5-6. Gone Fishing criteria.

Then I establish the action **Auto reply to message** in the Action Entry dialog box, as shown in Figure 5-7 to finish the statement.

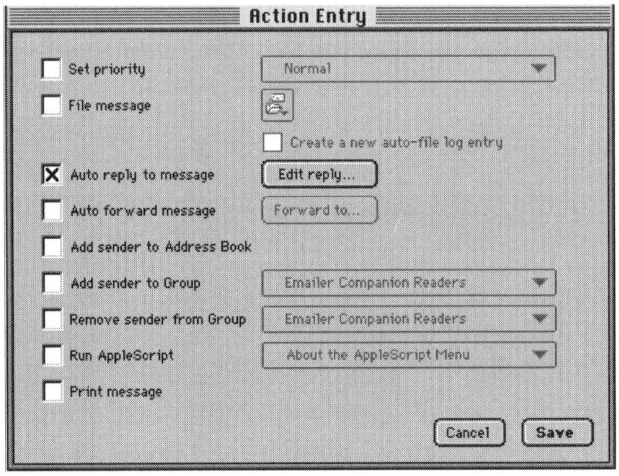

FIGURE 5-7. Gone Fishing action.

Another step is still required. I have to give Claris Emailer something to reply with, so I press the **Edit reply** button to open a dialog box in which I can create a suitable message, as shown in Figure 5-8.

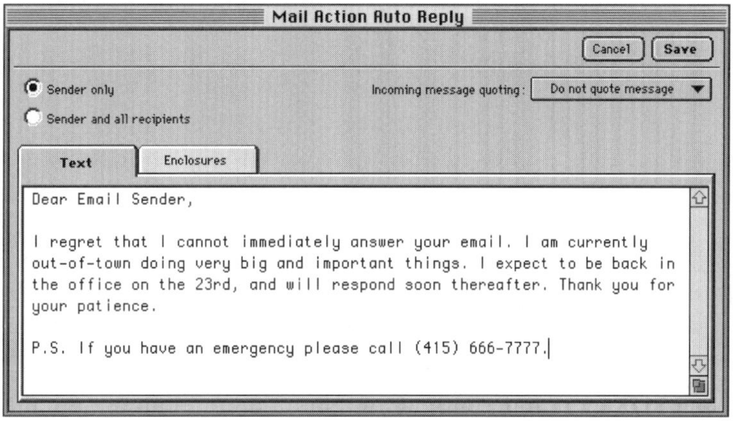

FIGURE 5-8. Auto Reply message.

Now my email is covered until I return from Canada with my quota of Northern Pike. Of course, this is not an action I want performed all the time, so I click on its item in the Mail Actions List to disable it until the next time I am on the way to the airport.

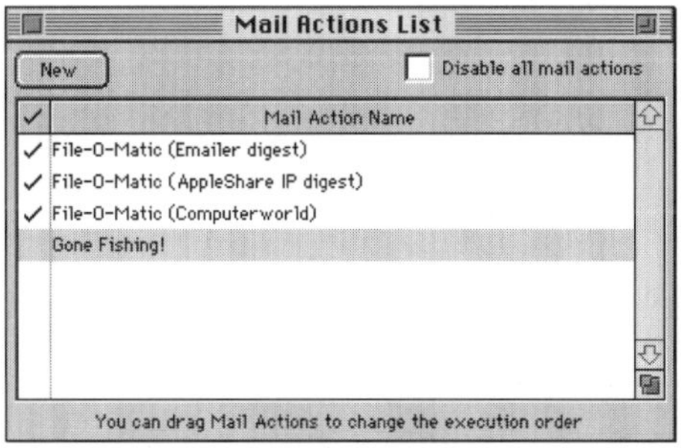

Buck Passer

Another nice thing about mail actions: The proverbial buck need not stop here. Instead, you can pass it to other recipients.

Have you ever had clients, customers, or acquaintances who waste a lot of your time? I thought so. Me, too. I depend on my secretary to screen their phone calls and determine if I should respond to them immediately. Often they are just as happy to talk to her. With this mail action I can also direct my secretary to screen my email.

First, I set the criteria. In this case it is "if the message's **From** field **Contains dufusmueller** . . ." (That is a fictitious name. No offense intended to any real Dufusmuellers out there.)

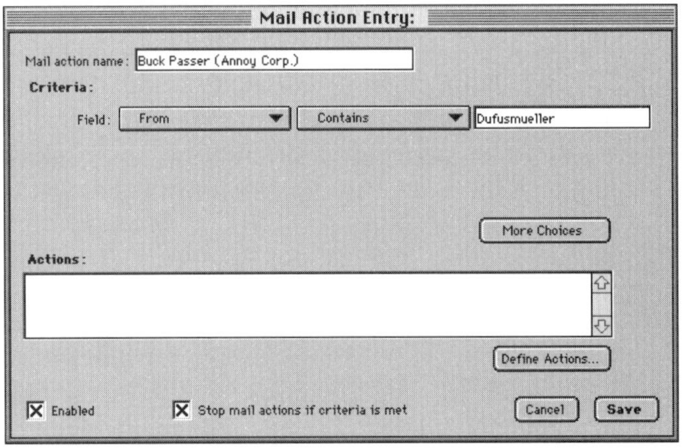

FIGURE 5-9. Buck Passer criteria.

Next, I complete the statement by choosing the **Auto forward message** action in the Action Entry dialog box, as shown in Figure 5-10.

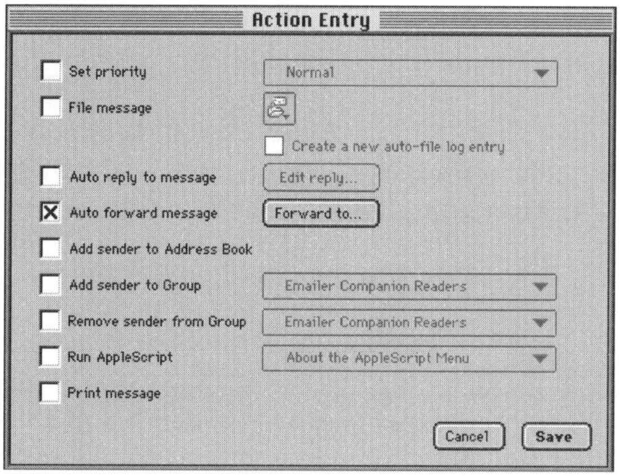

FIGURE 5-10. Buck Passer action.

I have to tell Claris Emailer where to forward the irritating little notes, so I press the **Forward to** button in the Actions Entry dialog box and enter my secretary's email address in the dialog box that results.

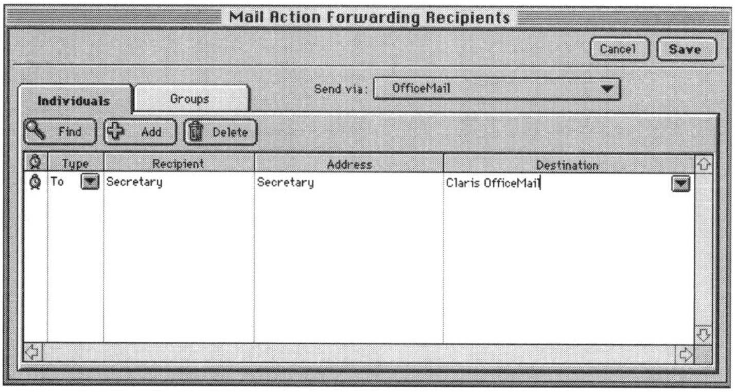

Now she can read it and let me know if it is important.

Let's reverse the idea. What if the email from a certain source is so important that you want to make sure someone responds to it even while you are away on important business (i.e., fishing)? This brings up an important point: Messages can be processed by multiple actions.

For example, imagine I have created a Buck Passer action to make sure that all email from Mr. Pompous of Big Bucks, Inc. is immediately forwarded to secretary.

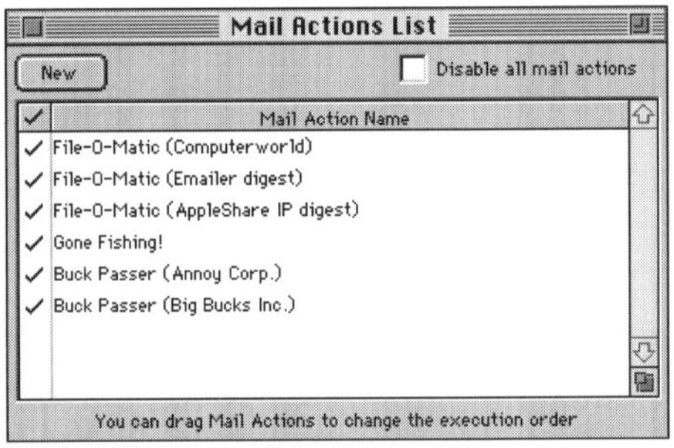

The order in which the action is listed in the Mail Actions List is significant. Remember that the criteria of my Gone Fishing action called for the processing of *all* incoming mail. If that action is listed before my Buck Passer routine, it will process any email coming from Mr. Pompous and my secretary will never know about it. Therefore, I need to list the Buck Passer action in the beginning in order for Claris Emailer first to see if any incoming messages are from Mr. Pompous. If so, it will forward them. If not, it will pass them on to the Gone Fishing mail action. You can change the order of these items by clicking on them and dragging them around in the Mail Actions List.

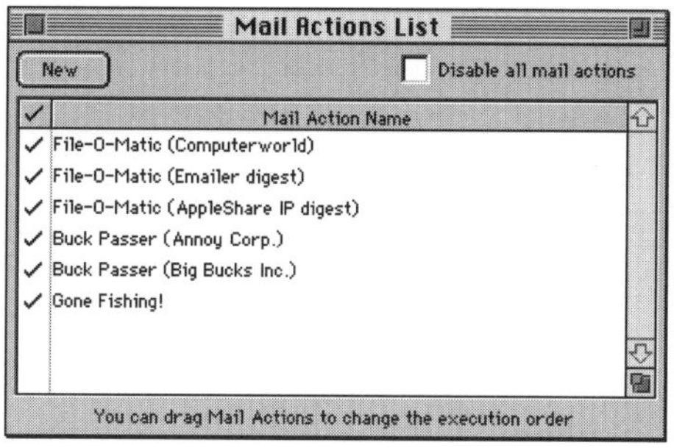

What if I want my secretary to get the message and I also want Mr. Pompous to get my Gone Fishing reply, just in case it takes a while for my secretary to get back to him?

As it stands now, Emailer will evaluate incoming email to determine if "pompous" is part of the From address field. If so, it will forward the message to my secretary and do nothing further with it, because the **Stop mail actions if criteria is met** check box in the Mail Actions Entry dialog box, shown in Figure 5-11, was selected by default when I created the routine. If I deselect this check box, the Buck Passer action will forward the message to my secretary, and then the Gone Fishing action will reply to it automatically.

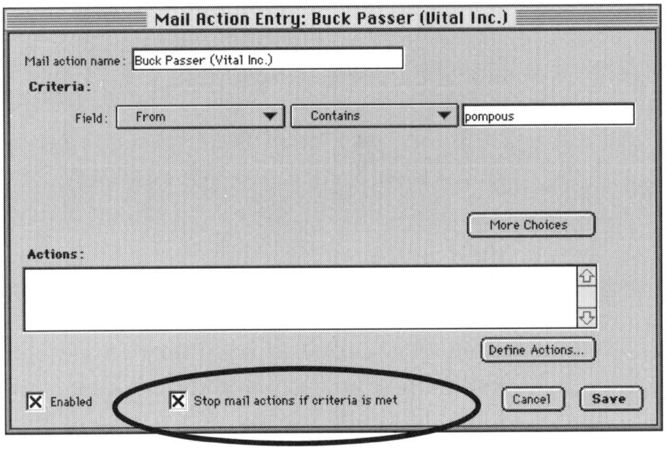

FIGURE 5-11. Stop mail actions if criteria is met check box.

Info Gleaner

In addition to processing email using multiple actions, Claris Emailer can process messages using multiple criteria within an action. Doing so requires a new type of criterion: The *test*. A test criterion provides for two actions, one for when the result is *true* and one for when it is *false*. It can be expressed abstractly like this:

```
If X is true, then do Y.
If X is false, then do Z.
```

I take advantage of this ability with an action that I use to search for key words in incoming email. Here is a somewhat esoteric but nevertheless impressive example of how it works.

I have an interest in earthquakes, which I guess is only natural when you live in San Francisco. Because of this, I subscribe to an earthquake notification service that sends me a message every time a temblor of magnitude five or higher is felt in the United States or one of magnitude six or higher is felt anywhere in the world.

I am interested whenever a major earthquake occurs, but not enough to read every message I get from the mailing list. I am concerned, however, whenever a major earthquake occurs near my friends or family members. I want to be alerted when this happens, so I set up what I call an Info Gleaner action, so-called because it will glean several pieces of information from a message and make a decision based on them.

To create this action I need to direct Claris Emailer to perform several tests on an incoming message, not just one. I can do this by pressing the **More choices** button in the Mail Actions Entry dialog box, which will modify the dialog box as shown in Figure 5-12 to permit me to enter up to 20 different tests for any message.

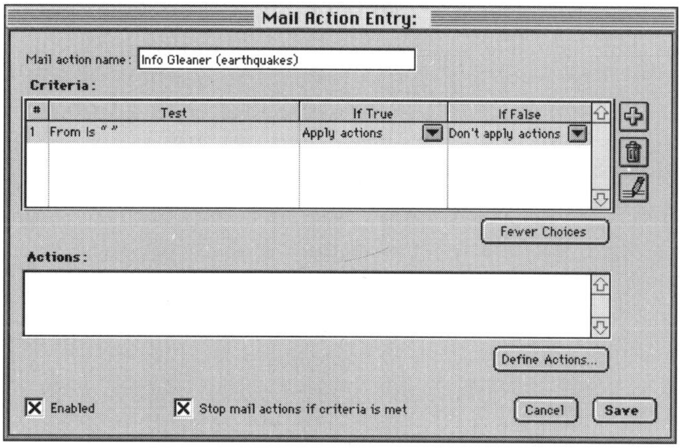

FIGURE 5-12. Mail Action Entry window with more choices.

If I press the **Fewer Choices** button, the dialog box will be returned to its former single-criterion state.

Like other dialog boxes in Claris Emailer, this one contains buttons for **Add** (+), **Delete** (trash can), and **Edit** (pencil).

First I limit my criteria to messages coming from the earthquake notification service. I can establish this test by pressing the **Edit** button or just double-clicking on the first line to open a Mail Action Criteria dialog box. This dialog box contains fields for the same type of data that I set in the Mail Actions Entry dialog box in the earlier examples.

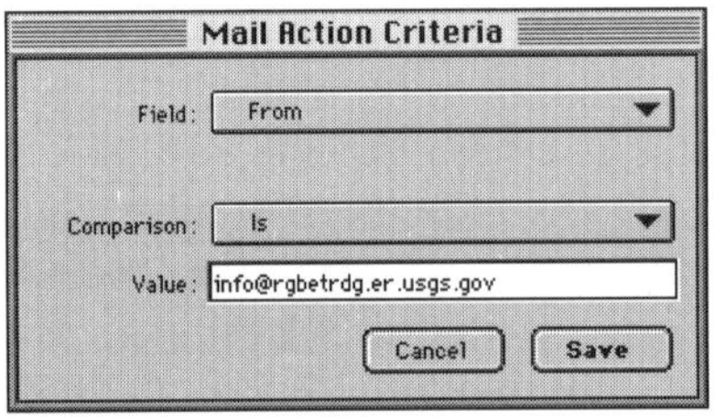

I make the first criterion "if the **From** field **is info@rgbetrdg.er.usgs.gov** . . ." In a more basic action I would press the **Define Actions** button after this to establish the "then" part of the statement. In using advanced criteria, however, I want Claris Emailer to go through a few more steps before performing the final action.

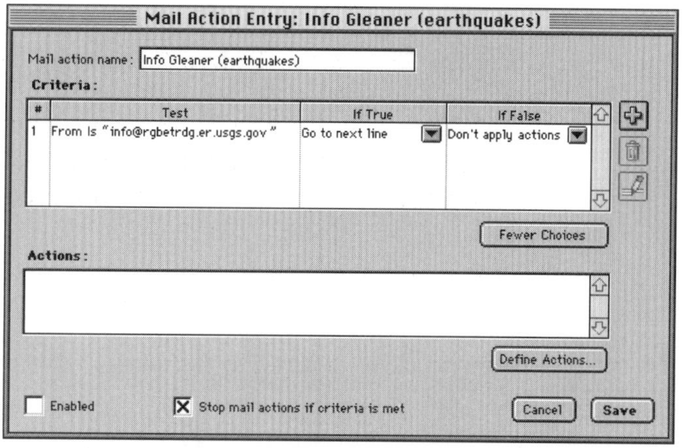

FIGURE 5-13. A test.

Each step must make provisions for both a true and a false answer. In this case, when the "if" statement is true, I direct Claris Emailer to continue processing the message by choosing **Go to the next line** in the pop-up menu under the If True heading. When the statement is false, there is no point in continuing to process the message, so I choose **Don't apply actions** in the pop-up menu under the If False heading. No further tests will be applied.

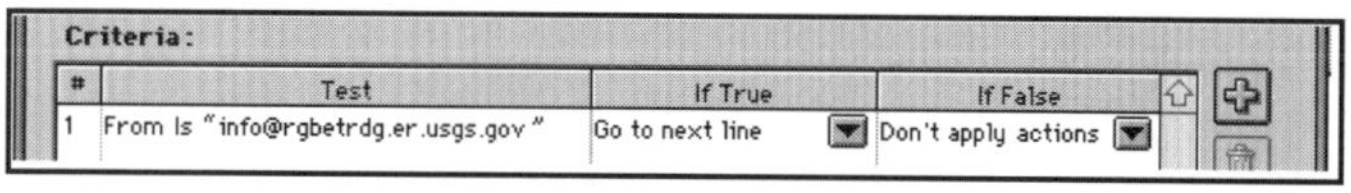

When messages come in from this mailing list, they contain information about earthquakes all over the world. The epicenters are identified by their latitude and longitude and the nearest town, city, country, or geographical feature.

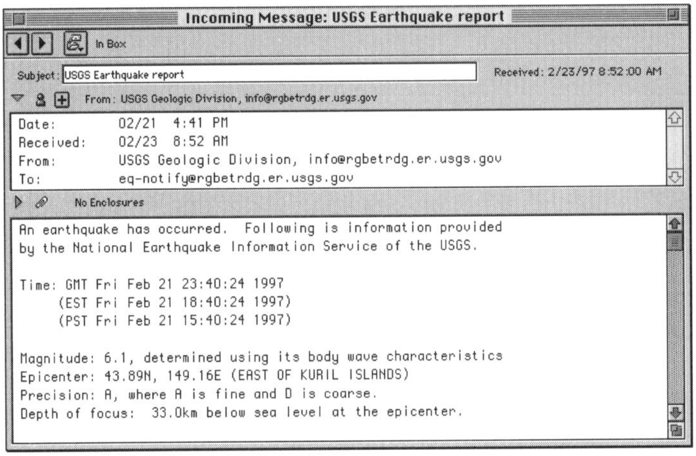

An earthquake of magnitude six or greater in Chile does not concern me much. An earthquake of the same magnitude in California, where I live and have relatives, does. So does an earthquake in Shanghai, China, where I have friends. I want Claris Emailer to do something special with messages containing either the word "California" or "China."

To do this, I make the next test "if the **Message body Contains** 'California,' then **Apply actions** [which are as yet unspecified]. If it does not, **Go to the next line** and the next test." My third test is "if the **Message body Contains** 'China,' then **Apply actions**. If it does not, **Don't apply actions**." At that point there is no need to examine the message further.

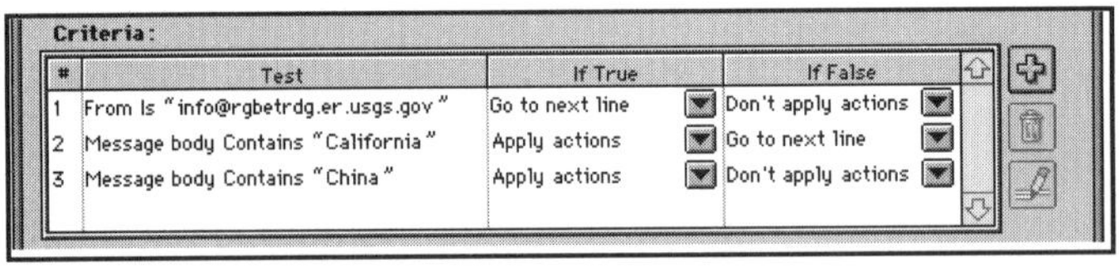

Once I have applied all the tests necessary to glean the information I want, I tell Claris Emailer how I want the appropriate messages handled. In this case, I want to be alerted by the special nature of the message, so I select the **Set Priority**

check box in the Actions Entry dialog box and pick "Urgent" in the pop-up menu.

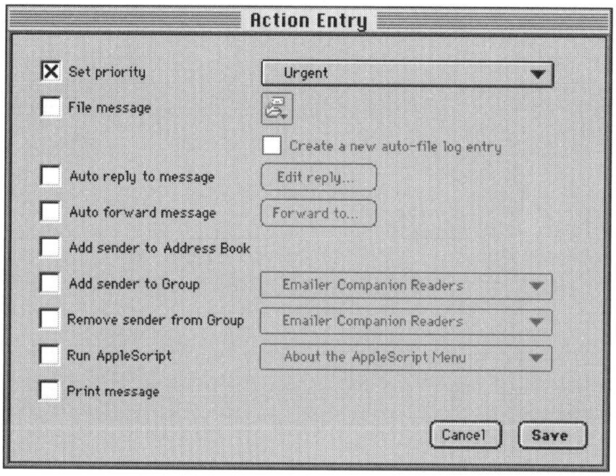

FIGURE 5-14. The final action.

Now the messages of specific interest to me will be listed as "Urgent" in the Browser window.

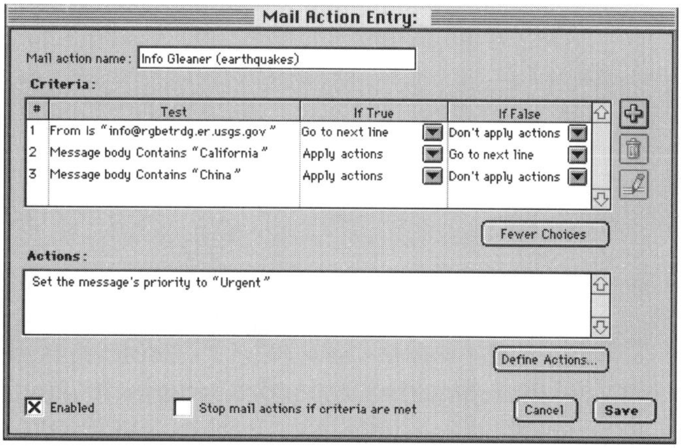

FIGURE 5-15. Info Gleaner mail action.

tip *Would you like to join the Major Earthquake Notification Service? You can sign up for it by visiting U.S. Geological Survey's WWW page. The URL is: "http://geology.usgs.gov/eq/eq_subscribe.html"*

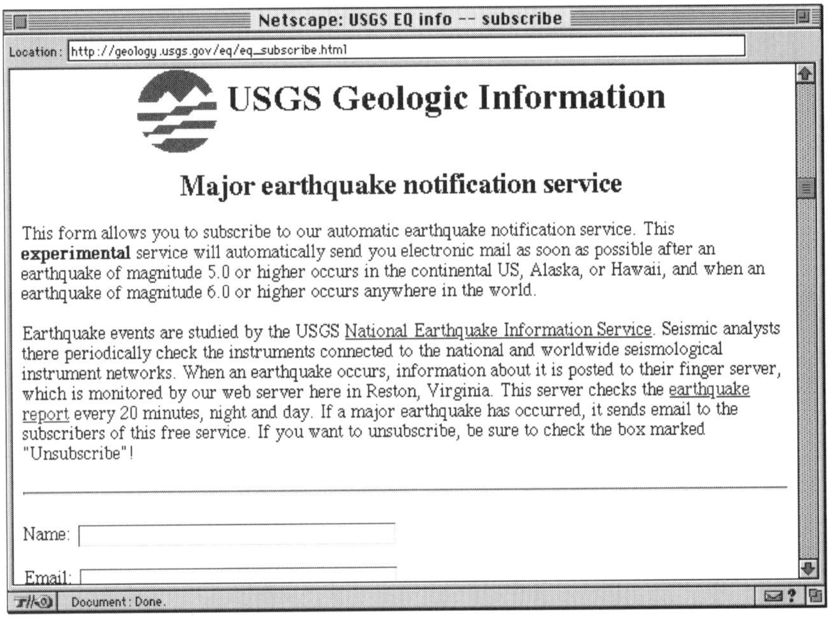

It is maintained by Peter Schweitzer, "pschweitzer@usgs.gov."

Email on Demand (EOD)

This routine is a good example of how several mail actions can be used in conjunction. It directs Claris Emailer to respond to certain message queries by returning specific files, much like a fax-on-demand system.

Here is how it works. You advertise the fact that interested parties can receive information about you or your organization by sending a message to your email address with the word "contents" in the Subject field. When such a message comes in, Claris Emailer replies to it by sending a list of possible documents that the recipient can request and further instructions for retrieving them. These instructions tell them which codes to use in their messages to obtain the information they want. Emailer uses these codes to reply with the correct documents. Call it a poor man's list server.

The first action you need to create is the one that will answer the initial query. Its criterion is "if the **Subject** field **is contents** . . ." The criterion is not case- sensitive, so it will work if the sender types "contents," "Contents," "CONTENTS," or even "CoNtEnTs."

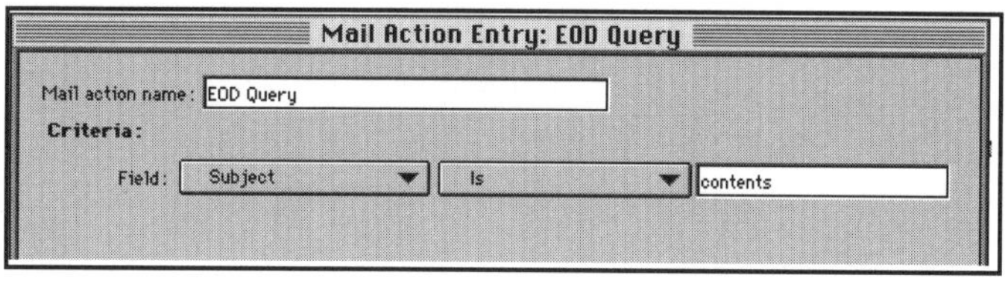

There are two resulting actions. The first requires that the **Auto reply to message** check box be selected in the Actions Entry dialog box as shown in Figure 5-17. Here press the **Edit reply** button to create a message that will be returned to the sender of the query, as shown in Figure 5-16. In the message provide codes for the documents that can be requested. Be sure these codes are fairly obscure and therefore unlikely to show up in unrelated email. Also provide specific instructions for how to request these documents. For example: "To receive any of these documents, please send a message to 'trdell@smtp.trdell.com' with the codes of the documents you want in the body of your message."

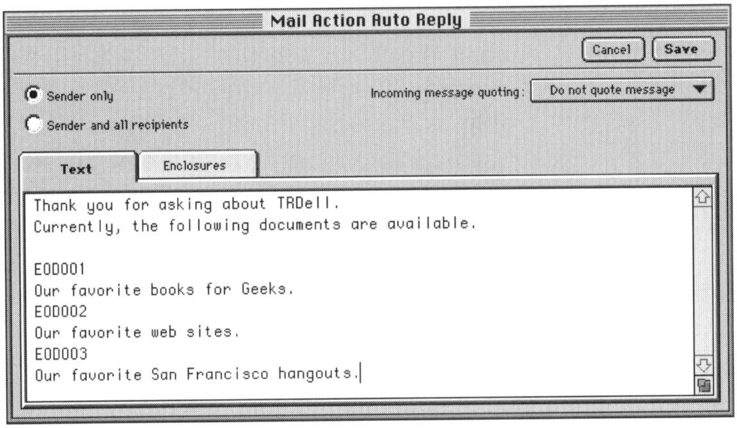

FIGURE 5-16. EOD contents reply message.

Naturally you are interested in the people who are interested in you or your organization. Why not keep track of who has sent you queries? To do this, first create a group in your Address Book named something appropriate, like "EOD Queries." Next, select the **Add sender to Group** check box in the Actions Entry dialog box, as shown in Figure 5-17. Choose your newly created group in the pop-up menu.

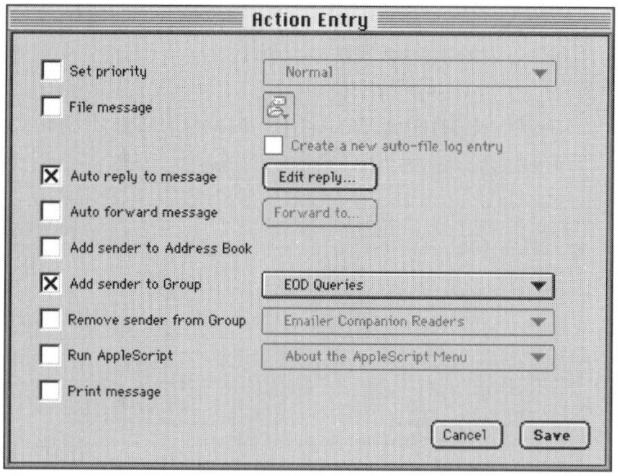

FIGURE 5-17. EOD actions.

Now you have a routine that will not only accept queries and reply with the EOD contents message but also build a database of addresses for all those who have requested information. This group will come in handy later when you want to send out announcements or bulk email.

Now comes the second part of the process, sending out the requested documents. I recommend that you create actions for each code that you have assigned to your documents. Their criteria would be in the form "if the **Message body** field **Contains EOD001** . . . "

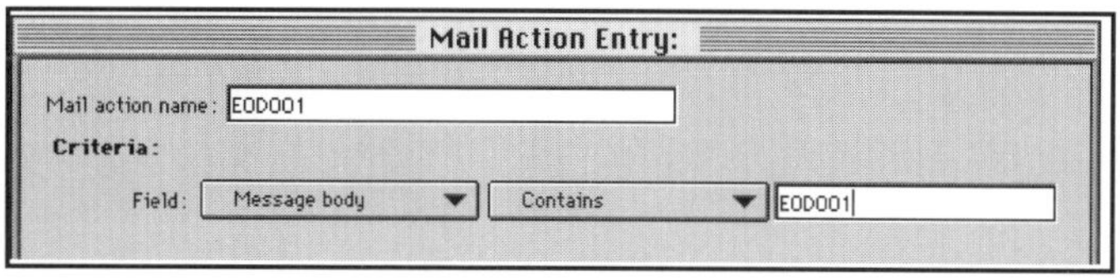

This routine also requires that the **Auto reply to message** check box be selected in the Actions Entry dialog box. When you press the **Edit reply** button to create the reply message, you can put the text of the requested document into the message body. This works fine for short documents or those that do not require formatting.

Another thing you can do is type a cursory note for the reply message, as shown in Figure 5-18.

FIGURE 5-18. EOD reply.

Then send the requested document along as an enclosure, as shown in Figure 5-19. This works well for large text documents or documents with formatting or graphics content such as an Adobe Acrobat or PostScript file.

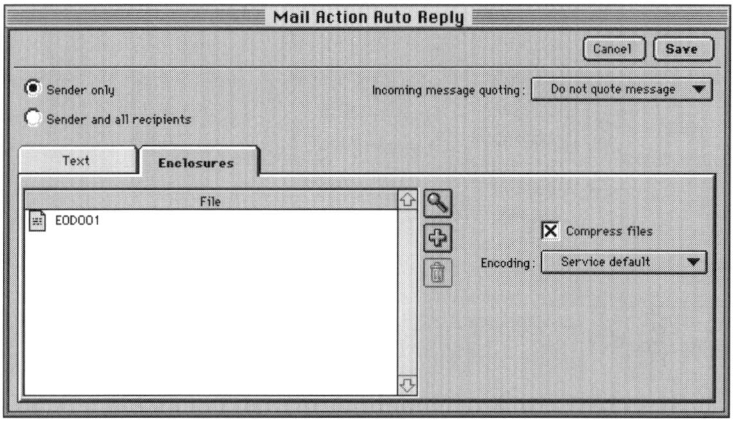

FIGURE 5-19. EOD enclosure.

Create as many email-on-demand actions as you need and put them in sequential order in the Mail Actions List. Be sure to enable the **Stop mail actions if criteria is met** check box only in the last one. The sender might request multiple documents, so you will want each message passed through the entire email-on-demand list.

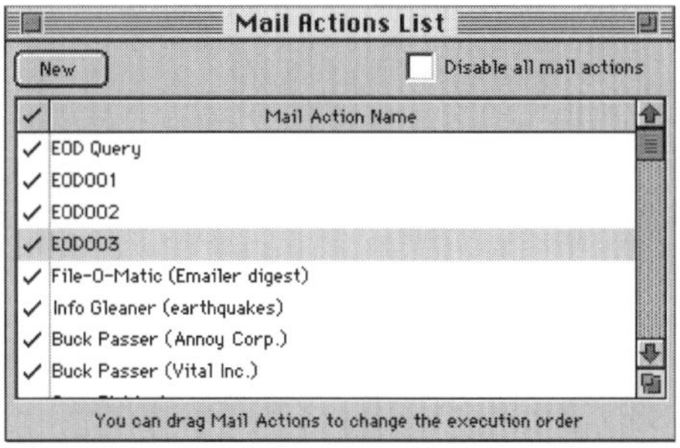

Spam Be Gone

Bulk email, or "spam," can be a real annoyance. Claris Emailer users are especially susceptible to this deluge of digital garbage because we usually have multiple email accounts. I cannot tell you how many times I have had myself removed from a mailing list that knew me at one address, only to find myself on this list again under a different address. Spam Be Gone is a domain name filter designed to automatically spit out a negative response whenever I get bulk email from a source I do not like. It works for all my accounts, including all four America Online screen names.

To create this routine, we return to the **More Choices** button in the Mail Actions Entry dialog box. Here we can copy and paste each domain name coming from a bulk emailer that we want to leave us alone, as shown in Figure 5-20. If the statement is true, **Apply actions**. If not, **Go to the next line** and see if the address comes from the second domain name.

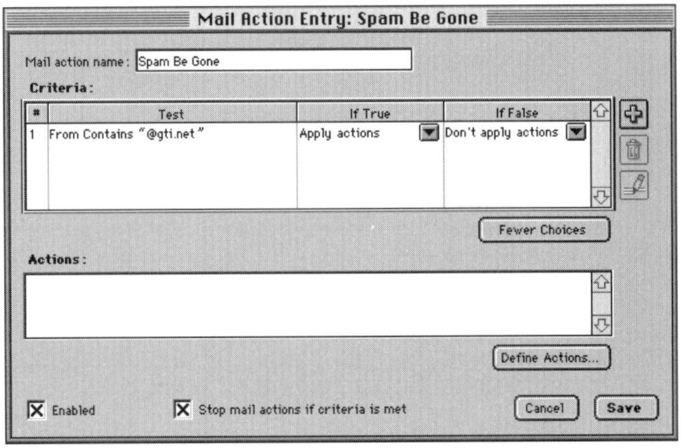

FIGURE 5-20. Spam Be Gone criteria.

Here is a likely candidate for Spam Be Gone, wouldn't you say (Figure 5-21)?

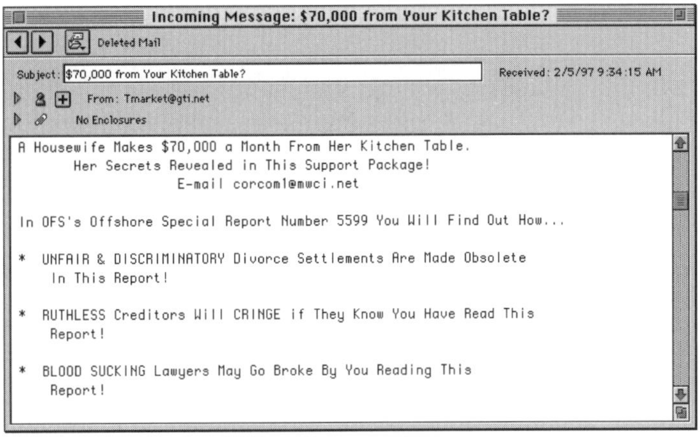

FIGURE 5-21. Possible candidate for Spam Be Gone.

How about this one (Figure 5-22)?

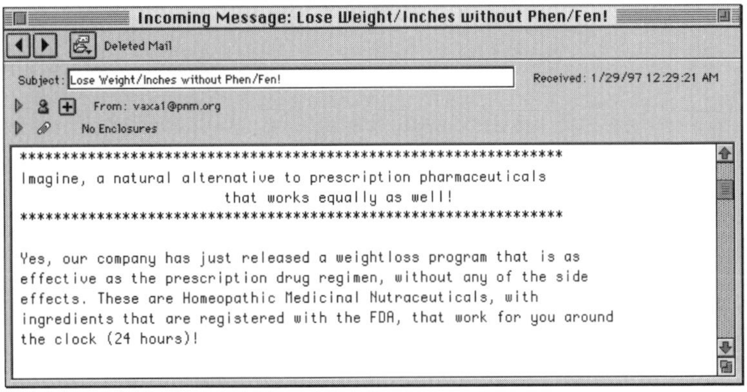

FIGURE 5-22. Another likely candidate for Spam Be Gone.

Maybe this one too (Figure 5-23)?

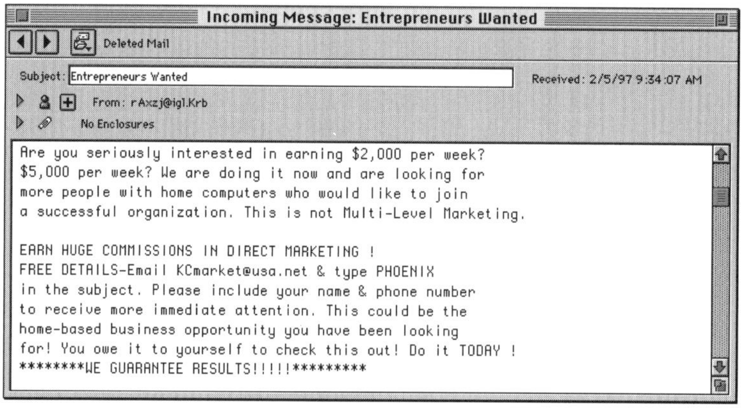

FIGURE 5-23. Oh, please.

In all fairness I should mention that I have found useful information in bulk email from time to time. I even look forward to some of it. But when the email is so far out of my areas of interest as to be ridiculous, I consider it a Spam Be Gone candidate.

Fortunately for us, most bulk emailers include instructions for getting off their mailing lists, which most often involve replying with a message that contains "remove" or "unsubscribe" in the Subject or Body fields. To take advantage of this, use the **Auto reply to message** check box in the Actions Entry dialog box, and create a reply message containing the key words, as shown in Figure 5-24.

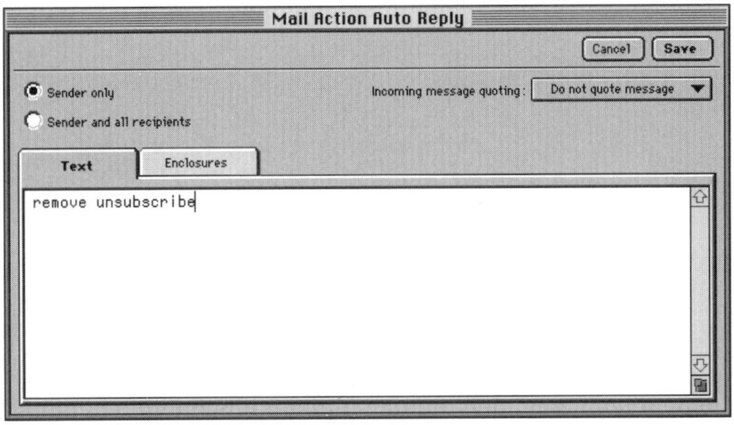

FIGURE 5-24. Remove from list key words.

Other bulk emailers do not provide such instructions, but here is a little trick you can try on them. Pretend your address does not exist by typing in something like what you see in Figure 5-25.

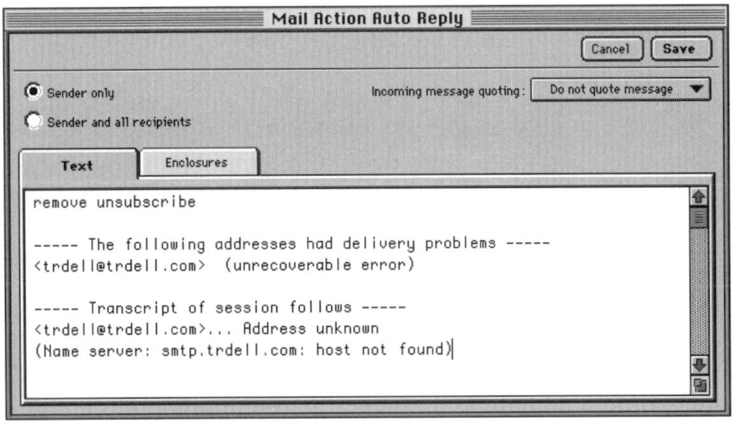

FIGURE 5-25. Alice doesn't live here anymore.

With luck, the email administrator will think that yours is just another bad address and will remove you from the mailing list.

What if neither of these approaches works? Why, then you will be sending a reply to each and every piece of junk email that comes in from a given domain name! How annoying for the sender! Gosh, maybe they will get angry and remove you from the mailing list. Oh, darn!

I hope these samples have interested you in using Claris Emailer's mail actions. They are a great feature.

Sharing Mail Actions

Once you have come up with some nifty mail actions, why not share them with other Claris Emailer users? You can export mail actions and exchange them by highlighting the action you want to exchange in the Mail Actions List window and selecting the **Save as file** command under the **File** menu bar item.

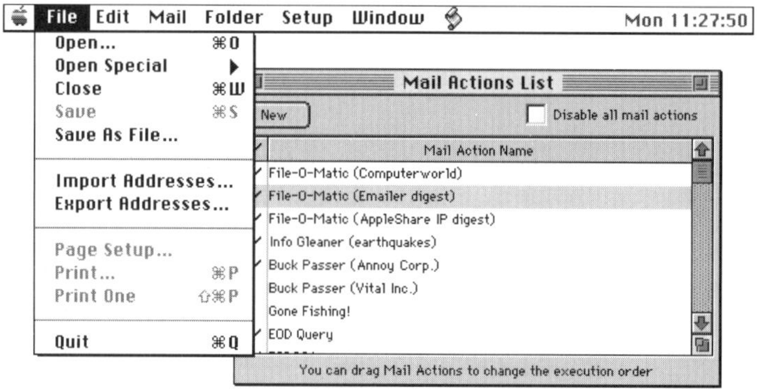

This will give you a file that you can email to other users, who can import the action into their Mail Actions List by dragging and dropping it into the Mail Actions List window.

A Couple of Preferences

A couple of defaults can be set for mail actions which pertain to automatic replies and automatic filing. You can set them by selecting the **Preferences** command under the **Setup** menu bar item, and then highlighting **Mail actions** in the Preferences window that results, as shown in Figure 5-26.

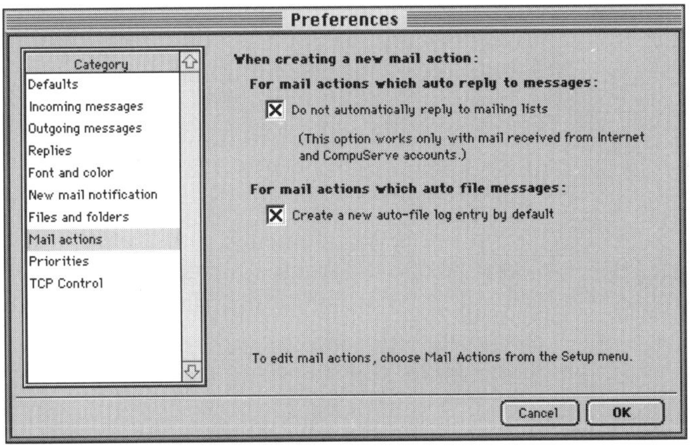

FIGURE 5-26. Mail Actions Preferences.

The first check box affects Internet and CompuServe accounts and determines whether or not Claris Emailer will be permitted to respond to mailing lists. The second check box determines whether or not the **Create an entry in the Logs folder** check box is selected by default when you enable the **File message** check box in the Actions Entry dialog box.

Summary

Claris Emailer permits you to automate many repetitive tasks using *Mail Actions*. Mail Actions are established in the Mail Actions List and can be used to prioritize, file, reply to, forward, and print incoming messages. They can also be used to automatically save addresses to the Address Book. Mail Actions are broken down into two parts. The *criteria* determine when and if any action will be performed. The *actions* determine what will be done with the email. It is possible to establish unlimited criteria, or *tests*, within a single mail action. A message can also be processed by more than one mail action.

Mail Actions can be used to launch AppleScripts. I will talk about that further on.

6

Making the Connection

Several types of computer-to-computer connections can be used to send and receive messages through Claris Emailer. On a LAN, Claris Emailer can use the Macintosh's built-in AppleTalk to communicate with an OfficeMail server. It can also use TCP/IP to communicate with internal POP mail hosts and with America Online and external POP mail hosts through a LAN-to-Internet link.

Off the LAN, Claris Emailer uses a modem to connect mobile users with America Online, CompuServe, or an ISP's mail host, the last accomplished with TCP/IP over *Point-to-Point Protocol (PPP)*. Claris Emailer can even use a RF modem to communicate with RadioMail's Internet email over the airwaves.

If all went well with Easy Setup, which was covered in Chapter 2, you are already using some of these connection methods. This chapter is for those who ran into trouble with Easy Setup or who wish to change their configurations or who are curious about the setup options. It should also be useful to administrators deploying Claris Emailer throughout their organization.

Connecting with AppleTalk

AppleTalk is a protocol created by Apple Computer to permit communications between one Macintosh and another or between a Macintosh and a printer. A *protocol* can be thought of as a digital language used by computers to communicate with each other. Although they might not be aware of it, most Macintosh owners are familiar with three AppleTalk implementations.

The best known implementation is *LocalTalk,* a cabling scheme any Macintosh computer (and even the Apple II) can use. It requires that you install a network transmitter/receiver, or *transceiver,* which plugs into the printer port on the back of the Macintosh.

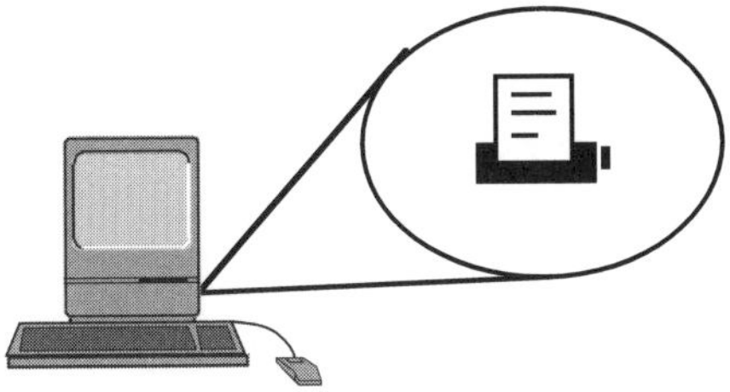

FIGURE 6-1. LocalTalk transceivers are attached to the printer port.

Special shielded cabling is then run between this transceiver and another transceiver attached to a printer or Macintosh. Several devices can be attached this way in what is called a *daisy chain*. The most common variation on LocalTalk is *PhoneNet*, a system designed by Farallon Computing that permits the use of inexpensive, flat telephone cable between the transceivers.

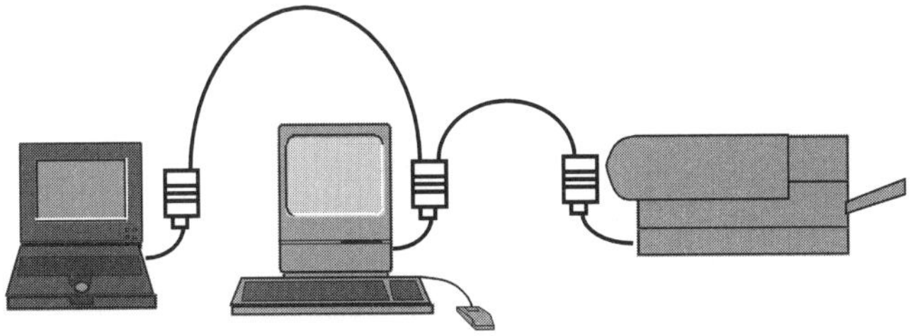

FIGURE 6-2. A typical LocalTalk daisy chain.

The LocalTalk signal is powered by the Macintosh. It provides a reliable system that has even been used to create impromptu networks between PowerBooks on airplanes.

The second implementation is *EtherTalk*, which supports the use of AppleTalk on an *Ethernet* network. Ethernet is a standard that can be used with twisted-pair cabling, which looks like telephone wiring, only thicker, or with coaxial cabling, which looks like the stuff that runs to your television set but has different electrical properties. You will hear Ethernet's various types referred to as *Thicknet, Thinnet, 10BaseT* and *100BaseT* (or *Fast Ethernet*). Macintoshes can use a transceiver appropriate to the Ethernet cabling type, which is attached to their built-in Ethernet ports. Older machines can have an Ethernet *Network Interface Card (NIC)* installed in them.

FIGURE 6-3. Ethernet transceivers are plugged into the Ethernet port or their own NICs.

In the case of coaxial cabling, the Ethernet signal is powered by the computer. In the case of twisted-pair cabling, it is most often powered by a device called a *hub*. Either way, Ethernet, at its slowest, is 44 times faster than LocalTalk and can be used over greater distances.

The last familiar implementation of AppleTalk is *AppleTalk Remote Access*. This is a specially tuned version of AppleTalk designed to run over telephone wires—actual telephone wires this time—and to be used with modems. With it you can do things like telecommuting, accessing all of your LAN's services from miles away.

FIGURE 6-4. ARA works over modems, which are attached to the modem port.

There are two AppleTalk technologies available on the Macintosh. The older of the two has been dubbed "Classic Networking." To use it you simply attach the appropriate transceiver to your Macintosh and then select its interface in the Network control panel.

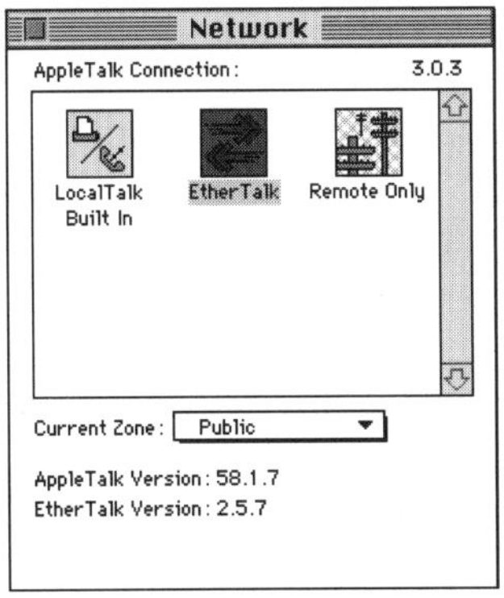

The newer of the two is *Open Transport*. To use it you attach the appropriate transceiver to your Macintosh and then select its interface in the control panel named for the protocol you wish to use, such as AppleTalk.

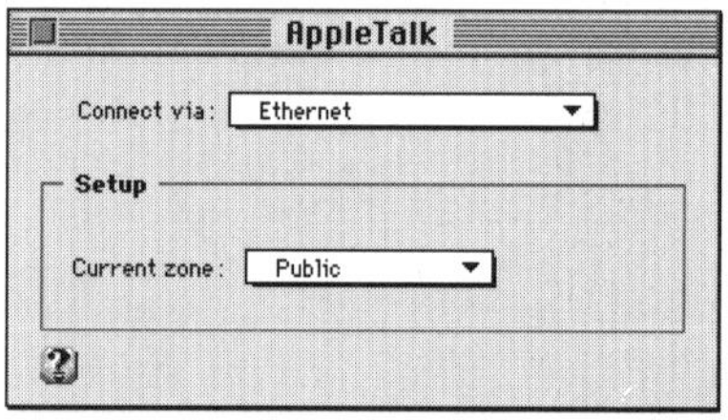

Protocols like AppleTalk require computers to use a unique number in communicating on a network, just as a building must have a unique number to receive postal mail. Such numbers are called *network addresses* and *node addresses* and are analogous to street addresses and zip codes.

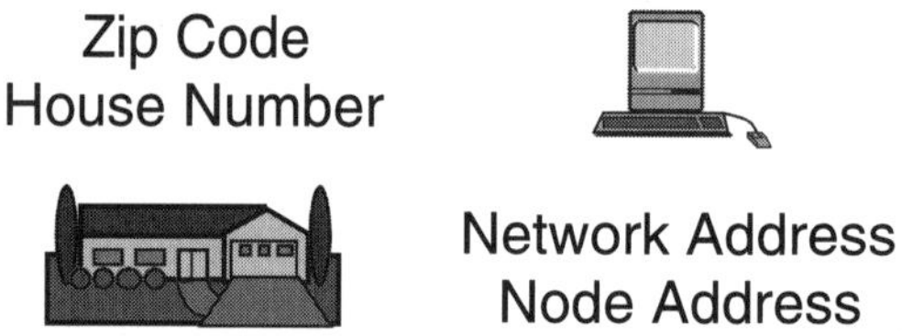

Computers running AppleTalk consult with each other and choose their own network and node numbers through a process called *dynamic addressing*.

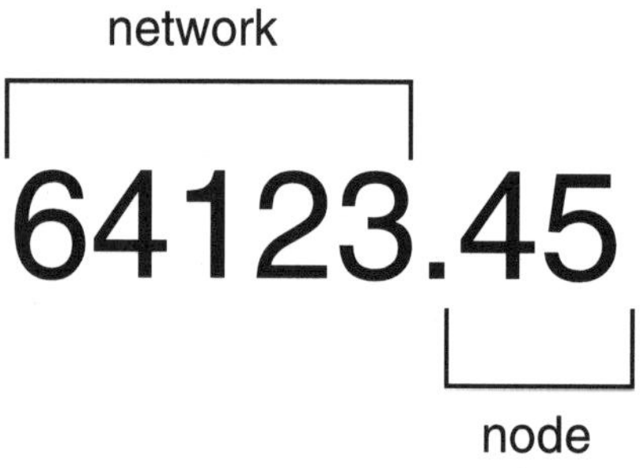

AppleTalk communications can be initiated with the Chooser, which is located under the **Apple** menu bar item.

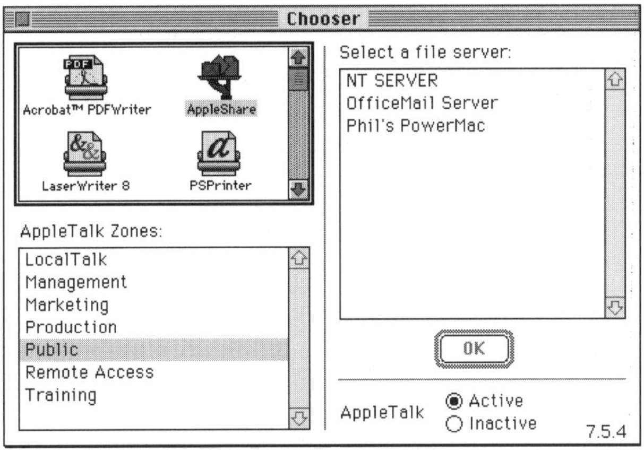

FIGURE 6-5. The Chooser.

On smaller networks, the Chooser window contains two panes. The one on the left contains icons for printers and network services; the one on the right contains the names of computers and printers running on your network. Choose an icon on the left and you will see the available network devices on the right.

On larger networks, the Chooser often contains one additional pane for AppleTalk *zones*, as shown in Figure 6-5, which are used to gather network devices into groups to make them easier for you to find. For instance, your network administrator might put all of the computers on one office floor into one group, so you do not have to look at a building-wide list of hundreds of computers just to find the printer down the hall. Choose an icon in the upper left, then choose a zone in lower left, and you will see the available network devices on the right.

Once on an AppleTalk network, you can use the East Setup procedure detailed in Chapter 2 to locate and communicate with an OfficeMail server. If your network has zones or multiple OfficeMail servers, you will need to ask your network administrator which one is for your use.

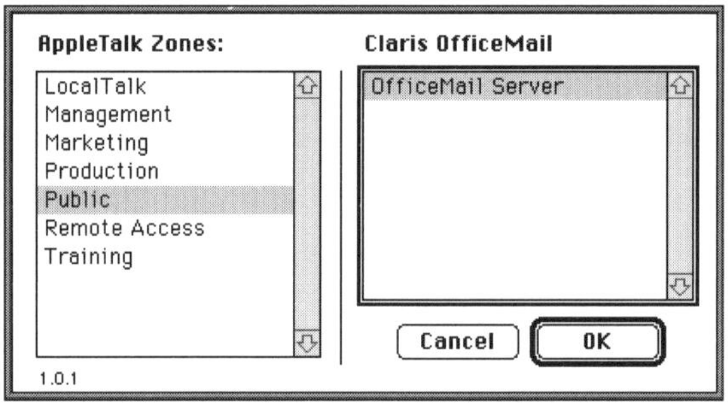

Using ARA

When you are away from the LAN, you do not have to lose access to your OfficeMail server. If your network is designed to support ARA dial-up access, you can run AppleTalk over a modem connection. Ask your network administrator about this possibility.

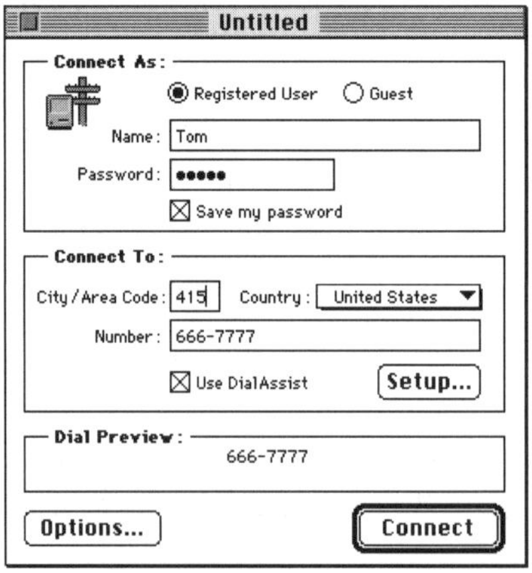

FIGURE 6-6. Opening an ARA connection.

Using ARA, you can access your office email as simply as if your computer were actually on the LAN.

NOTE *If you decide to use ARA, make sure that your network administrator has given you and other dial-in users access to the zone in which your Office-Mail server resides.*

Connecting with TCP/IP

AppleTalk is sufficient for most communications between Macintosh computers. Macs and Claris Emailer can also communicate with other types of computers using the ever-more-universal language of the Internet: TCP/IP.

TCP/IP was made a standard component of the Mac OS beginning with System 7.5. Prior to that, it was available as an addition. Like AppleTalk, it comes in two varieties: Classic Networking, called *MacTCP*, and Open Transport, called TCP/IP.

As with AppleTalk, each computer on a TCP/IP network must be given a unique network address and *host* (node) address. These are collectively called the *IP address*.

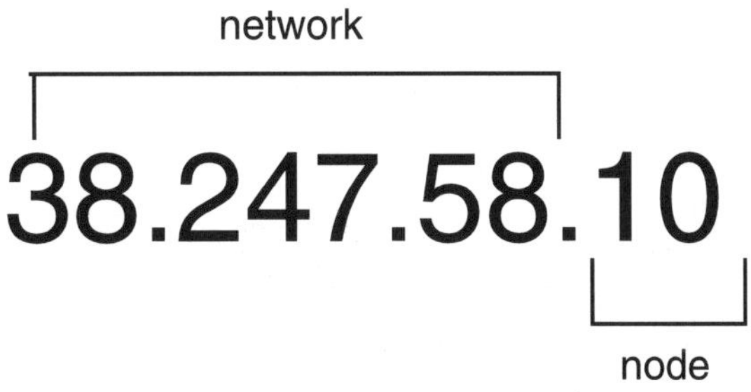

Computers do not negotiate these addresses among themselves, as they do with AppleTalk. Instead, each computer is given an address by a network administrator through *static addressing*. As you might imagine, if the administrator makes a mistake and gives the same address for two hosts on the same network, there will be problems. For this reason, it is important that you be careful when configuring TCP/IP. This is no place for trial and error!

If you are on a LAN connected to the Internet, its IP addresses must be unique, not just for all the hosts on your local network but for hosts throughout the whole world. Instead of coming from a local network administrator, they are assigned by a central authority called the *InterNIC*.

Wherever you get your IP address, here is how you will use it to configure your TCP/IP connection.

Using MacTCP

If your Macintosh is running under Classic Networking on an Ethernet network, you may use this procedure. Before you can start, you will need to ask the following of your network administrator or ISP:

Which addressing method should I use—*manual, server,* or *dynamic?*

You can write it down here: ______________________________.

If manual addressing is being used, what is my IP address?

You can write it down here: ______________________________.

What is the IP address of my gateway router?

You can write it down here: ______________________________.

What is my Subnet Mask?

You can write it down here: ______________________.

What are the IP addresses of my *Domain Name Service (DNS)* servers?

You can write it down here: ______________________.

You can write it down here: ______________________.

What are the domain names of my DNS servers?

You can write it down here: ______________________.

You can write it down here: ______________________.

Once you have this information, open the Network control panel from the **Control Panels** item under the **Apple** menu bar item. (If you do not see a Network control panel, then the Macintosh is probably running Open Transport. You can skip ahead to the next section).

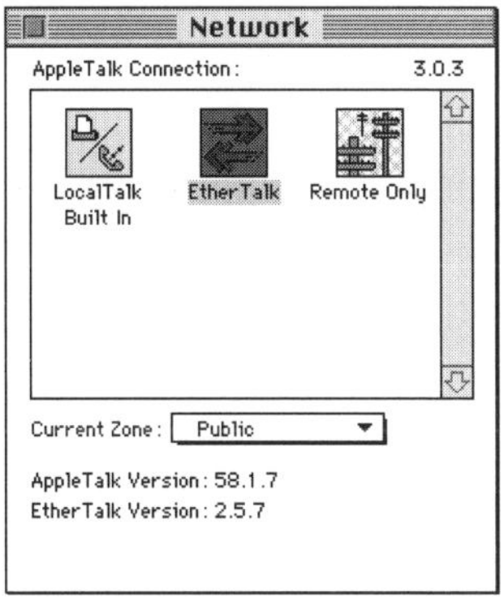

Let's assume your organization has an Ethernet LAN, as most do. Here you select the **EtherTalk** interface. If you are on a network with zones, you choose your zone in the Current Zone pop-up menu. Click on the box in the upper left of the title bar to close the window.

Next, open the MacTCP control panel from the **Control Panels** item under the **Apple** menu bar item.

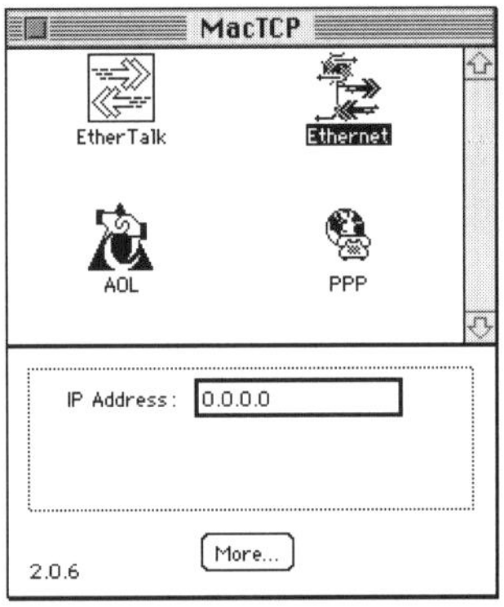

Make sure that the **Ethernet** interface is selected. Do not select **EtherTalk** here. (That is AppleTalk over Ethernet.) Next, press the **More** button at the bottom.

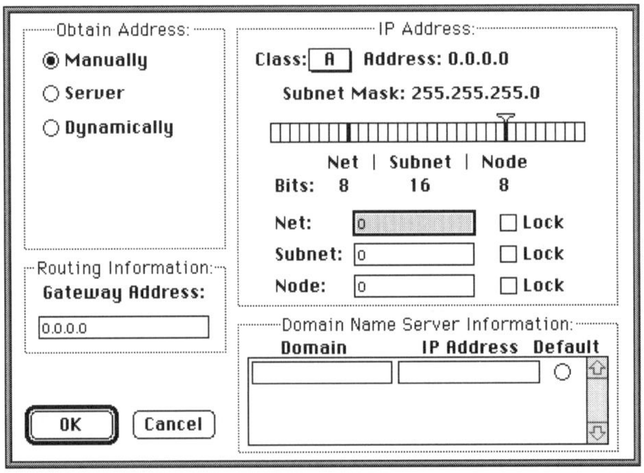

FIGURE 6-7. MacTCP Administrator window.

In the MacTCP Administrator window that appears, choose either the **Manually**, **Server**, or **Dynamically** radio button as directed by your network administrator or ISP. For this example, I will use **Manually** because it is the most complicated.

Next, type the gateway router's IP address in the Gateway Address field.

The Subnet Mask will probably be **255.255.255.0**. Move the lever beneath the Subnet Mask field to change this number if necessary.

Finally, type the domain names and IP Addresses of your network's DNS servers into the Domain Name Server Information fields.

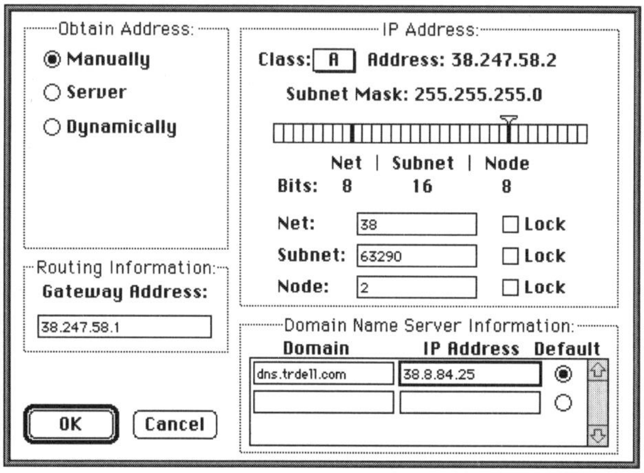

FIGURE 6-8. Configured MacTCP Administrator window.

When you are done, press the **OK** button to return to the MacTCP control panel's window.

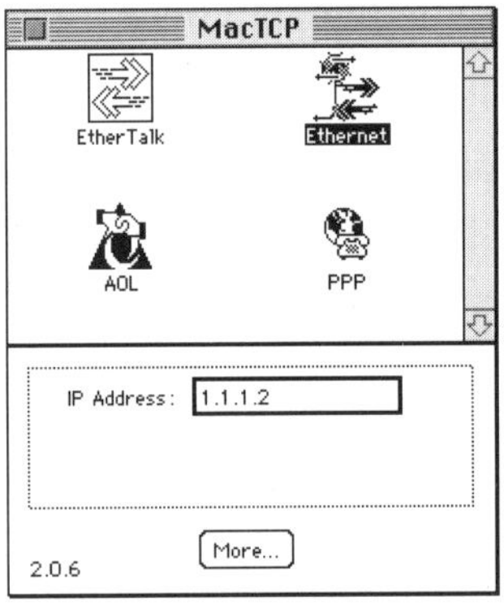

What you do next will depend on the instructions given to you by your network administrator or ISP. If you are using the manual addressing method, you may type your Macintosh's unique IP address in the IP Address field. When you are done, close the control panel and restart the Macintosh.

If you are on a LocalTalk LAN, the procedure varies somewhat because the LocalTalk scheme does not directly support TCP/IP.

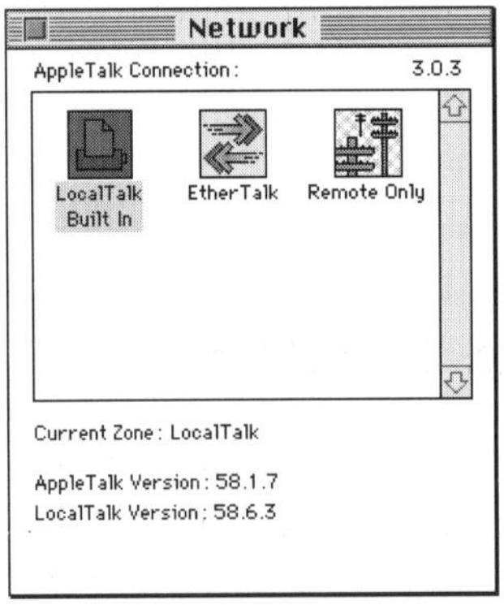

Computers on LocalTalk must use an AppleTalk-to-IP gateway. Under this system, the LocalTalk computer speaks to an AppleTalk gateway, which in turn translates that network traffic into IP and forwards it over Ethernet or a telecom connection. IP gateway software can run on a server machine, or it can be built into an Internet router.

In connecting to the Internet over LocalTalk, the MacTCP configuration information is the same. However, when you return to the MacTCP control panel at the end of the process, you will select the LocalTalk interface. A pop-up menu appears beneath it in which you will choose the zone that contains the IP gateway.

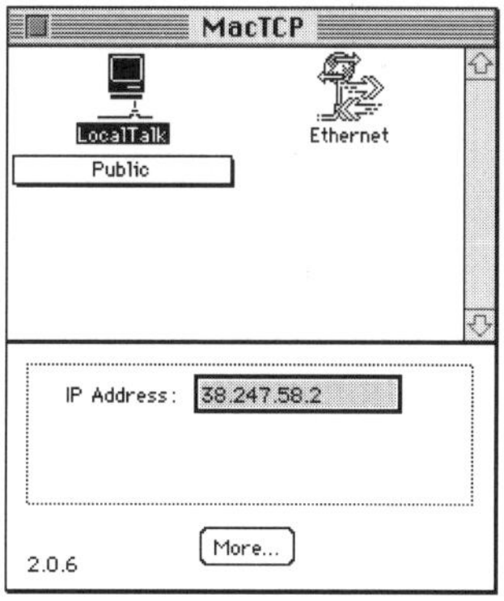

When you close the control panel, the Macintosh will be given an IP address by the IP gateway. You might need to restart.

Working with TCP/IP under Open Transport

As easy as it is to configure MacTCP, Open Transport makes it even easier. First, however, you will still need to get information from your network administrator or ISP.

Which addressing method should I use—*manual, BootP, DHCP,* or *RARP?*

You can write it down here: ______________________________.

If manual addressing is being used, what is my IP address?

You can write it down here: ______________________________.

What is the IP address of my gateway router?

You can write it down here: ______________________________.

What is my Subnet Mask?

You can write it down here: ______________________________.

What are the IP addresses of my DNS servers?

You can write it down here: ______________________________.

You can write it down here: ______________________________.

What are the domain names of my DNS servers?

You can write it down here: ______________________________.

You can write it down here: ______________________________.

Assuming you are on an Ethernet network, first open the TCP/IP control panel from the **Control Panels** item under the **Apple** menu bar item. (If you do not see a TCP/IP control panel, the Macintosh is probably running Classic Networking.)

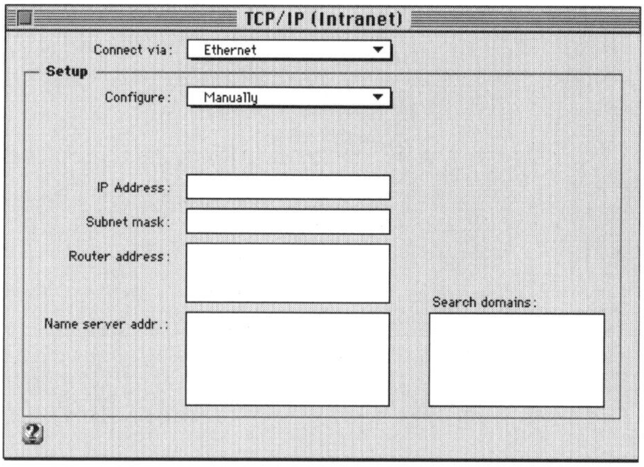

FIGURE 6-9. TCP/IP control panel.

Choose the **Ethernet** interface in the Connect via pop-up menu. Depending on what your network administrator or ISP has told you, you might choose **Manually** in the Configure pop-up menu. In the IP Address field, type your Macintosh's unique address. Do not forget to type the Subnet Mask in the Subnet Mask field.

Finally, type the gateway router's IP address in the Router Address field and the IP addresses and domain names for your network's DNS servers in the Name server address and Search domain fields, respectively.

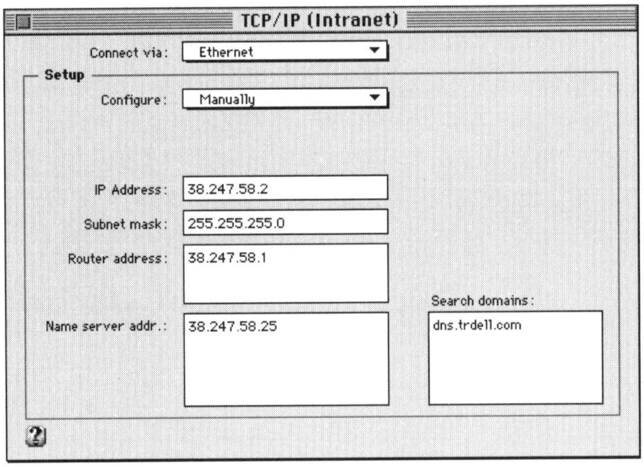

FIGURE 6-10. Configured TCP/IP control panel.

Next, close the window. When asked if you want to save the changes to the configuration, press the **Save** button. You usually do not need to restart the Macintosh.

If your computer is on LocalTalk, you will need the services of an IP gateway. In this event choose **AppleTalk (MacIP)** in the Connect via pop-up menu. Open Transport will deduce that you need to use a MacIP server, as shown in the Configure pop-up menu, but you will need to press the **Select Zone** button to tell it where to find it. Open Transport will get the other information from the IP gateway.

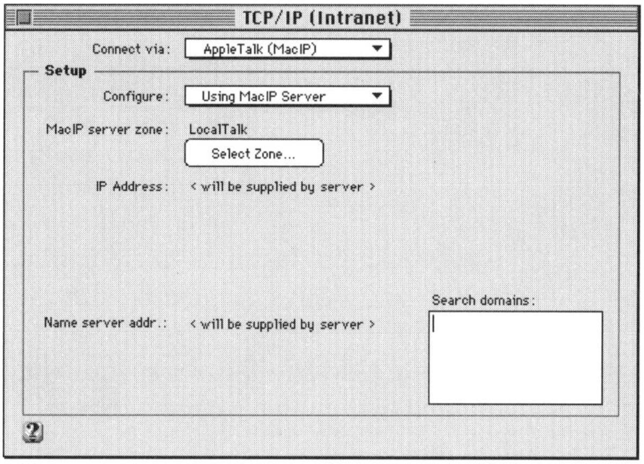

FIGURE 6-11. TCP/IP control panel configured for IP gateway.

Next, close the window. When asked if you want to save the changes to the configuration, press the **Save** button. You usually do not need to restart the Macintosh.

Working with MacPPP

Up to this point I have assumed you are going to use Claris Emailer's TCP/IP functions on a LAN, but it is just as likely that you will use it over a modem connection. To do so, you need to add one extra process to enable your network traffic to pass through the telephone system.

ISPs can accommodate dial-up access using either *Serial Line Interface Protocol (SLIP)* or PPP. The latter is the more common connection type. Think of PPP as a telecommunications bridge over which TCP/IP travels, much as ARA is a bridge over which AppleTalk travels.

If you are using Classic Networking, you can add PPP capabilities to you your Macintosh with a simple freeware application called *MacPPP,* distributed by the University of Michigan and Merit Network, Inc. MacPPP is composed of a system extension and a control panel.

MacPPP must be configured in addition to, not in lieu of, MacTCP. Go back and follow the steps in the *Using MacTCP* section before continuing here. The one difference in that configuration will be that you choose the **PPP** icon in the MacTCP control panel instead of **EtherTalk**, **LocalTalk,** or **Ethernet**.

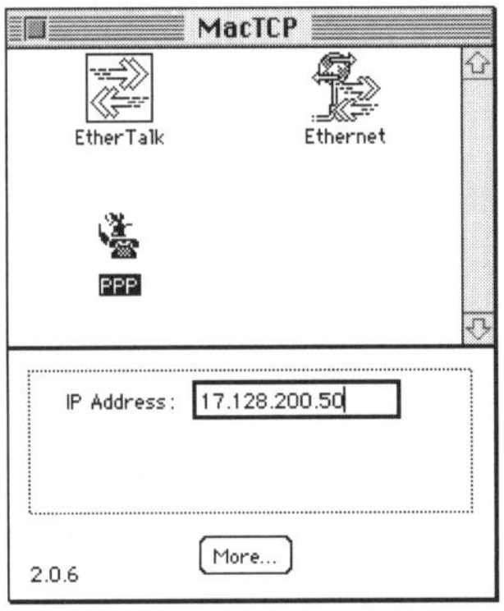

In addition to the MacTCP configuration information, you will need to get two more things from your network administrator or ISP:

What is the local telephone number?

You can write it down here: ______________________________.

What is my login password?

You can write it down here: ______________________________.

WARNING!

But then make sure to keep this book in a secure place so nobody else gets hold of it!

To configure MacPPP, open the Config PPP control panel from the **Control Panels** item under the **Apple** menu bar item.

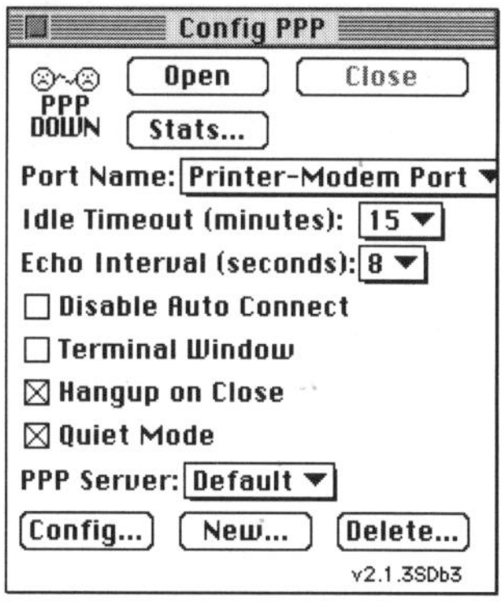

First, choose the port on which you have attached your modem in the Port Name pop-up menu. If you have an internal modem, it will show up here as well.

After the time specified in the Idle Timeout pop-up menu has elapsed and there has been no activity on the line, MacPPP will automatically close the connection. This will save you from being billed for online time that you are not using. Choose a reasonable number here.

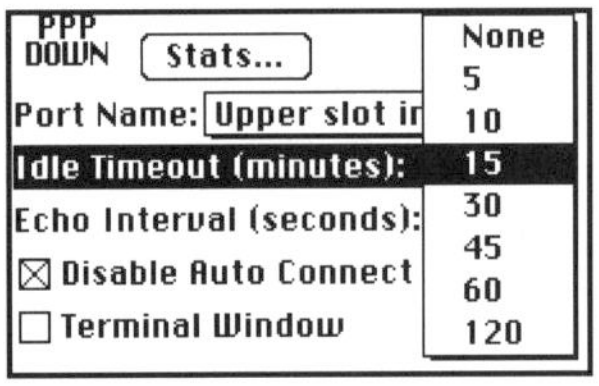

If you deselect the Quiet Mode check box, you will receive a warning dialog box before MacPPP quits the connection.

MacPPP uses a *Line Control Protocol (LCP)* echo request to find out whether its connection is still functional or has been dropped by the PPP server. MacPPP will send out these requests at the interval specified in the Echo Interval pop-up menu. It assumes that the link is down if the PPP server does not respond after three tries. I suggest you make the intervals long, since it is not uncommon for PPP servers to be so busy that it takes them a while to respond.

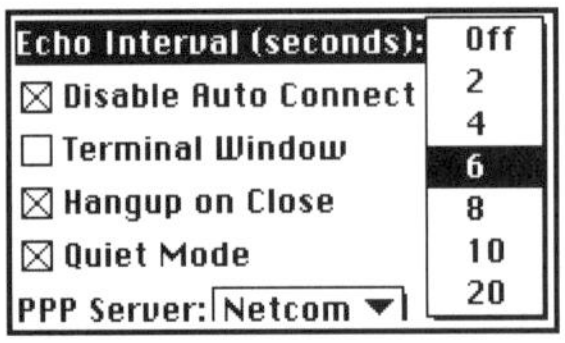

I would not recommend leaving the Disable Auto Connect check box selected. If you permit automatic connections, Claris Emailer will be able to dial out on its own to get your email according to the schedule you configured. Otherwise, it will need you to initiate the connection each time by pressing the Open button in the MacPPP control panel.

Selecting the Terminal Window check box directs MacPPP to bring up a basic terminal emulator window when it connects with the PPP server. You will almost always leave this unchecked. If you do not, MacPPP will ignore all of your preconfigured phone number and modem settings and you will be forced to use the command line interface to type in each command.

The Hangup on Close check box directs MacPPP to hang up the modem when the PPP session ends so that other services, such as ARA or fax software, can use it. Select this.

Next press the **New** button and name the connection in the resulting PPP server name dialog box.

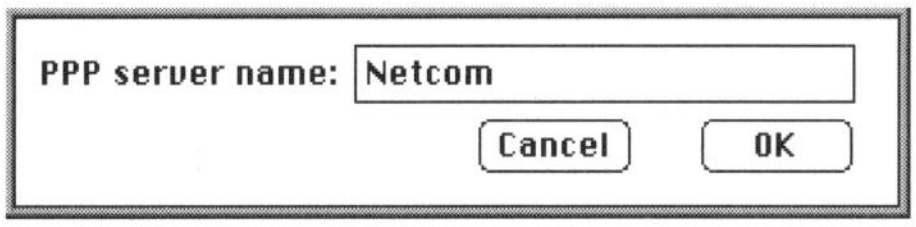

The new name will appear in the PPP Server pop-up menu.

Once you have returned to the MacPPP control panel window, press the **Config** button. You will need to enter information that is appropriate for your modem and PPP account here.

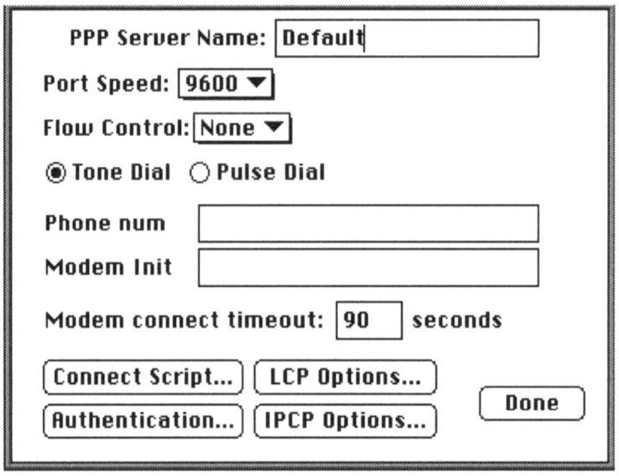

You might need to consult the manual that came with your modem to determine what to choose in the Port Speed pop-up menu. If you have a 14,400-Bps modem, it can often achieve speeds of 57,600 Bps with data compression. You can set the port speed as high as 230,000 Bps if your modem and Macintosh can support that speed. (The Macintosh Serial port is limited to 38,400 Bps.)

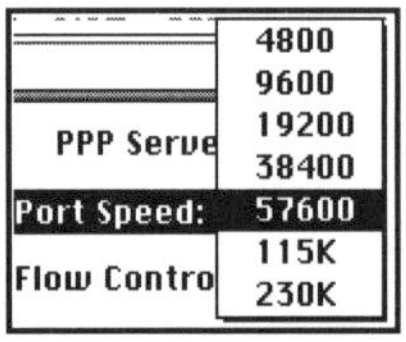

If you are using a modem that is faster than 9,600 Bps, it will probably come with a *hardware handshaking* cable that permits it to work at the higher speeds. If you have such a modem, choose **CTS & RTS (DTR)** in the Flow Control pop-up menu, unless your network administrator or ISP tells you otherwise.

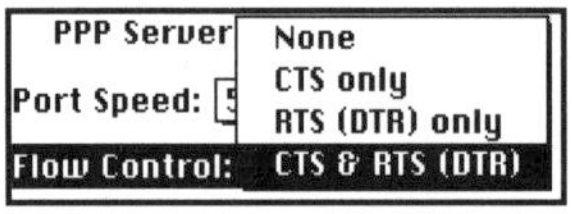

In addition, you might need to type "&D0" in the Modem Init field to tell the modem to ignore the *Data Terminal Ready (DTR)* signal. This is necessary because some high-speed modems will attempt to use the DTR wire inside the modem cable to signal that the device should hang up. The Macintosh wants to use this line for a *Request To Send (RTS)* signal instead. Disabling DTR with this command permits this.

You might want to add other commands here as well. The command "&F" will initialize the modem with its presumably optimum factory settings. The command "M0" will turn off the annoying modem speaker. Consult your manual for details.

Type the phone number of your organization's or ISP's PPP server into the Phone num field.

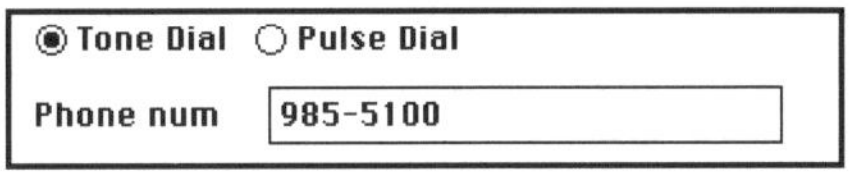

What you type in the Modem connect timeout field determines how many seconds MacPPP will keep trying to make a connection before it gives up.

You may or may not need to create a special login script. If your network administrator or ISP gives you one, click the **Connect Script** button and enter its variables. These vary with the PPP server, so there is no point in going into it here. Be aware, however, that the "\t" command causes MacPPP to enter terminal mode, in which case you would need to enter your login name and password manually.

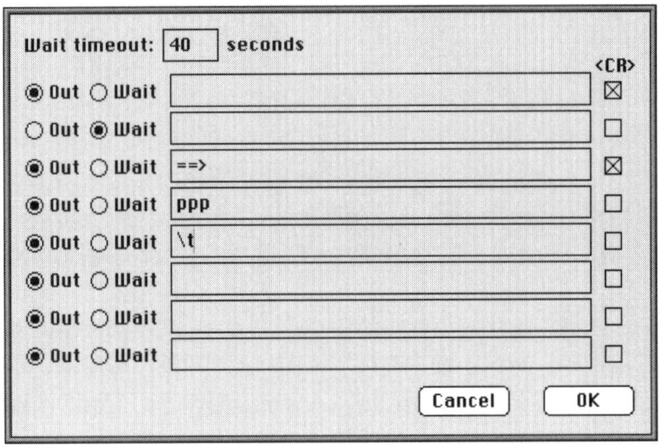

FIGURE 6-12. MacPPP login script.

I suggest you avoid this type of login script. Instead, have the login name and password information presented to the PPP server automatically each time so that Claris Emailer can make connections by itself. Enter this data in the fields accessed through the **Authentication** button. Here you may also establish the number of times MacPPP will try to reconnect after it gets a busy signal and at what intervals.

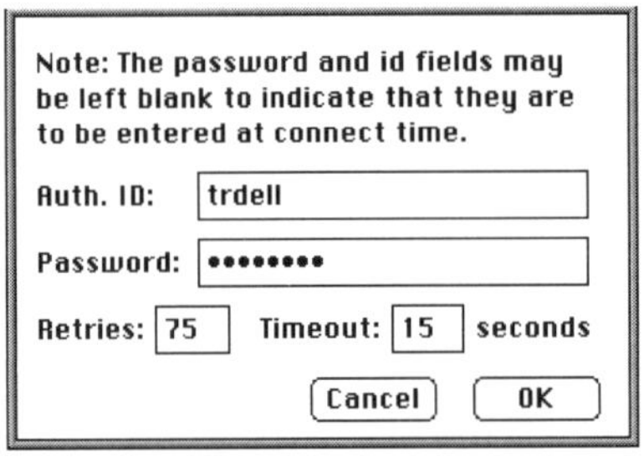

If your network administrator or ISP has given you a static IP address (manual addressing), select the **IPCP Options** (IP Control Protocol) button and enter it in the Local field.

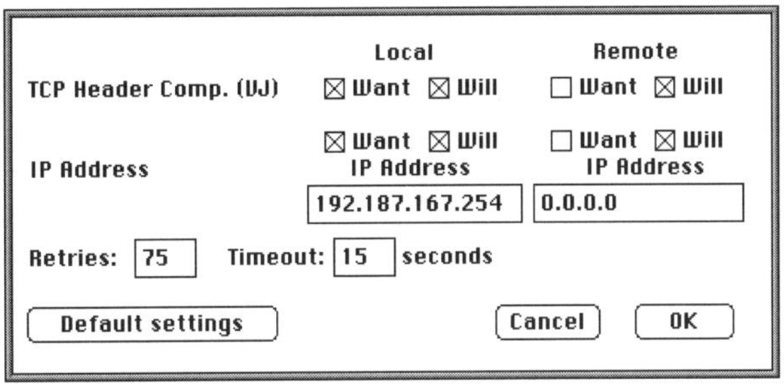

Be careful. If you were not given a static address and you do this, MacPPP will not open a connection unless the PPP server accepts the address you typed in. If you have problems, try letting the PPP server provide the IP address by leaving the field with the default setting.

It is best to leave the LCP and IPCP options alone unless otherwise directed. They relate to how PPP negotiates its connection with the PPP server.

When you have completed these steps, close the Configuration window by pressing the **Done** button.

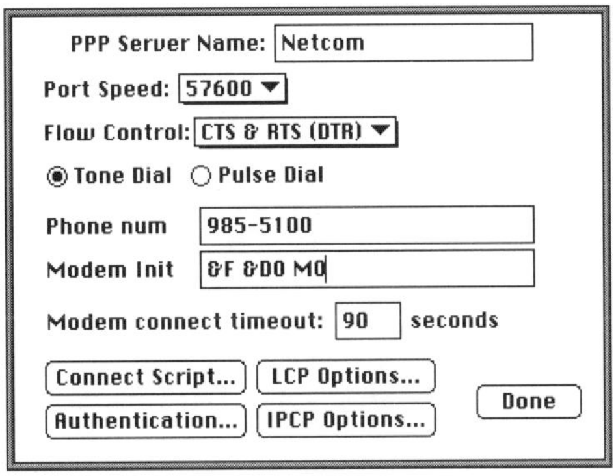

When you return to the MacPPP control panel window, test the connection by pressing the **Open** button. A dialog box will appear to show the connection's progress. Once the connection is established, the Config PPP window changes to reflect it—PPP up!

You should not need to use the MacPPP control panel to connect like this again. Once it is configured, all you have to do is boot up Claris Emailer and it will establish the PPP connection automatically in the background.

Using Open Transport/PPP

If your Macintosh is running under Open Transport, you can also use the MacPPP control panel as I have just described. A better choice, however, is Apple's own Open Transport/PPP, which can be used with System 7.5.3 and newer versions. Either way, you will still need to get these things from your network administrator or ISP and then add them to the TCP/IP configuration information I described in *Working with TCP/IP*:

What is the local telephone number?

You can write it down here: ______________________________.

What is my login password?

You can write it down here: ______________________________.

WARNING! *But then make sure to keep this book in a secure place so nobody else uses it!*

Open Transport/PPP needs to be installed after Open Transport TCP/IP. Once installed, it makes a new option, **PPP,** available to you in the Connect via pop-up menu. It also adds the choice of **Using PPP Server** to the Configure pop-up menu.

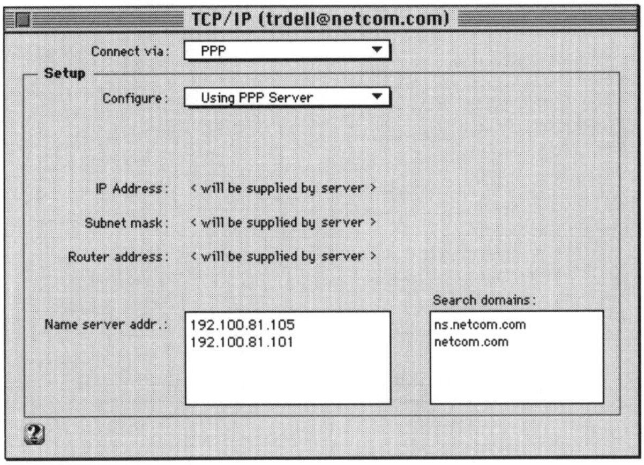

FIGURE 6-13. TCP/IP control panel configured for PPP.

Once you have TCP/IP configured according to instructions, you can choose the PPP control panel from the **Control Panels** item under the **Apple** menu bar item to enter the PPP server's phone number.

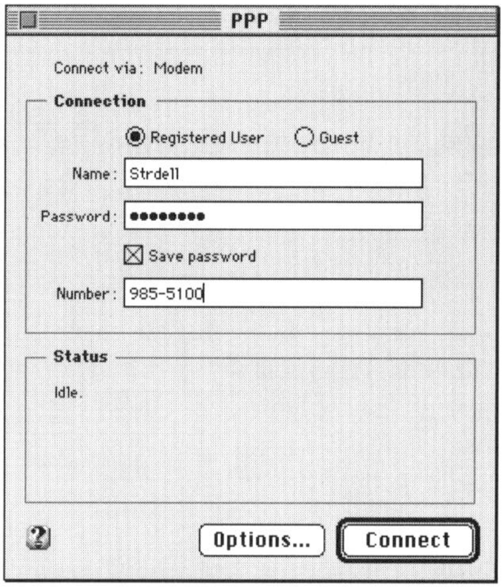

FIGURE 6-14. PPP control panel.

I recommend that you add your login name and password here and then select the **Save password** check box so that Claris Emailer can dial out on its own. Press the **Connect** button to test the connection. The Status field will stop reading "idle" and start showing connection statistics.

In addition to MacPPP and Open Transport/PPP, you may also use FreePPP or MacSLIP to make your connection. These are configured in much the same way. Follow the instructions in their accompanying "read me" files for specifics.

Connecting with Modems

One of the factors that has made email viable in the 1990s is the increased speed of data transfer over telephone lines. This has been made possible by ever-faster modems. No means of communications will succeed for long when its users are cut off from it for extended periods. How do you rely on it? Thanks to modems and online service providers, your email is as close as the nearest telephone. You need never be cut off from it for very long. (If you use RadioMail you can even dispense with the telephone!)

For practical purposes, a modem connection can be used in the same manner as a LAN connection once it is established. However, there is another layer of complexity in working with modems. In order to create a connection over most telephone lines, the modem must transform *digital* data into analog sounds. Our *analog* telephone system was designed to carry voices, not computer data, so an entire industry had to be developed to make both possible. Before we move on to further Claris Emailer configuration instructions, it will help you to know some of the terminology used in this industry.

First of all, we are talking about analog telephone systems here. These are installed in most homes throughout the US and were not designed with data in mind. In contrast, the newer digital telephone systems, such as those used by *Integrated Services Digital Network (ISDN)*, were designed to carry both voice and data.

The measure of how many parts of a character (a letter or number) can be sent or received in a second is defined as *Bits per second (Bps)*. The measure of how many characters can be sent in a second is defined as *Characters per second (Cps)*. For purposes of measurement it is generally assumed that each character transferred is made up of one *start bit*, eight bits for the character, and one *stop bit*, for a total of 10 bits. Using this measure, you can send 30 characters in a second with an old 300-Bps modem. Of course, few people still use modems that slow. Newer ones are generally described in terms of *kilobits per second (Kbps)*, such 33.6 Kbps (33,600 Bps).

Many people use Bps synonymously with *Baud rate*, but the two terms are not really the same. The Baud rate is the number of frequency changes made per second, which may or may not equal the Bps.

When buying a modem you might be confused by all the modem protocol standards. These are easier to evaluate when you know what they are for. They fall into four categories: *modulation, error correction, data compression,* and *file transfer.*

Modulation Protocols

Modulation protocols are the techniques used to encode digital data as analog signals. These protocols have evolved a lot over time.

When 300-Bps modems were commonplace in the US, they generally adhered to the Bell System's Bell 103 standard. Next came the Bell 212A standard, which supported a revolutionary 1,200 Bps, and then came the end of the Bell System monopoly. What filled the vacuum both in the US and abroad were the standards of the French-based *Consultative Committee for International Telephony and Telegraphy,* or *CCITT* (the *Comite Consultatif Internationale de Telegraphique et Telephonique,* if you prefer). CCITT is part of the Geneva-based *International Telecommunications Union (ITU).* Its standards have evolved roughly as follows:

- **V.21:** A 300-Bps data modulation standard, adopted in 1964, that is essentially the same as Bell 103.
- **V.23:** A 1,200-Bps data modulation standard adopted in 1964.
- **V.22:** A 1,200-Bps data modulation standard like Bell 212A adopted in 1980.

- **V.22bis:** A 2,400-Bps data modulation standard that permits modems to fall back to a slower but more reliable 1,200-Bps speeds on noisy lines. Adopted in 1984, it was the first CCITT standard to be accepted in the US.

- **V.32:** A 9,600-Bps/4,800-Bps data modulation standard adopted in 1984.

- **V.32bis:** A 14,400-Bps modem standard, adopted in 1991, that permits fallback to speeds of 12,000 Bps, 9,600 Bps, 7,200 Bps, and 4,800 Bps.

- **V.34:** A 33,600-Bps/28,800-Bps data modulation standard adopted in 1994.

The "bis" designation is for a secondary version of a protocol; "ter, " for a third version. Although it is difficult no to, don't confuse these data modulation standards with V.17, V.21, V.27ter, and V.29 fax standards.

The fallback speeds become important in a couple of instances. The first is when you have poor-quality phone lines. When a lot of errors are apparent, the modems will drop back to slower, but more stable, transmission speeds. The second is when your modem is faster than those of your service provider. The idea is that you can still connect at lower speeds and vice versa, which assumes that both ends have multi-speed modems that integrate the different modulation methods and components into single units.

Here is where knowing which standards your modem supports is important. If you have a 9,600 Bps modem and your service provider has a V.32 modem, you can communicate at 9,600 Bps, right? Not unless your modem also supports V.32. If it is one of the older U.S. Robotics or Hayes V-series that does not support V.32, the connection you get will be at a measly 2,400 Bps!

Error Correction Protocols

The data modulation standards I just described pertain to a modem's base speed, but if telephone lines are of poor quality you can expect a lot less. To achieve and sustain high-speed transmissions, modems use error correction protocols. Under these protocols, the sending modem forwards data in packets that include an error-control value and the receiving modem then recalculates the value. If it is the same as what the sending modem transmitted, it accepts the packet. If not, it asks the sending modem to send the packet again.

Another set of standards is associated with these techniques. In addition to those of the CCITT, there are protocols created by Microcom, Inc., and later incorporated into the CCITT, known as the *Microcom Networking Protocols (MNP).*

- **MNP 2, MNP 3, MNP 4:** These are the most basic error-checking techniques.
- **V.42:** This technique uses an error correction protocol called *Link Access Procedure for Modems (LAPM)*. If this techniques fails, it will fall back to MNP 2–4.
- **MNP 10:** This is an error correction protocol that works well with cellular phones or particularly bad cabling. It is also the method used by Apple Remote Access.

Remember, for any of these techniques to work, the modems at both the sending and receiving ends must adhere to the same standards.

Data Compression Protocols

Error correction protocols are vital in maintaining high-speed connections, but it is the data compression protocols that make the highest speeds possible. A data compression protocol does not change the number of data bits transmitted or the number of signal transitions that occur in a given period of time. Instead, their data compression algorithms remove repetitive bits to increase the content of the bit stream. Here too we find standards from both the CCITT and MNP:

- **MNP 5:** This technique compresses data by as much as 2:1. It requires the presence of MNP 2-4 error correction.

  If you are dialing in to download files that have already been compressed with StuffIt or PKZip, MNP 5 will actually slow the process as it tries to further compress them. This is one situation in which you might want to disable it.

- **MNP 7:** This technique compresses data by as much as 3:1.

- **V.42bis:** This technique uses the Lempel Zev algorithm to compress data by as much as 4:1; it requires the presence of a LAPM connection. V.42bis is not compatible with MNP 5, but if the modem cannot make a connection with this protocol, it will attempt MNP 5.

Here too, if you are downloading files that have already been compressed with StuffIt or PKZip, further compression will be redundant. V.42bis is smart enough to know this, and if it detects a compressed file, it sends it on untouched.

Data compression techniques grow more sophisticated all the time. Under optimum conditions, they can boost a 28,800-Bps modem's transmission rate to 57,600 Bps and a 33,600-Bps modem's transmission rate to 115,200 Bps or even 230,000 Bps. By way of comparison, LocalTalk is 230,400 Bps.

Impressive as that may sound, it still pales in comparison to ISDN, which can permit a base speed of 128,000 Bps and, with data compression, 512,000 Bps. Unfortunately, not all household telephone cabling can handle ISDN, and the service itself is not widely available. In the near future, however, most of us can look forward to *Asymmetrical Digital Subscriber Lines (ADSL)* and speeds measured in Megabits per second!

File Transfer Protocols

File transfer protocols also provide error detection and correction, but only during a file transfer. They do not help if you are reading your email or conferencing online with someone. Following are the most common file transfer protocols.

- **XModem:** This is the first and most commonly used public domain protocol. It provides error detection and correction by resending the problem portion of the transfer.

- **YModem:** This variation of XModem sends an additional block of information, prior to a file transfer, that contains the file name and size and information about its last modification. Having the name sent with the file data permits files to be sent in batches.

- **YModem G:** This variation of YModem works in conjunction with modem error correction protocols. The file transfer protocol issues no acknowledgments at the receiver end itself, so data can be downloaded more quickly. If an error is detected, however, the file transfer is aborted with no attempt made at error recovery.

- **ZModem:** Probably the best choice among the various public domain protocols, this one allows for batch file transfers and can actually recover from a crash. When you dial back in, the transfer continues from where you left off.

- **MacBinary:** For Macintosh users only, this protocol combines the Finder information block, data fork, and resource fork into a single file.

Modem Workings

Whether or not they are made by pioneer Hayes Microcomputer Products, most modems make use of the Hayes *AT Command Set* and are designated "Hayes-compatible." The AT Command Set is a control language used to enable and disable the various capabilities of intelligent modems. The "AT" refers to "attention," which is the first command sent to a modem in an *initialization string*. A few commands every modem user should be happy to know about pertain to the device's speaker.

- **M0**: Speaker off at all times

- **M1**: Speaker on until connection established

- **M2**: Speaker on at all times

- **M3**: Speaker off during dialing but on until connection established

- **L0**: Speaker volume low
- **L1**: Speaker volume low (less "low," I guess)
- **L2**: Speaker volume medium
- **L3**: Speaker volume high (to annoy co-workers and neighbors)

The AT commands you use will vary according to your exact modem hardware and in accordance with the directions of your service provider. Most modem's manuals do a good job of listing the options.

One last thing before we move on to using this information with Claris Emailer. Ever wonder what those nifty blinking lights on the front of the modem mean?

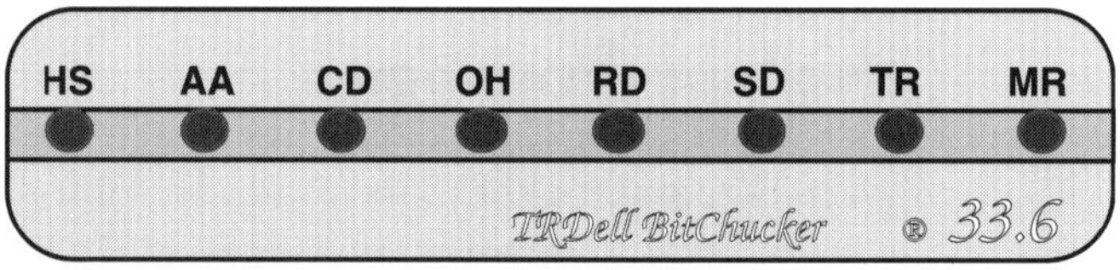

- **HS**: High Speed operation mode
- **AA**: Auto Answer incoming calls
- **CD**: Carrier Detect, signal received from remote modem
- **OH**: Off Hook
- **RD**: Receiving Data
- **SD**: Sending Data
- **TR**: Terminal Ready for communications (your computer)

- **MR**: Modem Ready for communications

Working with Service Providers

If you have an America Online and / or CompuServe account, you may recall supplying some modem configuration information to Claris Emailer during Easy Setup. This information can be modified at any time, or you can create additional configurations for other modems and locations.

To edit your Claris Emailer accounts, choose the **Service Providers** item under the **Setup** menu bar item to open the Service Providers List window. Double-click on any listing to look at the configuration settings associated with the service provider.

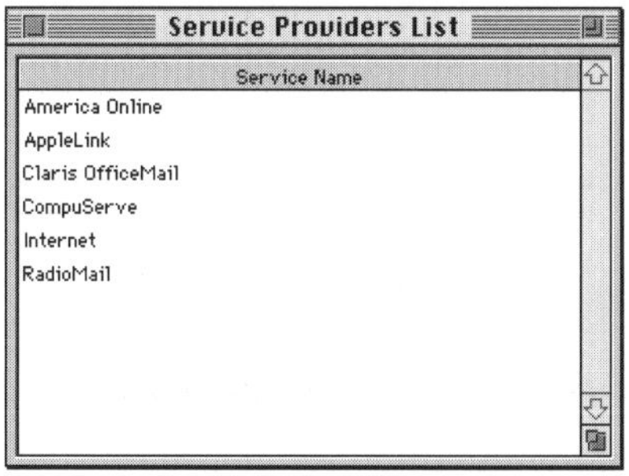

You can also highlight the service that you want to work with and choose **Edit Service** under the **Edit** menu bar item, if you prefer.

America Online

AOL permits access to its service either with a modem or over a LAN. To establish these settings, open the America Online Service Entry dialog box.

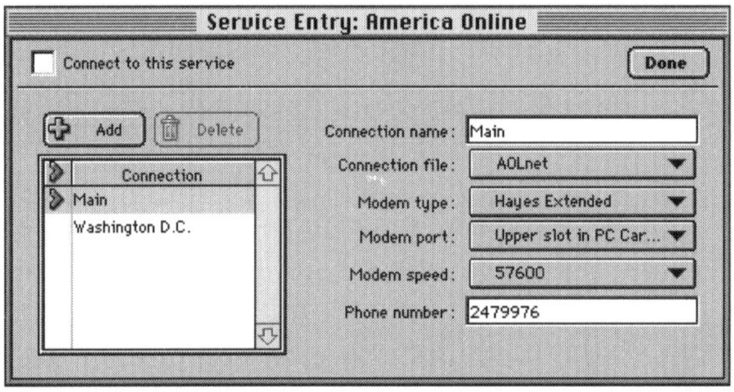

If you established a connection to AOL using Easy Setup, the **Connect to this service** check box will be enabled. Uncheck it whenever you want to suspend communications with the service provider.

You might want to collect your AOL email from multiple locations. These locations can be established in the pane at the left of the Service Entry dialog box using the **Add** (+) button. The options you created when you ran Easy Setup are listed under the name "Main" by default. You can add configurations for home, office, school, or other cities you visit while on the road. You can also add configurations for different types of modems or LAN access. Whichever listing has the arrow before it is currently active, just as in other Claris Emailer lists.

Here is an example of how this works. When I am at my San Francisco office I connect to AOL over a LAN-to-Internet connection by selecting **TCP/IP** in the Connection file pop-up menu.

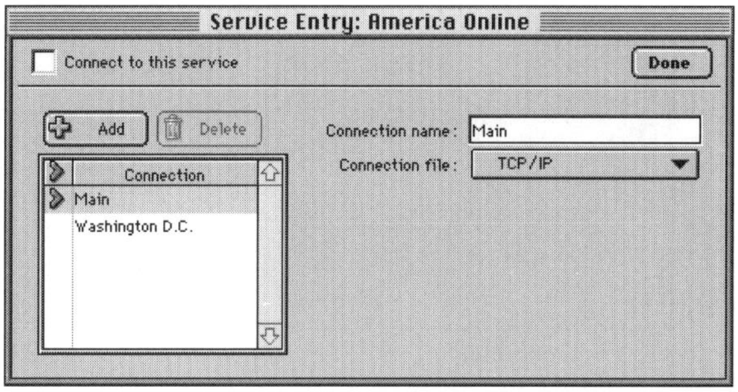

Claris Emailer then falls back on my MacTCP or Open Transport settings to communicate with the service provider.

WARNING!

You cannot use ***TCPack for AOL*** *here. That communications tool works only with the AOL client. Trying to use it will cause errors that may be unrecoverable.*

When I am at home, I connect using a modem. To set this up I first copied the Setup information from my AOL software to Claris Emailer.

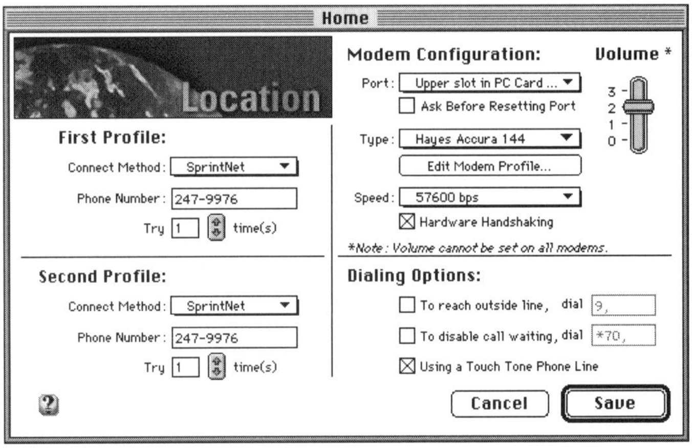

FIGURE 6-15. Settings dialog box in America Online software.

In San Francisco, AOL subscribers connect using SprintNet. To enable this, I choose **Sprint** in Claris Emailer's America Online Service Entry dialog box Connection file pop-up menu.

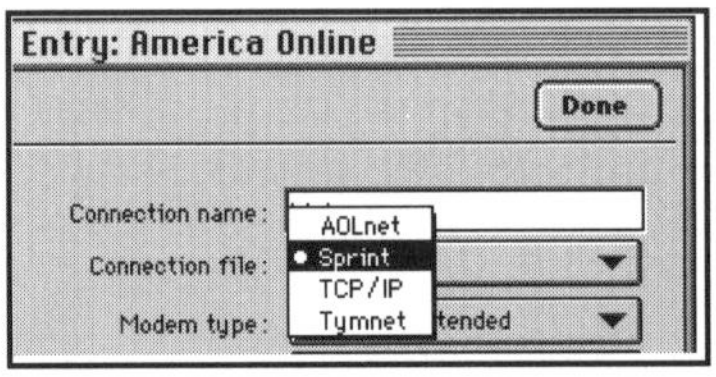

Surprisingly, the modem in my PowerBook is not listed among the choices in the Modem type pop-up menu. (Hey, it was on sale). Like most modems, however, it is Hayes-compatible.

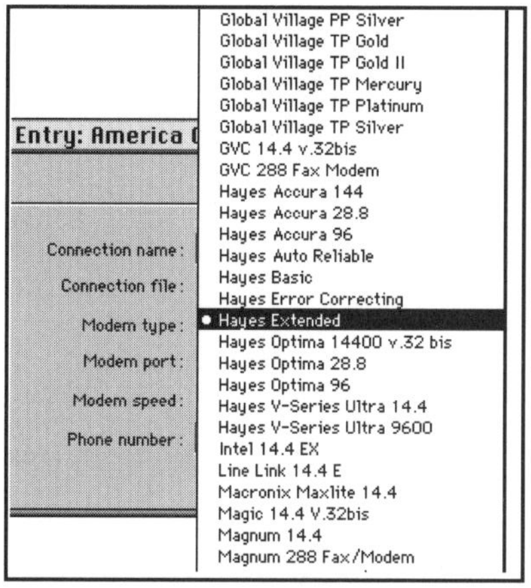

My modem is an internal PC Card, so I choose **Upper slot in PC Card module** in the Modem port pop-up menu to select it.

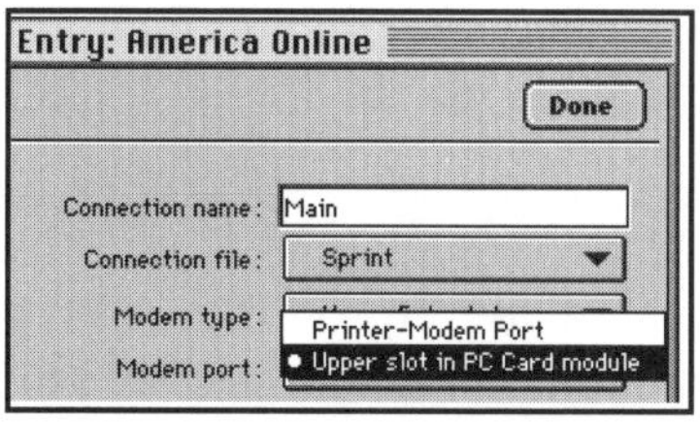

With compression, I am supposed to get 57,600 Bps out of my modem. I choose the highest possible setting in the Modem speed pop-up menu because I know my multi-speed PC Card will drop back to lower speeds if necessary.

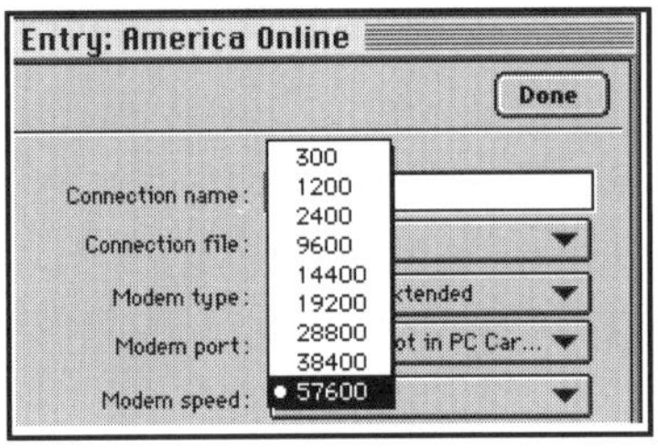

Finally, I take the local access number from my AOL software (see Figure 6-14) and type it into the Phone number field.

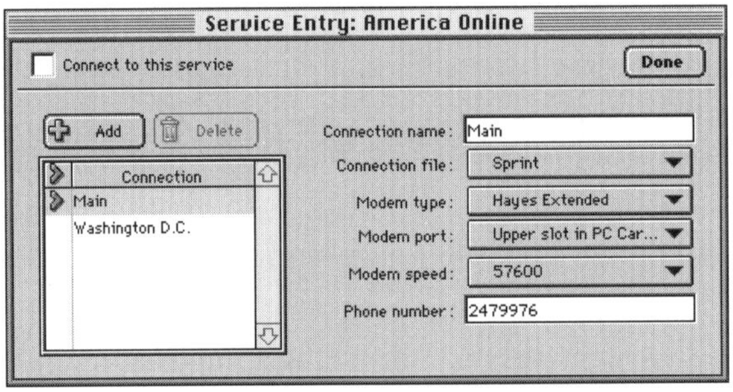

Now I can gather my AOL email quickly and automatically from home without ever booting up the AOL software. Back in the office, I select **TCP/IP** in the Connection file pop-up menu again. Claris Emailer will remember my "Sprint" settings.

When I am away from both home and office, I set up additional entries for the AOL local access numbers in other cities. For instance, to prepare for a trip to Washington D.C., I first logon to AOL and find out what dial-up numbers are local to my hotel (Keyword "Access").

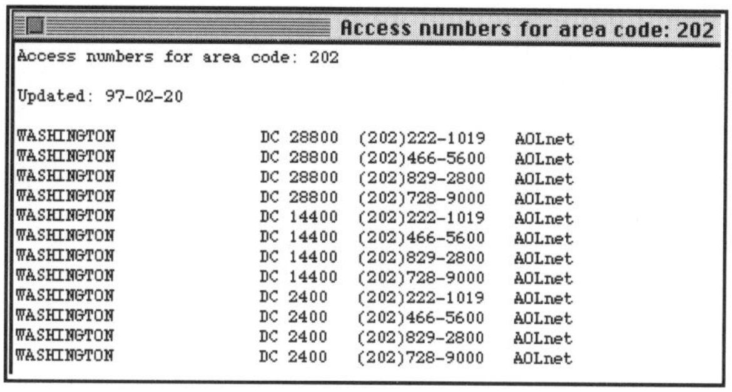
Access numbers for area code: 202

Access numbers for area code: 202

Updated: 97-02-20

WASHINGTON	DC	28800	(202)222-1019	AOLnet
WASHINGTON	DC	28800	(202)466-5600	AOLnet
WASHINGTON	DC	28800	(202)829-2800	AOLnet
WASHINGTON	DC	28800	(202)728-9000	AOLnet
WASHINGTON	DC	14400	(202)222-1019	AOLnet
WASHINGTON	DC	14400	(202)466-5600	AOLnet
WASHINGTON	DC	14400	(202)829-2800	AOLnet
WASHINGTON	DC	14400	(202)728-9000	AOLnet
WASHINGTON	DC	2400	(202)222-1019	AOLnet
WASHINGTON	DC	2400	(202)466-5600	AOLnet
WASHINGTON	DC	2400	(202)829-2800	AOLnet
WASHINGTON	DC	2400	(202)728-9000	AOLnet

FIGURE 6-16. Looking up AOL local access numbers.

Then I use the **Add** (+) button to include "Washington D.C." information in the America Online Service Entry dialog box.

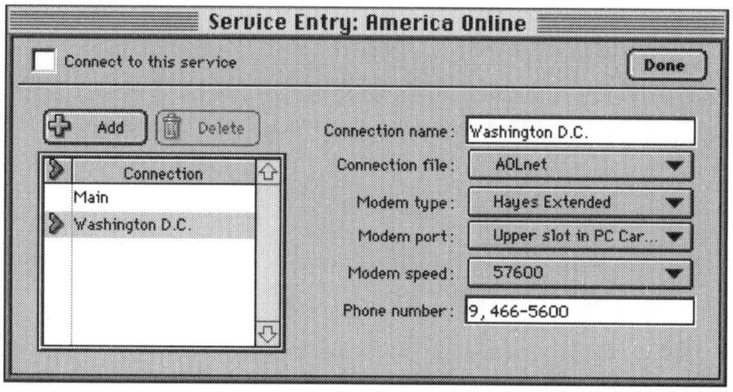

Now when I check into my hotel I can immediately check my email as well.

CompuServe

The CompuServe Service Entry dialog box is configured in much the same manner as the America Online Service Entry dialog box.

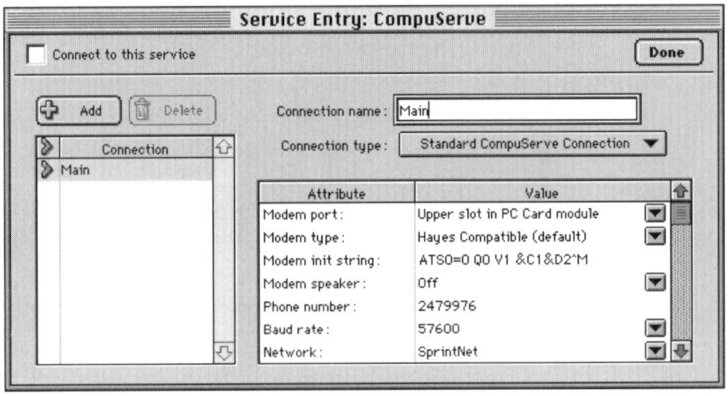

There are a few differences. Notice, for instance, that you are shown the modem initialization string associated with the device you choose in the Modem type pop-up menu. These settings will work in most circumstances, but you can have even greater control over your modem's operations by choosing **Mac Comm Toolbox Connection** in the Connection type pop-up menu.

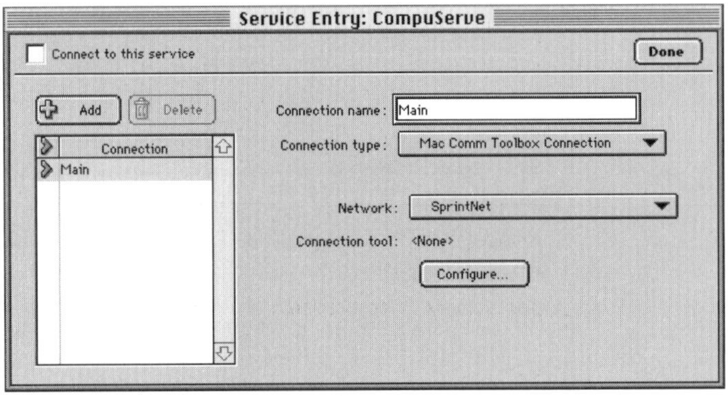

The Macintosh Communications Toolbox is a feature of the Mac OS that permits software developers to create applications without having to write their own modem connection files each time. The Comm Toolbox supports different tools for different hardware within its architecture. Several of these tools are installed by Claris products such as Claris Emailer and ClarisWorks.

To make use of the most commonly used modem tool, press the **Configure** button.

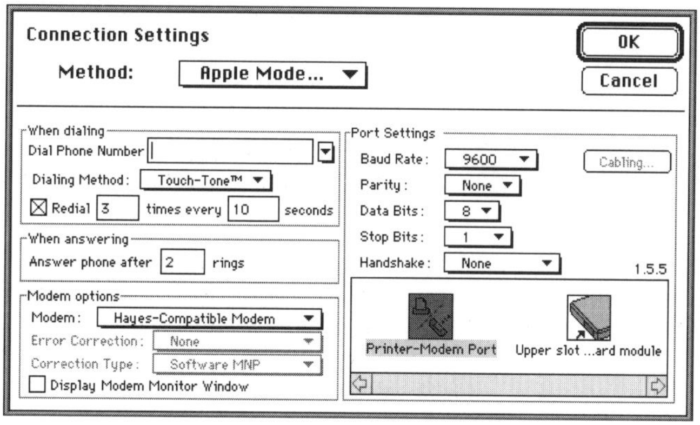

The **Apple Modem Tool**, shown to the left, chosen from the **Method** pop-up menu in the Connection Settings window, gives you many options for fine-tuning your modem configuration. You should recall the function of many of these settings from the last section of this chapter, but the pop-up menus of the Port Settings pane requires further explanation.

In the Baud rate pop-up menu you can establish the ultimate speed of your modem.

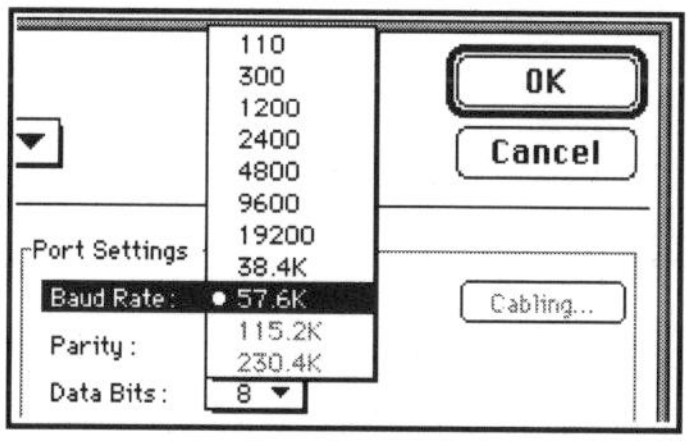

I do not envy anyone who must choose 110 Bps here! Carrier pigeons are faster.

In the Parity pop-up menu you can establish which method will be used by the modem to ensure ungarbled data transmission. Most Macintosh computers and mainframe-based services do not use parity, so **None** will be your likely choice here.

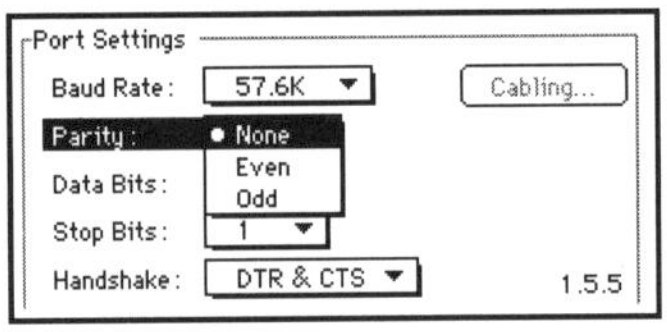

In the Data Bits pop-up menu you can designate how many bits make up a character being sent. This is almost always **8**.

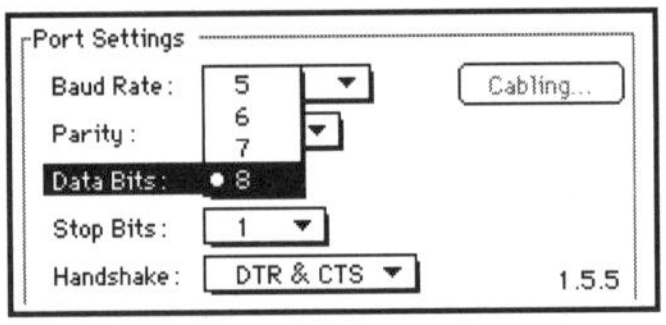

In the Stop Bits pop-up menu you designate how many bits will be used to mark the end of a character during transmission. This is almost always **1**.

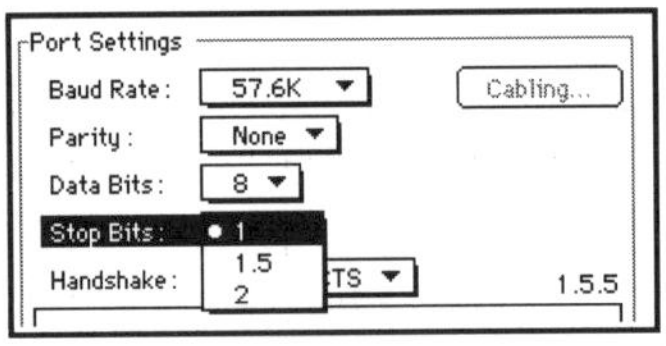

You will often see and hear these modem settings referred to collectively as "8-N-1," meaning eight data bits, no parity, and one stop bit.

The Handshake pop-up menu refers to *flow control,* or the process of regulating the stream data moving between sending and receiving computers. Some online services use the software control method XON/XOFF so that one modem does not transmit data faster than the other modem can receive it. If you are using a modem that is faster than 9,600 Bps, it will probably come with a hardware handshaking cable. *Data Terminal Ready (DTR)* and *Clear To Send (CTS)* make use of this cabling.

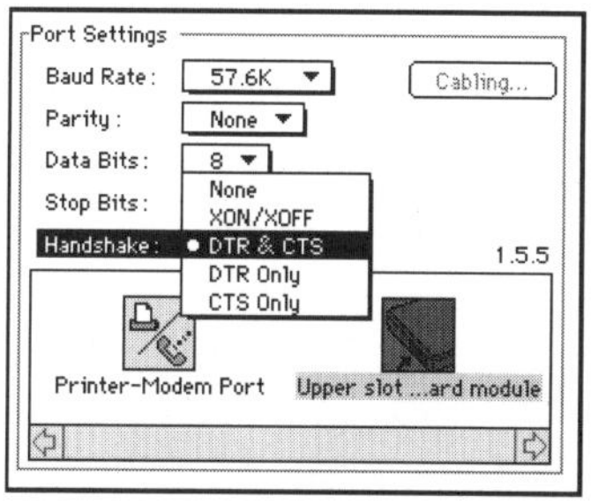

Press the **OK** button when you are done working in the Connection Settings window.

Why bother with all this? Take a look at the Network pop-up menu . . .

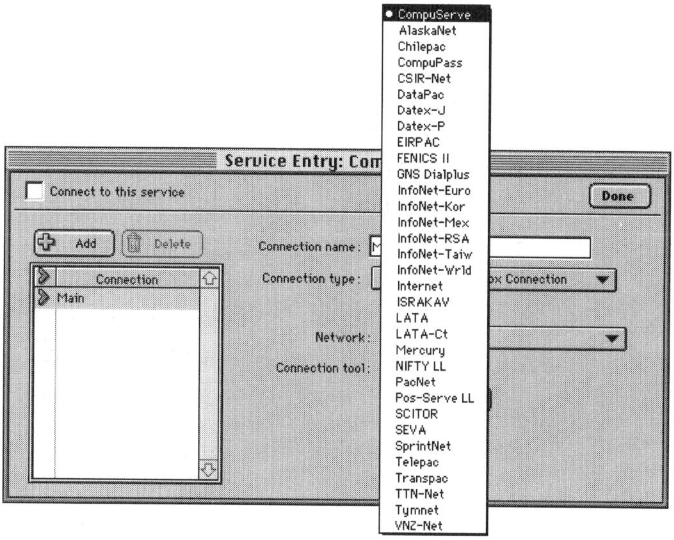

CompuServe is an international online service provider that can be accessed through a great many telecommunications systems. By providing this level of control over your modem connection, Claris Emailer ensures that you will have the best possible chance of getting your email throughout the world!

As with America Online you can connect to CompuServe over the Internet, but it takes a few more steps to set up than does America Online. First select **Mac Comm Toolbox Connection** in the Connection type pop-up menu and Internet in the Network pop-up menu.

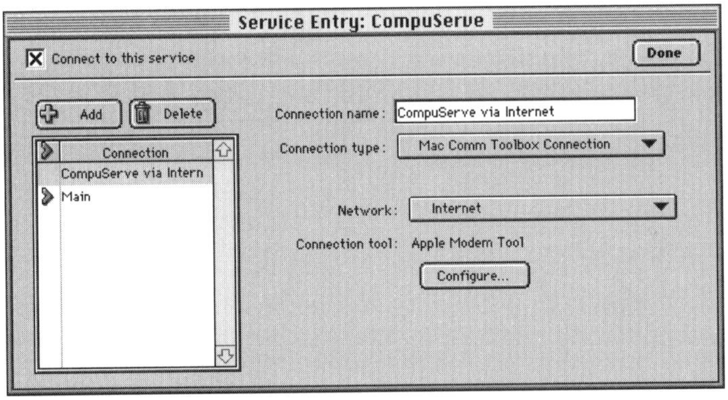

Press the **Configure** button to open the Configuration Settings window. Here, choose **CompuServe TCPack** from the Method pop-up menu to make sure "gateway.compuserve.com" is entered in the Address/Name field.

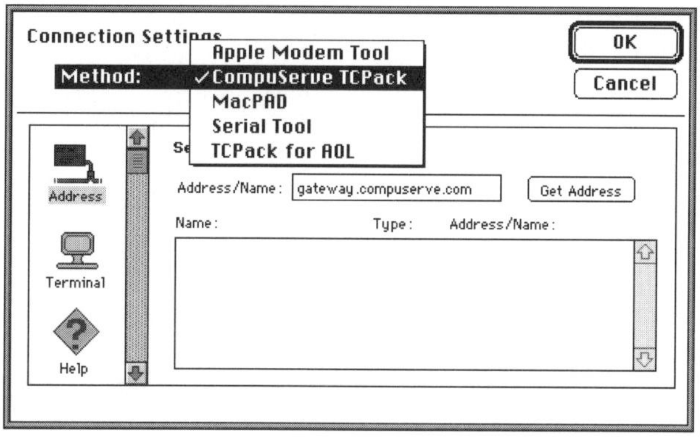

The CompuServe TCPack is installed by the CompuServe Information Manager Installer. You might need to modify its default settings depending on your location. Select the **Help** icon to see further details.

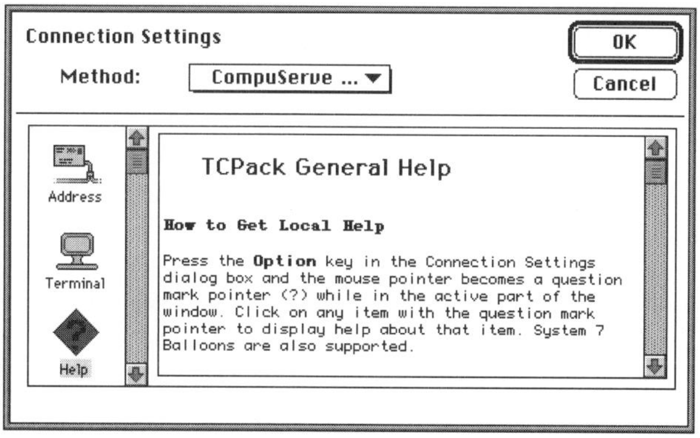

Press the **OK** button when you are done.

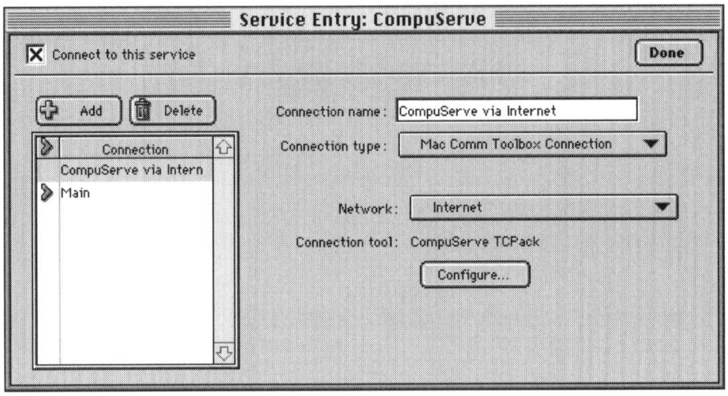

If the CompuServe TCPack is not installed on your Macintosh, select the **TCP Tool** from the Method pop-up menu of the Configuration Settings window instead. Next, enter "gateway.compuserve.com" in the Address field and choose the **Telnet** option.

Internet, OfficeMail, and RadioMail

Because they do not require direct use of a modem, the last three services are not configured beyond Easy Setup in the Service Providers List. All that is determined here is whether or not you will connect to these services.

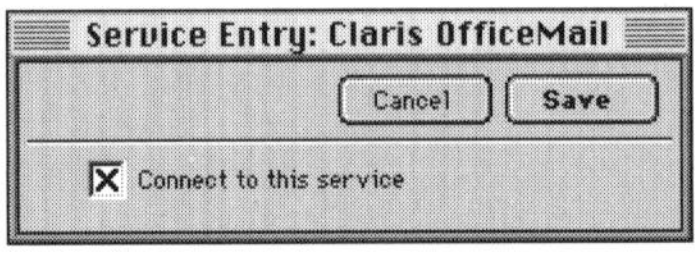

If you select the **Connect to this service** check box, the service in question will be available in Claris Emailer's Schedule and Connect Now windows. To configure these services, go to the Accounts List (which will be discussed further in Chapter 7).

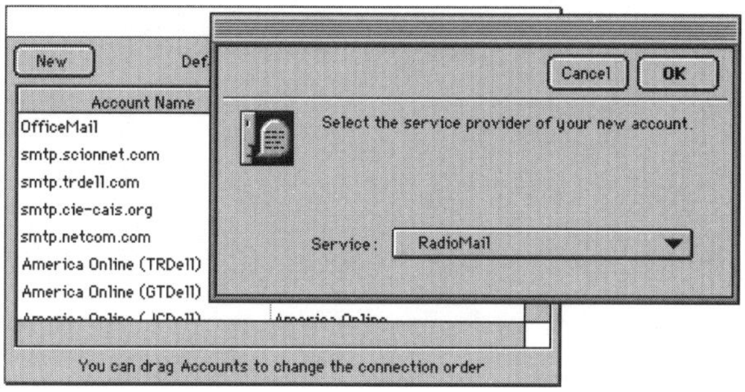

Locations List

Claris Emailer gives you a Locations List so that you do not have to reconfigure the Service Providers List each time you change locations. This is particularly helpful to travelers. It can be opened by choosing **Edit Locations** in the fly-out menu of the **Current Location** command under the **Setup** menu bar item.

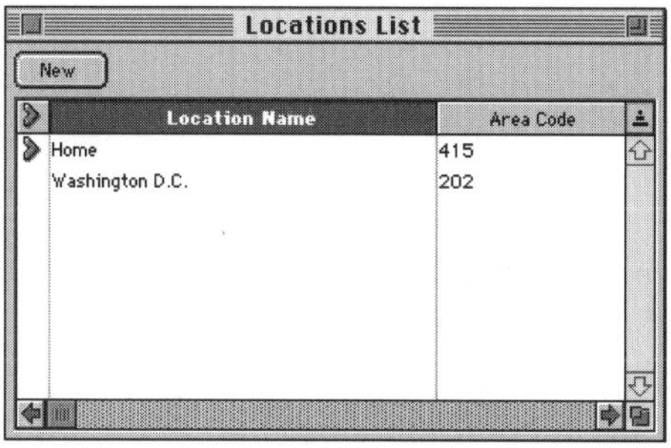

Here, press the **New** button to open a Location Entry dialog box, in which you can add the name and area code of the location to which you are traveling.

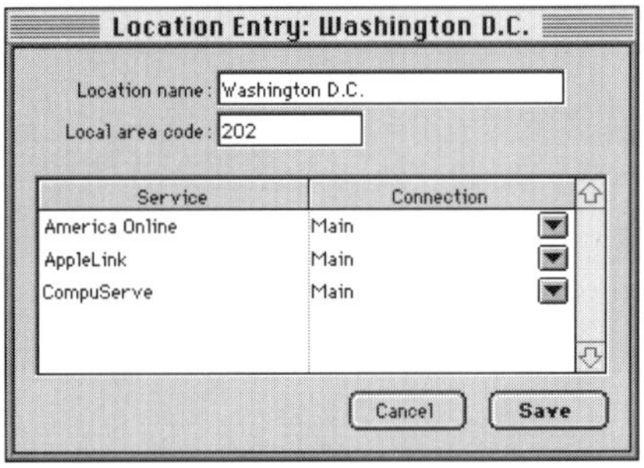

Listings for America Online and CompuServe are also found here. By clicking on the pop-up menus in the Destination field, you can change or edit their Service Providers List entries.

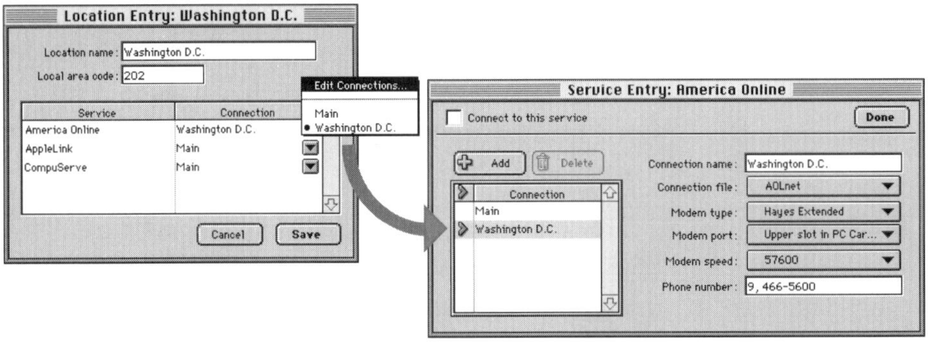

After you set up the configurations for a given location once, switching between one and another is as simple as choosing its designation from under the menu bar.

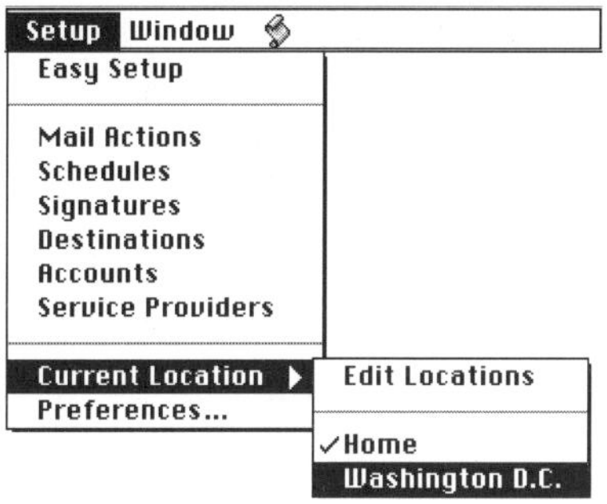

AppleLink

You might have noticed "AppleLink" in some of this book's illustrations.

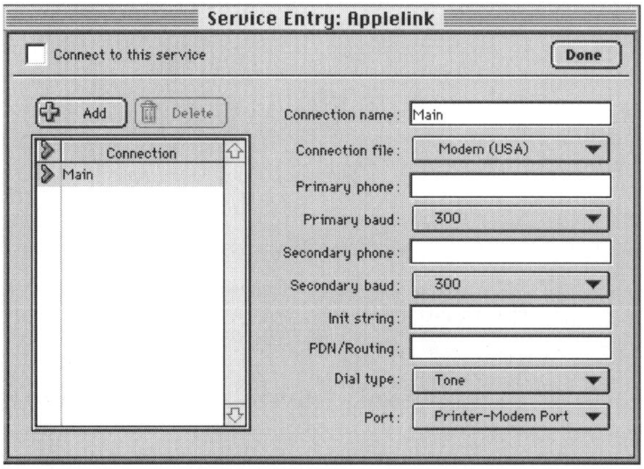

Earlier in the decade when America Online had just a few thousand subscribers and CompuServe was dominated by "DOS heads," the online refuge of Macintosh developers and fans was AppleLink—Apple's own internal online service that offered email and bulletin boards to serious "Mac heads." Around the time Claris Emailer version 2.0 was created, Apple decided to pull the plug on AppleLink. It has since been supplanted by the newer and cheaper WWW. Rather than eliminate a feature that could be useful to many Claris Emailer users, Claris left it in there during AppleLink's last few weeks, but there is no point in documenting it because it no longer exists.

A similar fate befell Apple's eWorld, which was accessible through Claris Emailer 1.0.

So, where does the dedicated Mac addict turn today? In my opinion Apple's offerings on the WWW are far more interesting than what came before, and they are cheaper to use. One of my favorites is the eWorld-like "build your own Web page" site. Check it out at "http://myhome.apple.com/home/welcome/guest."

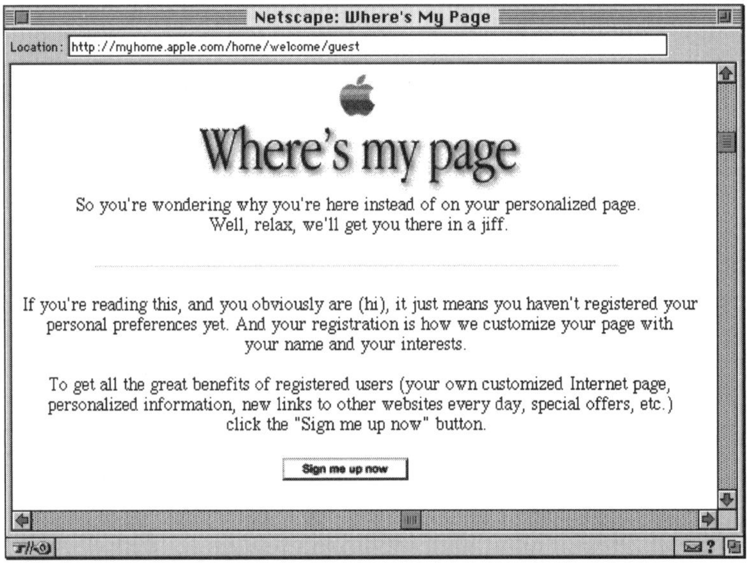

FIGURE 6-17. Apple on the WWW replaced eWorld and AppleLink.

Summary

On a LAN, Claris Emailer can use AppleTalk to communicate with an OfficeMail server over LocalTalk, Ethernet, or ARA. It can use TCP/IP to communicate with OfficeMail, internal POP mail hosts, and, through a LAN-to-Internet link, with America Online and external POP mail hosts. The Macintosh can use either of two types of OS-level networking software: Classic Networking or Open Transport. Under Classic Networking, LAN-based TCP/IP is configured in the MacTCP control panel, and IP for dial-up connections is supported by MacPPP. Under Open Transport, LAN-based TCP/IP is configured in the TCP/IP control panel, and IP for dial-up connections is supported by Open Transport/PPP.

Using an analog modem, Claris Emailer enables Macintosh users to communicate with America Online, CompuServe, and the Internet from multiple locations. It also supports the use of RF modems to communicate with RadioMail's Internet email over the airwaves.

7

Customizing Claris Emailer

Once you have run Easy Setup and familiarized yourself with Claris Emailer's Browser, message forms, and Address Book, you will know all you need to know to send and receive email successfully. Claris Emailer was designed to be powerful but simple. You can have faith that the application's default settings will work best in most situations.

After you have worked with Claris Emailer a bit, you may find that you want to customize its functions. In this chapter I will give you the run-down on the application's preference settings, with which you can tailor Claris Emailer to suit your own work style.

Like many Claris applications, Claris Emailer supports AppleScript, which allows you to customize Claris Emailer's workings further, creating your own helper applications to automate repetitive tasks. I will show you that, too.

Using Application Preferences

You can modify the way Claris Emailer performs some of its most basic tasks by selecting the **Preferences** command under the **Setup** menu bar item. In the Preferences window that opens, select the settings you wish to modify in the contents pane on the left.

Defaults

The **Defaults** preferences control the actions Claris Emailer will perform when it first boots up, whether or not certain dialog boxes will be displayed while you are working, and what page setup will be used in quick printing.

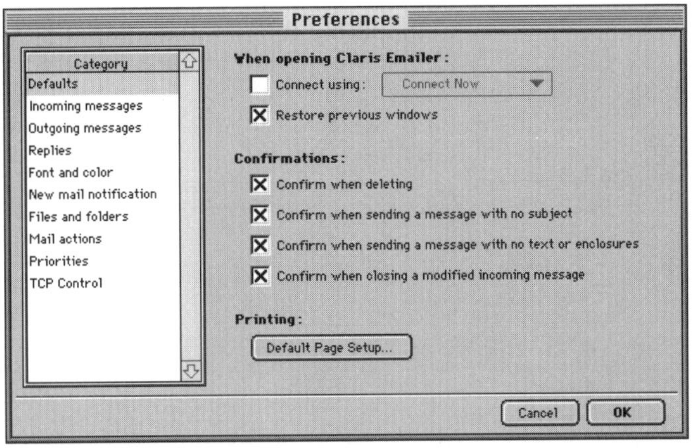

FIGURE 7-1. Defaults Preferences window.

Selecting the **Connect using** check box enables a pop-up menu in which you can tell Claris Emailer to open the **Connect Now** dialog box when it first launches, or connect automatically using one of your schedules.

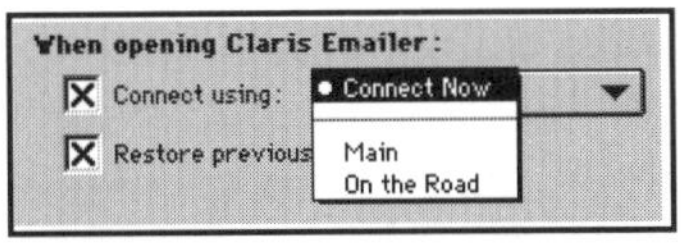

If you have disabled your schedules in the Schedules List window, this setting will not override it.

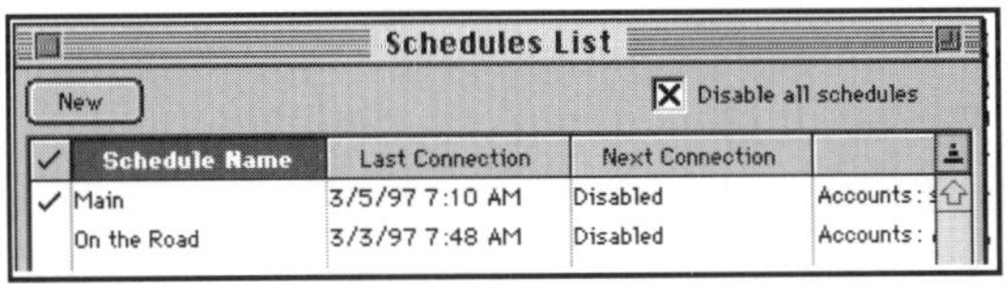

If you select the **Restore previous windows** check box here, the location to which you have dragged any windows before quitting Claris Emailer will be the same location in which the window reappears when it is booted up later. This can be handy if you like to have that Browser zoomed out "just so."

Be cautious about deselecting items in the Confirmations field's check boxes.

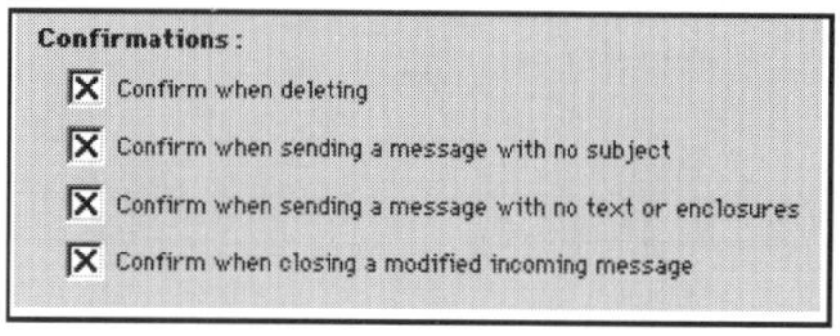

It is probably a good idea to enable the **Confirm when deleting** check box because there is no "undo" for this command and it is easy to get it mixed up with the harmless process of moving messages to the Deleted Mail folder.

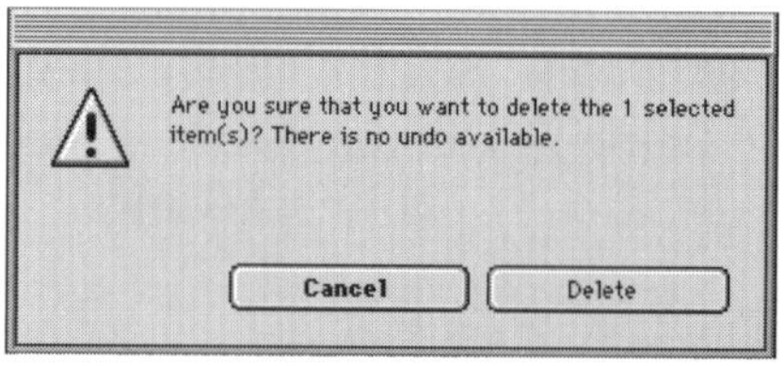

You can safely deselect the check boxes **Confirm when sending a message with no subject** and **Confirm when sending a message with no text or enclosures** in most cases. Be aware, however, that some email systems require contents in these fields and your messages will be returned if you leave fields blank.

I think it is best to have all these check boxes selected to serve as the warnings they were intended to be. If you find them annoying, simply hold down the **Option** key to override them. For example, if you choose several items in your Deleted Mail folder and press the **Delete** button while holding down the **Option** key, you will not be interrupted by the warning dialog box.

Use the **Default Page Setup** button to establish the parameters of your typical print jobs.

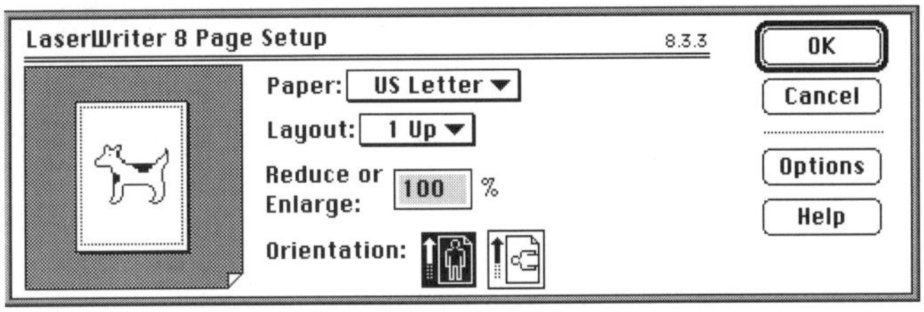

These are the settings Claris Emailer uses when you select the **Print One** command from the Toolbar **Print** button's pop-up menu or from under the **File** menu bar item.

Incoming Messages

Incoming messages preferences tell Claris Emailer what to do when it receives enclosures and new email as well as messages you are done reading.

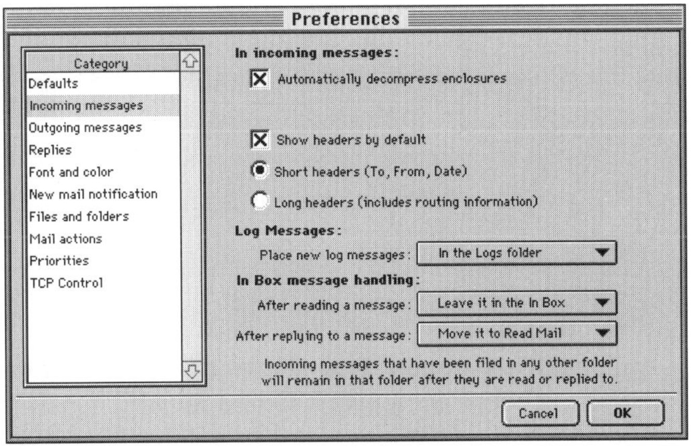

FIGURE 7-2. Incoming messages Preferences window.

If you select the **Automatically decompress enclosures** check box, Claris Emailer will use Aladdin's StuffIt to "unstuff" enclosures that have been sent to you. This happens in the background so it will not interrupt your work. Low hard drive space, however, will generate an error dialog box if the size of the decompressed file exceeds the space available.

If you deselect the **Show headers by default** check box, a typical incoming message will look like this:

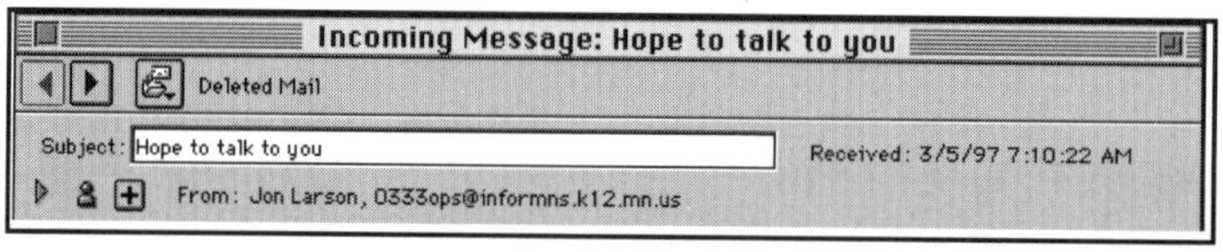

You will see who the message's sender was, and that is all you will see.

If you select the **Show headers by default** check box and choose the **Short headers** button, it will look like this:

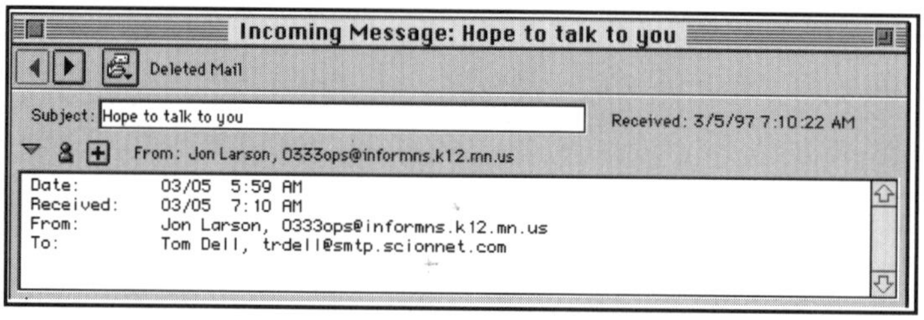

You will see who sent the message, who got it, and what time it was sent and received.

If you select the **Show headers by default** check box and choose the **Long headers** button, it will look like this:

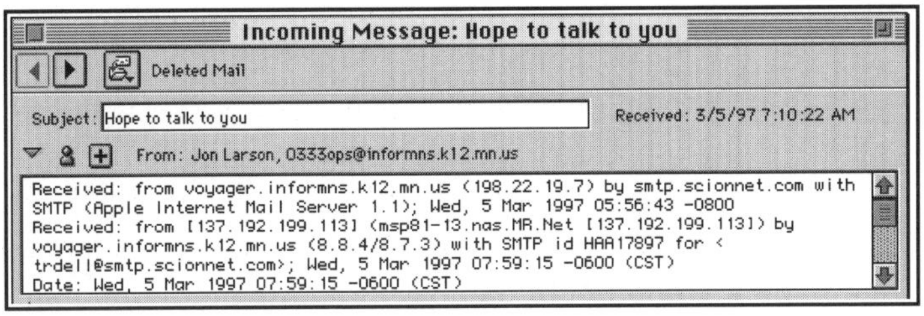

You will see who sent it, when it was sent, and the Cyberspace path it took in getting from point A to point B, your In Box.

Do not be confused here. The **Show headers by default** check box does not control either radio button. It only determines whether or not the headers window will be visible when you open an incoming message in the In Box folder. The header information you chose with the radio buttons is still available when you deselect the **Show headers by default** check box, but you must click on the triangle to expand the header field to see it.

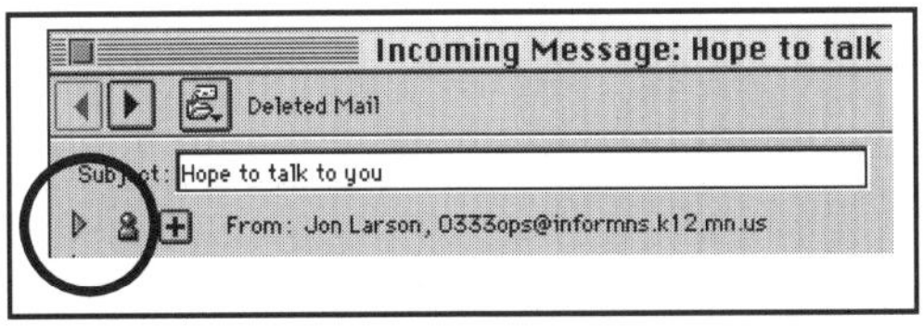

Since I want as much viewing space for the message as possible, I deselect the check box. I also choose the **Short Headers** button. If I want to see more after I have expanded the header field of a particular message, I can always choose the **Show Long Headers** command under the **Mail** menu bar item.

In the Log Messages field and its pop-up menu, you can decide whether to have log messages stored in the Logs folder or dropped into the In Box.

If you find that communications errors are common, let the Connection Log messages pile up in the Logs folder. When you have many accounts you will probably experience errors, albeit temporary ones. Connection Log messages can fill up your In Box in a hurry when a mail host is too busy to respond at a given time of day, or when your modem keeps encountering a busy signal.

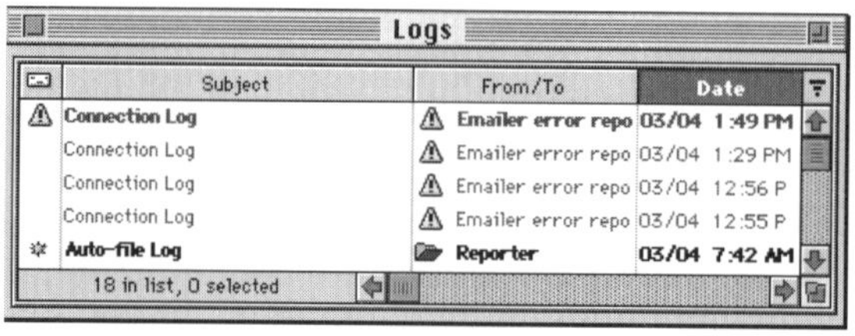

If you find that communications errors are rare, you might as well have these novelties dropped into your In Box. This setting is also handy when you want to know about it each time one of your auto-filing Mail Actions is triggered. For that to work, you must remember to choose the **Create a new auto-file log entry** check box when you create your Mail Actions, as I showed you in Chapter 5.

In the In Box message handling field's first pop-up menu you can decide to have messages you have read left alone, moved to the Read Mail folder, or moved to the Deleted Mail folder. In the latter case this does not mean that the files are actually deleted, it just means that they are put in the Deleted Mail folder. You still have to use the **Delete** command (manually or automatically) to really be rid of them for good.

In the In Box message handling field's second pop-up menu you can decide whether to have messages you have replied to left alone, moved to the Read Mail folder, or moved to the Deleted Mail folder.

These settings only pertain to your In Box. They do not affect any messages that you might file first, either manually or through Mail Actions, and then read or reply to.

I have several accounts and it is not at all uncommon for one or more mail server to be too slow to respond when Claris Emailer queries it, resulting in a Connection Log error message. I have auto-filing Mail Actions set up but I do not feel I need to know each time that something gets filed. For these reasons I choose to have log messages filed in the Logs folder.

When I read a message, I may not have time to respond to it immediately. So I leave it in the In Box to serve as a reminder. When I do reply, however, that is another story. I do not need messages wasting space in my In Box. I could have them moved to the Read Mail folder, but once I have replied to a message, that reply is as important to me as the original message when I am trying to recreate a chain of events. Since I have Claris Emailer copy an original message into a reply message by default, I can look in the Sent Mail folder to get a message containing both parts. I therefore use the In Box message-handling field's pop-up menu to direct Claris Emailer to toss replied-to messages in the Deleted Mail folder.

Outgoing Messages

Outgoing messages preferences tell Claris Emailer what to do when you send enclosures and new email and how to handle messages you have finished writing.

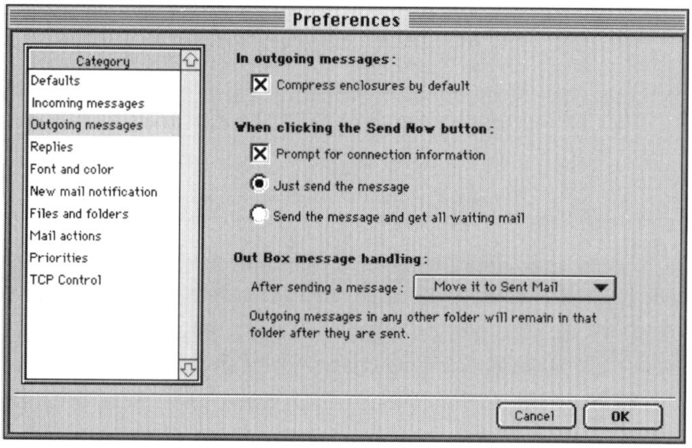

FIGURE 7-3. Outgoing messages Preferences window.

If you select the **Compress enclosures by default** check box, Claris Emailer will use StuffIt to "stuff" enclosures when you send them. You can override the preference by deselecting the **Compress Files** check box in the Enclosures field of a message form.

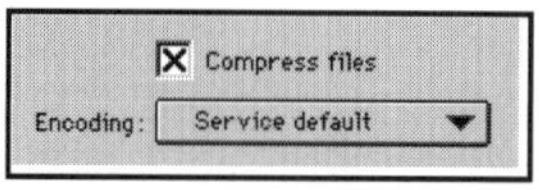

This has nothing to do with encoding, and it really pertains only to other Macintosh users because they are the ones who use StuffIt. If you exchange files mostly with PC or UNIX users, you might as well leave this unchecked. Also, if you are sending files to other Macintosh users who do not use

Claris Emailer, make sure they have StuffIt. Claris Emailer installs the StuffIt Engine System Extension itself.

If you select the **Prompt for connection information** check box in the "When clicking the Send Now button" field, you will be presented with a dialog box similar to the one you see when you use the **Connect Now** button. The buttons **Just send the message** and **Send the message and get all waiting mail** determine if both **Get** and **Send** check boxes will be enabled in this dialog box or only **Send**.

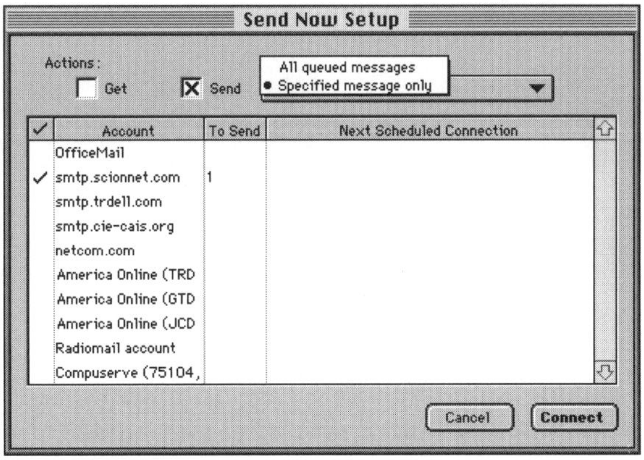

You can decide to send just the message you have finished writing, or that message along with any others waiting in queue, by using the Send Now Setup dialog box's pop-up menu.

This is an "as long as I'm here I might as well . . . " dialog box. While sending a message from one account, you might decide to check for a reply to a different message in a different account. If you do not use schedules, this feature can be most helpful.

I prefer to disable the dialog box and just send a message when I have finished writing it. I like to move on to the next task as soon as possible. I know that my schedule will be able to handle the rest. I can always override this feature temporarily by choosing the **Queue Message** button instead of the **Send Now** button.

The Out Box message-handling field's pop-up menu decides where messages you have just sent from the Out Box will be placed. You can leave them where they are, move them to the Sent Mail folder, or move them to the Deleted Mail folder.

I find it useful to keep the messages I have sent for a while, in case a question arises later and I want to review what I said. I could move the messages to the Deleted Mail folder, but then I would have to find them among all the other deleted items from my In Box. I could leave them in the Out Box and differentiate them from queued messages by the fact that those are all listed in bold face and have clock icons next to them. I cannot direct Claris Emailer to automatically clean out old messages in the Out Box, however. So my choice is the Sent Mail folder. It keeps my old outgoing messages separate from my old incoming email and can be cleaned out automatically.

These settings only affect messages that pass through the Out Box. If you file a message you are working on as a draft and then send it later, it will stay in the folder you sent it from.

Replies

In the **Replies** preferences window you direct Claris Emailer to perform special actions on the message form you use for replying to incoming email.

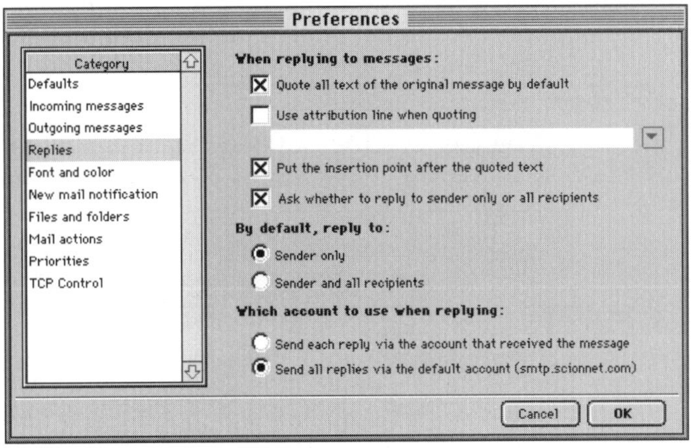

FIGURE 7-4. Replies Preferences window.

As I said earlier, I direct Claris Emailer to add the contents of an incoming message to the body of a reply message by default. This is done by selecting the **Quote all text of the original message by default** check box. If you deselect this, your reply messages will be a lot shorter, but what you say might be misunderstood if the recipient cannot remember what he or she said to elicit your response.

You can fine-tune this further by preceding the original message with something from the "Use attribution line when quoting" field. For instance, you might start off with "You said":

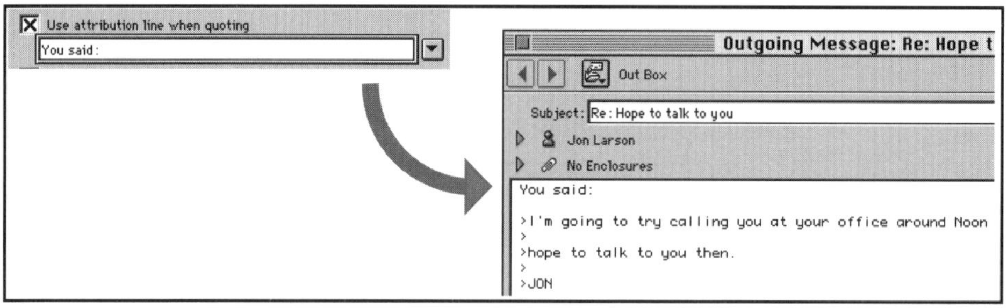

You can use the pop-up menu at the end of the field to add the sender's name and address and the date they sent the original message. For example, you could write "On <date>, <sender> (<sender address>) said":

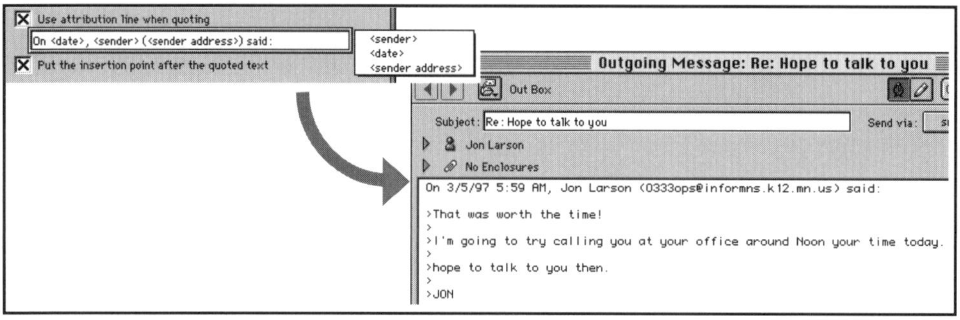

If you select the **Put the insertion point after the quoted text** check box, your comments will start after the previous message. When used in combination with the previous field, the attribution line is always placed above the original text and your reply is placed beneath the original text. If the messages you reply to are generally short, this is a useful feature because it puts your replies in a question-and-answer format. I should warn you, however, that many people find it tedious to scroll through nine paragraphs of their own question to get to your two- or three-word answer!

When you receive a message that has been sent to several people, you can tell Claris Emailer to address your reply to just the sender, or to the sender and everyone else who was sent the message, by using the buttons in the "By default, reply to" field. If you select the **Ask whether to reply to sender only or all recipients** check box, you are presented with a dialog box in which you choose between the two on a case-by-case basis.

In the last field you can decide to send your replies via the same account they came through or to have all email pass through just one account. If you have one account that is faster and more reliable than others, this a good candidate for the default in the Replies preferences window. You can always override this command in a message form's "Send via" pop-up menu.

Font and Color

The **Font and color** preferences window allows you to tell Claris Emailer which of your Macintosh's installed fonts you would like to see the email written in and how big it should be (up to 14 points).

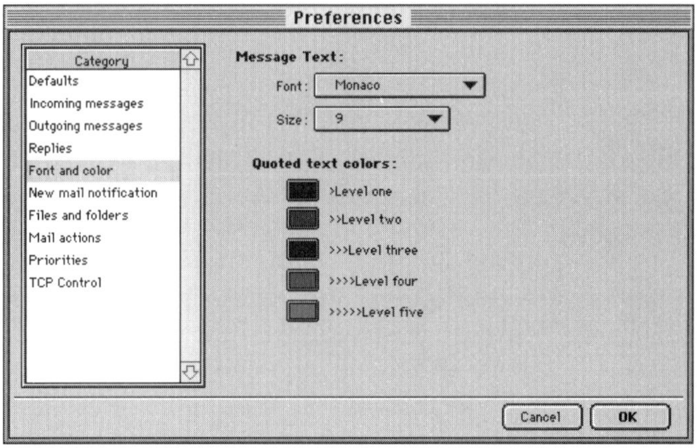

FIGURE 7-5. Font And color Preferences window.

If you find yourself squinting to read your email, avail yourself of this feature. It can make a real difference!

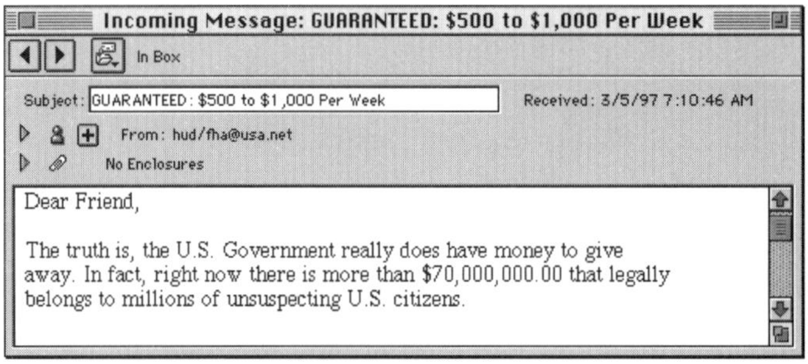

Be aware of one thing. If you plan to format your email using spaces you should stick with a *monospaced* typeface such as Monaco, Geneva or Courier. These allocate the same amount of space for each character regardless of their shape. The others, *kerned* fonts, make things look better by closing up space between thinner characters. An "i" takes up less space than an "m," for example. When you try to create pictures within the text that can really mess things up.

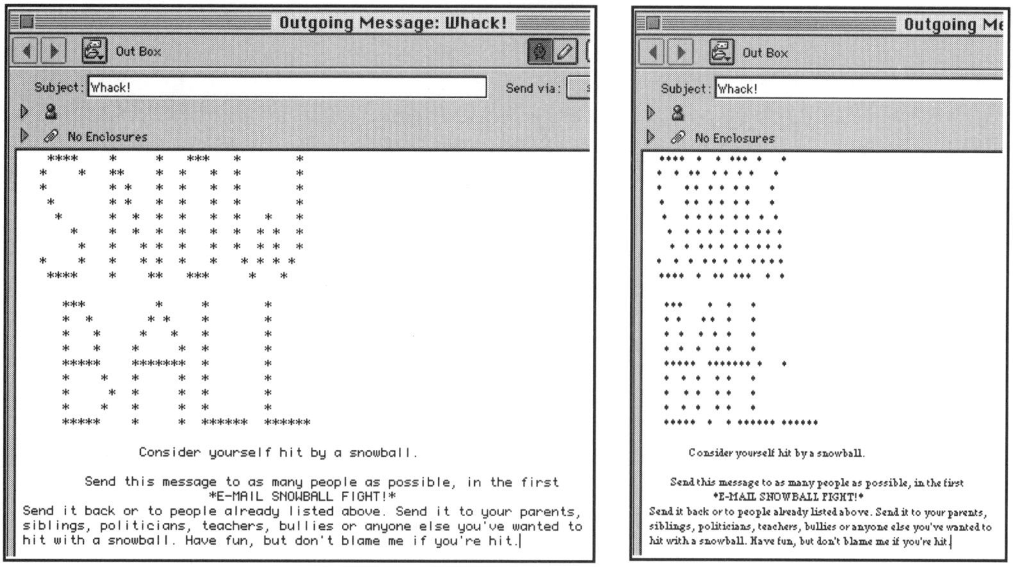

FIGURE 7-6. Monospaced font (Monaco) versus kerned font (Times).

When you choose to have the text from an incoming message copied into the message form of a reply message, Claris Emailer uses a number of greater than (>) symbols and a color to delineate comments hierarchically. This way you can read a message, reply to it, read a reply to your reply, reply again, and so on. You can keep this up for as many as five replies before Claris Emailer gives up on trying to order them for you. In the "Quoted text colors" field you can pick a color for each level using the Macintosh color wheel as illustrated in Figure 7-7.

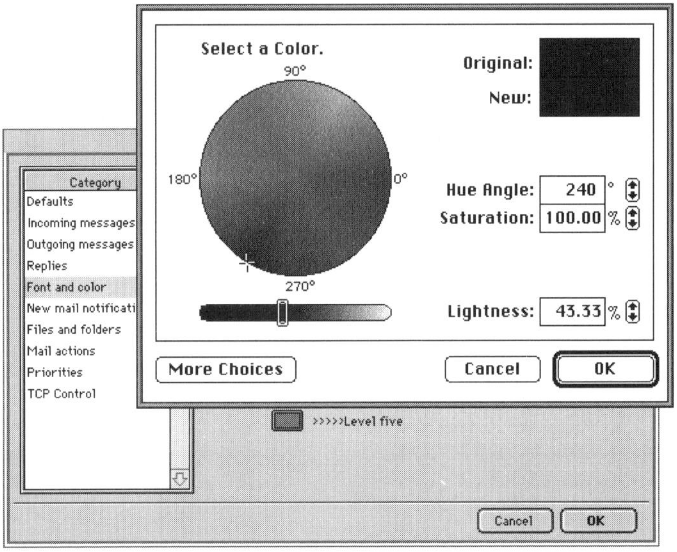

FIGURE 7-7. Choosing a color for quoted text.

New Mail Notification

In the New mail notification preferences window you can determine how Claris Emailer will inform you that new email has arrived.

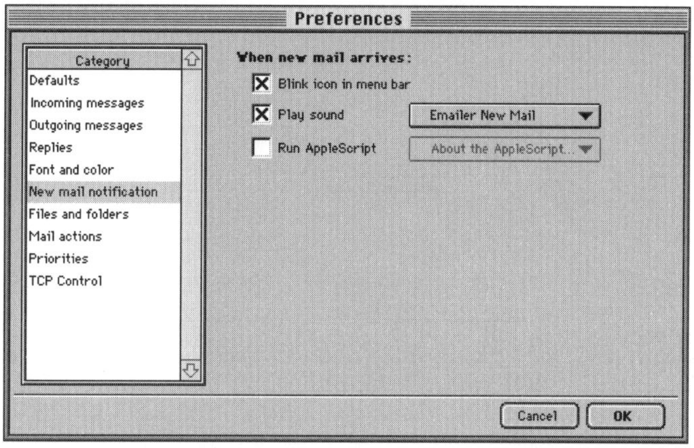

FIGURE 7-8. New mail notification Preferences window.

If you select the **Blink icon in menu bar** check box, Claris Emailer will call your attention to new email by blinking a little Claris Emailer icon (like the one to the left) over the Finder while you are working in another application.

You can have this accompanied by one of the sounds installed on your Macintosh if you choose the **Play sound** check box. Be careful which sound you use and how loud your Macintosh's volume setting is.

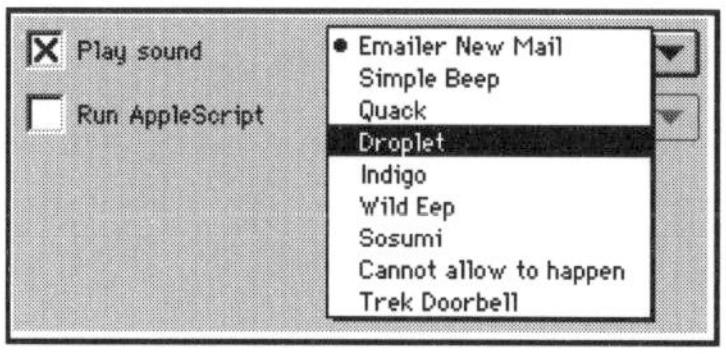

These two features make use of a little application that Claris Emailer installs in the "Startup Items" folder of the Macintosh's System Folder, called Notify Emailer Startup. Should you disable notifications (both here and in the OfficeMail Account preferences), this application is automatically removed.

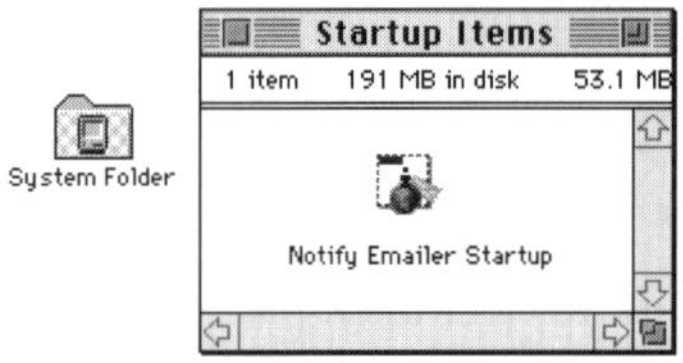

The last item in the New mail notification preferences window is a powerful feature that permits you to execute an AppleScript when new email comes in.

The only choice that makes sense here is **Speak Unread Mail**. This tells you verbally which folders you have unread email in—handy if you do a lot of automated filing. It can also read new messages in your In Box out loud. I will talk more about AppleScript further on.

Files and Folders

The Files and folders preferences window pertains to the actual Macintosh folder structure, not the folder structure within Claris Emailer's Folder List.

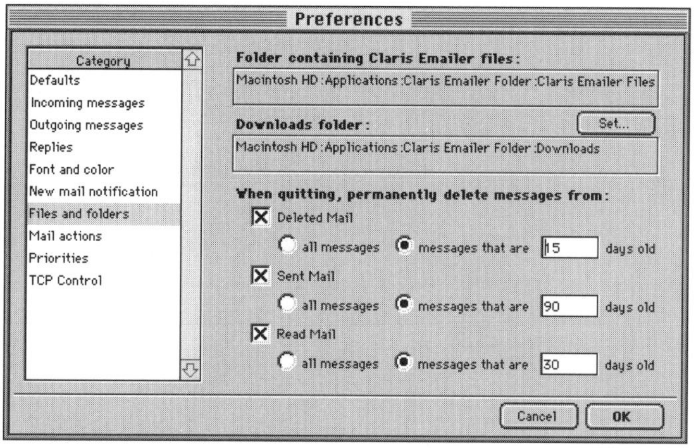

FIGURE 7-9. Files and folders Preferences window.

In the first field you can see where Claris Emailer keeps its Claris Emailer Files folder. In the second field you can tell Claris Emailer where you want it to put incoming enclosures. By default, Claris Emailer puts these files into the "Downloads" folder inside the Claris Emailer Folder. You can change this behavior. Use the **Set** button to open the Macintosh file selection dialog box and direct Claris Emailer to the folder of your choice.

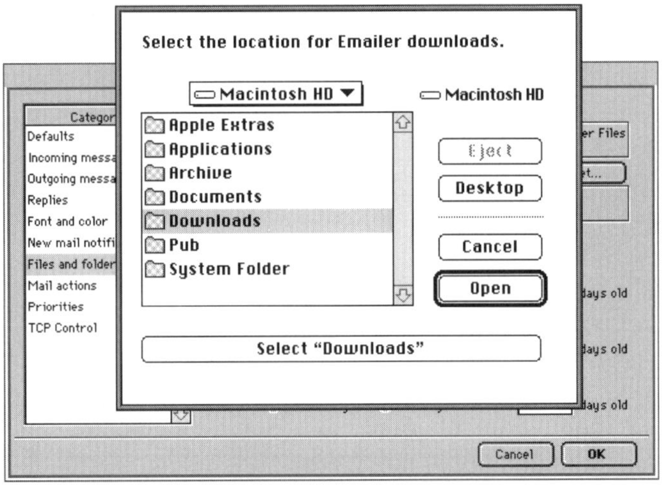

FIGURE 7-10. Show Claris Emailer where to put downloads.

You can quickly open either the Claris Emailer Files folder or the Downloads folder by choosing one of them in the fly-out menu of the **Open Special** command under the **File** menu bar item.

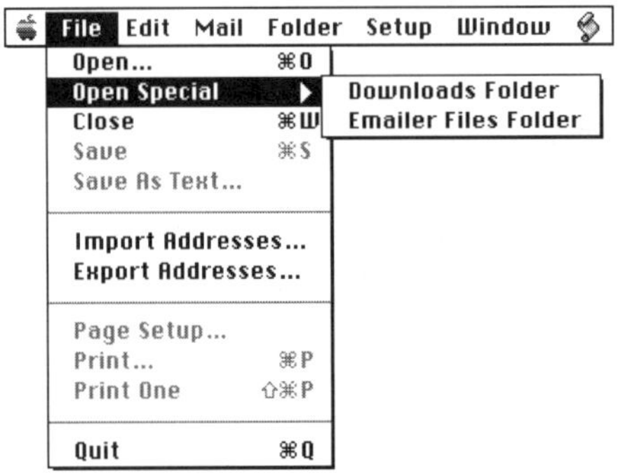

This window's next field contains, in my opinion, the most important preference settings Claris Emailer offers. These pertain to whether or not the application will be permitted to automatically delete some of your files and, if so, when. Such deletions are permanent.

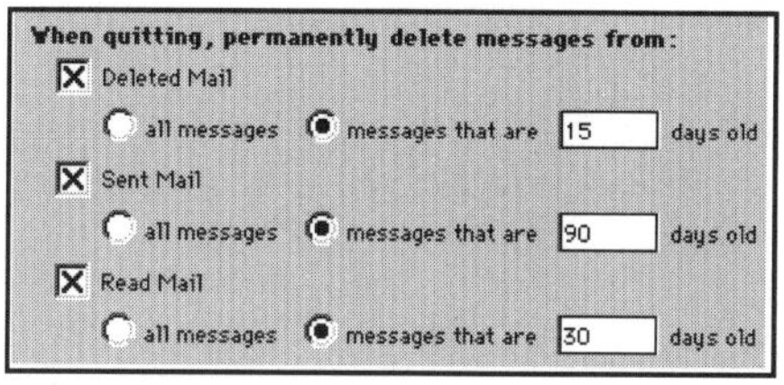

If you do not use these settings, you will have to remember to go through your Deleted Mail, Sent Mail, and Read Mail folders every so often to clean them out. Otherwise, Claris Emailer will eventually eat up all the hard drive space on your Macintosh!

I have Claris Emailer hold my sent mail and read mail for 30 to 90 days. That way I can always review something I said in the past or resend a message the recipient has lost. Deleted mail is mostly worthless to me. I let Claris Emailer hold it for a couple of weeks just in case I put something in the Deleted Mail folder by accident.

Mail Actions

The **Mail Actions** preferences window contains just two entries, only the first of which is important.

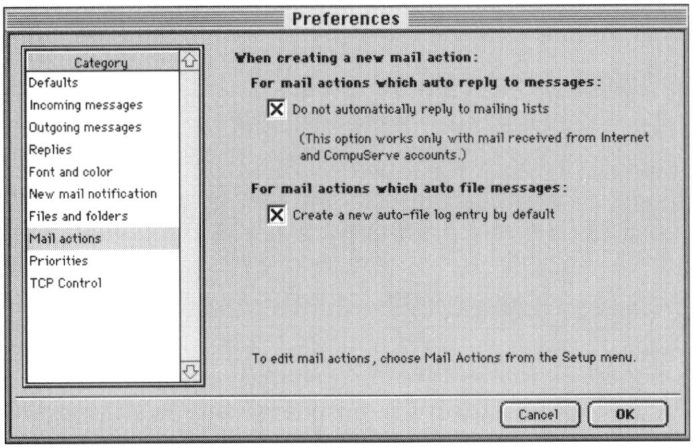

FIGURE 7-11. Mail Actions Preferences window.

If you have set up any mail actions that reply automatically to incoming messages, be sure to select the **Do not automatically reply to mailing lists** button. There is little point to telling all the members of a mailing list that, say, you are on vacation—over and over again. If you did, there would probably be some nasty messages waiting for you when you got home! This only pertains to Internet and CompuServe accounts.

In the earlier sections I explained that it is handy to be able to track email that has been handled by an auto-file Mail Action, but to do so you must make sure the **Create a new auto-file log entry** check box is used. The second check box in this window makes that the default condition.

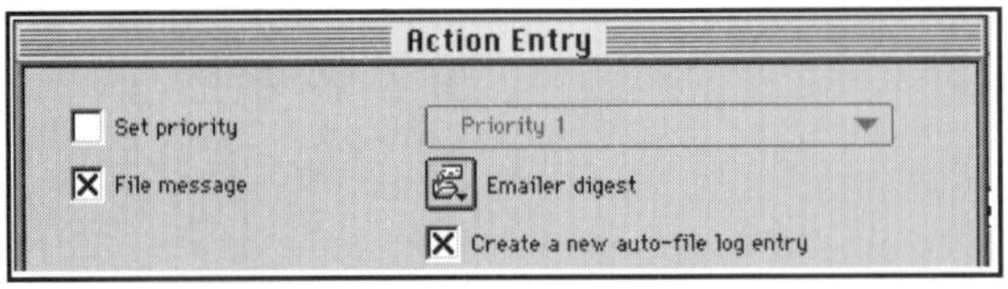

Priorities

What you type in the Priorities preferences window determines what color code you use for categorizing messages.

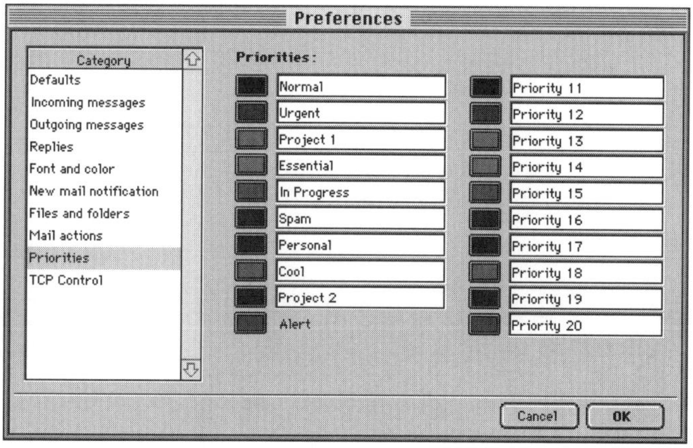

FIGURE 7-12. Priorities Preferences window.

The idea is to give you a method for ranking the relative urgency of email messages as they appear in the Priority column of the Browser.

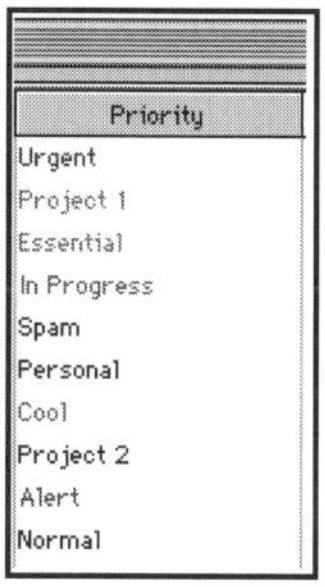

To give a message a priority, select it in the Browser and choose an item from the **Priority** fly-out menu under the **Mail** menu bar item.

Claris Emailer reserves one priority for itself, the red "alert." You can categorize your messages from relatively high to relatively low priority using the remaining fields. Alternately, you might associate certain priorities with certain addresses. Say that communications pertaining to "project X" get one priority and color, and every message from a given mailing list gets another. You can then use Mail Actions to ensure that these priorities get automatically assigned to incoming email. With 19 fields to work with, you have a lot of room for customization. You can also change these colors using the Macintosh color wheel.

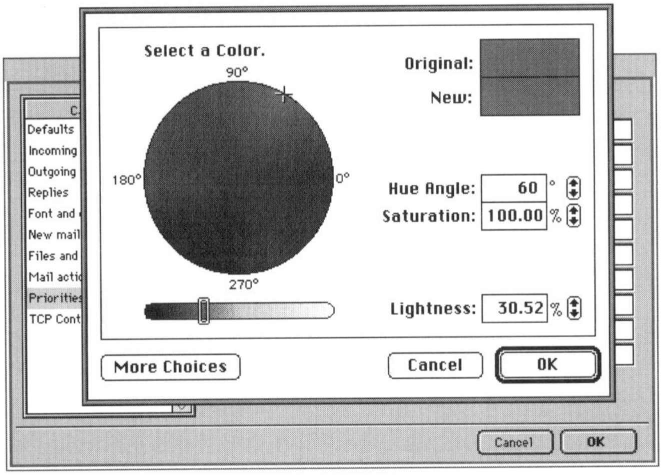

FIGURE 7-13. Setting a new priority color.

All incoming messages assume the first priority by default.

Your grading system may differ from that used by another email system or Claris Emailer user, so it only has significance for you. An exception would be if you have OfficeMail throughout your organization. In that case, standardizing priorities will work.

To stay consistent with the rest of my system, I use the same labeling scheme that the MacOS uses (as seen under the **Labels** menu bar item in the Finder). Of course, I could not resist a few labels of my own, such as "spam."

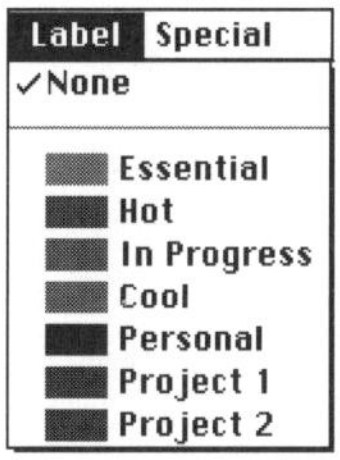

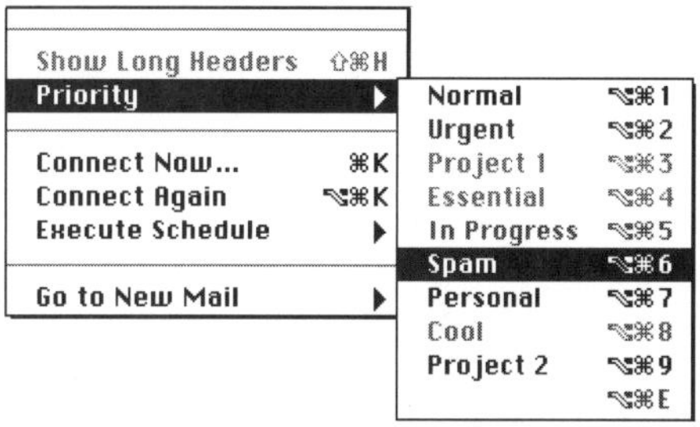

A friend of mine uses a "Top Secret" priority for some of his messages. Those get encrypted before they are sent out.

TCP Control

The TCP Control preferences window provides you with a tool for avoiding large online bills from your Internet dial-up service.

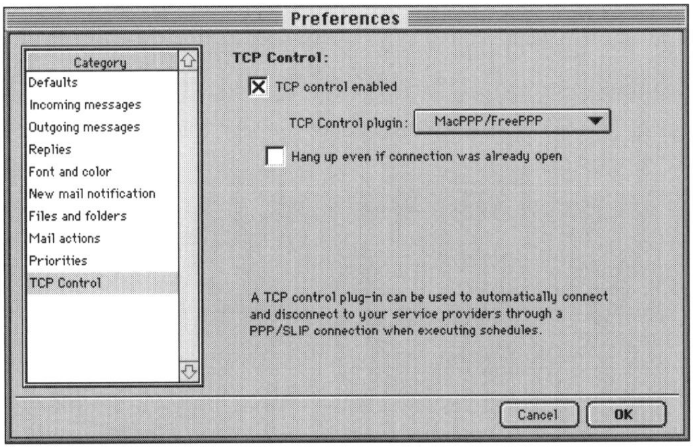

FIGURE 7-14. TCP Control Preferences window.

If you enable the **TCP control enabled** check box, the TCP Control plugin pop-up menu will make the **MacPPP/ FreePPP** option available to you. This plug-in gives Claris Emailer the ability to open and close your PPP connection without your intervention. If you choose the **Hang up even if connection was already open** check box, Claris Emailer will use an open PPP connection to transfer email and close it afterwards, even though it did not initiate the connection.

Using Account Preferences

In addition to the preferences you can specify for Claris Emailer as a whole, there are preferences associated with your accounts. To work with these, open the Account List by choosing the **Accounts** command under the **Setup** menu bar item.

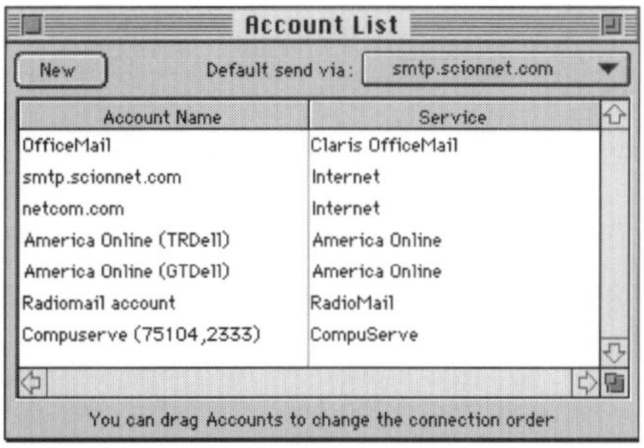

Here you can alter the default for each account, not just for each service provider. Double-click on an account's list item to edit it.

OfficeMail

The Account Entry window for OfficeMail contains two tabs besides the **Account Info** tab that you worked with during Easy Setup. Under the **Options** tab you can pick the default Signature file you want added at the bottom of messages sent from an account. You can also decide which encoding method will be used by default. Since you will be using OfficeMail to exchange messages primarily with Macintosh users, you will usually choose **BinHex** here.

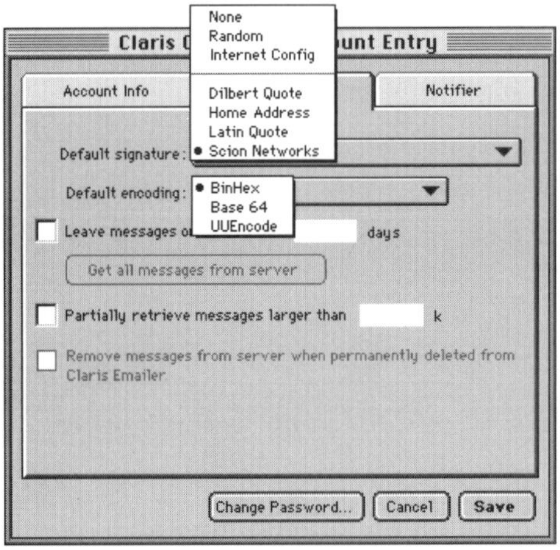

The OfficeMail server will store your new email only until you log in with Claris Emailer. After it passes the files over to you, it erases them from its own hard drive. You can alter this behavior by selecting the **Leave messages on server for X days** check box. In general, you do not want to use this feature because it will eat up hard drive space on both your Macintosh and the server. If you are experiencing problems with your Macintosh, however, having copies of your messages stored on the server can give you some peace of mind. It is also helpful if you log in to OfficeMail from multiple machines. If you use this feature, be sure to select the **Remove messages from server when permanently deleted from Claris Emailer** check box to make sure email you do not want anymore gets discarded. You can direct the OfficeMail server to download all your old messages again by pressing the **Get all messages from server** button.

The **Partially retrieve messages larger than X k** is particularly useful for PowerBook users connecting to their OfficeMail servers remotely over ARA. You might receive file enclosures that are so big that they would take a long time to download. You might just as well leave them on the server until you get back to the office. With this option set, you would be given the message but not the enclosure. A commonly used setting here is **512**.

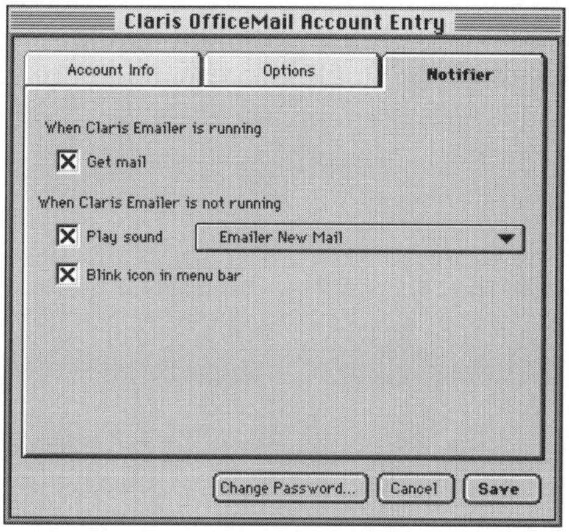

You can be informed about the arrival of new email even when Claris Emailer is not running. That is the job of the Notify Emailer Startup application, which I mentioned in the last section. How this is done is determined by what you select under the **Notifier** tab.

If the **Get mail** check box is selected, the OfficeMail server will pass new email to Claris Emailer and you will be notified as it comes in. If you do not select this, the OfficeMail server will not pass email to your Macintosh until you log in using a schedule or the **Connect Now** command.

The other settings under this tab work in the same way as those of Claris Emailer's **New mail notification** preferences window, as previously described.

Internet

Internet accounts have the same settings options as those used by OfficeMail. The exception is the **Connect using APOP** check box. Enable this check box only if your ISP or server administrator tells you to use authenticated POP.

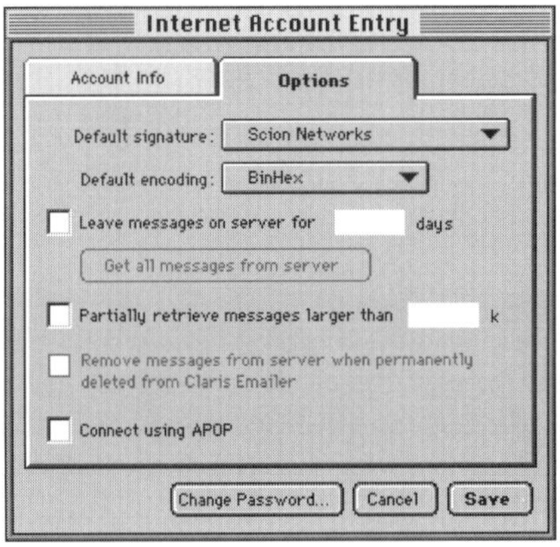

America Online, RadioMail

AOL and RadioMail accounts provide just one default settings choice, the Signature file.

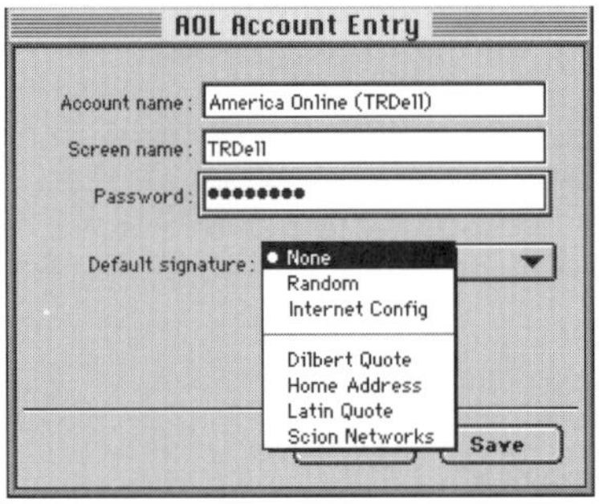

CompuServe

CompuServe accounts can be modified with regard to the default signature and whether or not your email should be left on the service provider's servers. In addition, you can direct Claris Emailer to ignore the messages CompuServe sends out during a connection to remind you that you are being charged for that connection.

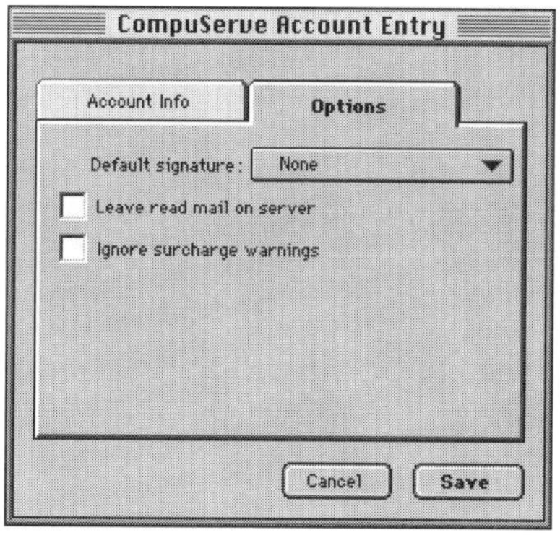

Using Internet Config

You might have noticed that "Internet Config" is one of your choices for the default signature. This refers to the Internet Configuration System, a nifty Macintosh freeware application made available by Peter N. Lewis and Quinn "The Eskimo." This application makes the lives of Macintosh users easier by reducing the number of times they need to enter various Internet preferences into various Internet applications. For instance, why should you have to enter your Internet email address into Claris Emailer, *and* Apple Cyberdog, *and* NewsWatcher, *and* Anarchie, and so on? You shouldn't and you don't. Enter this information once, and Internet Config and its System Extension makes the information available to all Internet applications.

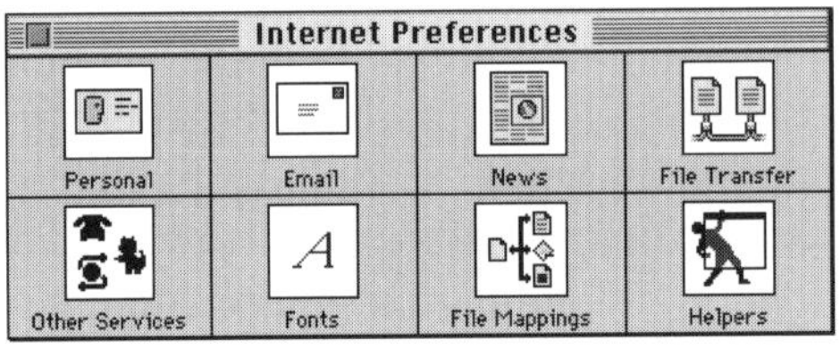

Among the settings Internet Config will remember for you is a signature.

An application must be "Internet Config aware" to take advantage of this. Fortunately, Claris Emailer is.

You can find this application at numerous sites on the Internet, including "ftp://ftp.share.com/internet-configuration" (in the U.S.), and "ftp.quinn.echidna.id.au/Others/Quinn/Config" (in Australia).

You can contact its authors at "internet-config@share.com."

Using AppleScript

Some Macintosh users never use AppleScript. Many do not know what it is for, and some think it just looks scary. That's a pity because it is yet another reason why the MacOS is more user-friendly than any other operating system currently produced.

At its simplest, AppleScript is a sort of macro language. Using an application called Script Editor you can "record" various actions you perform repetitively to a create a list, or *script*, of steps. After that, you no longer have to perform those steps. Instead, you play back the script and the Macintosh performs the actions without you so much as twitching a muscle.

If you have never used AppleScript before, take a minute to try it out. First, go to the Claris Emailer folder and select the Claris Emailer application. Next, select **Automated Tasks** under the **Apple** menu bar item and pick **Add Alias to Apple Menu** in the fly-out menu. AppleScript will launch, create an alias of Claris Emailer, and drop the alias into the "Apple Menu Items" folder inside the System Folder.

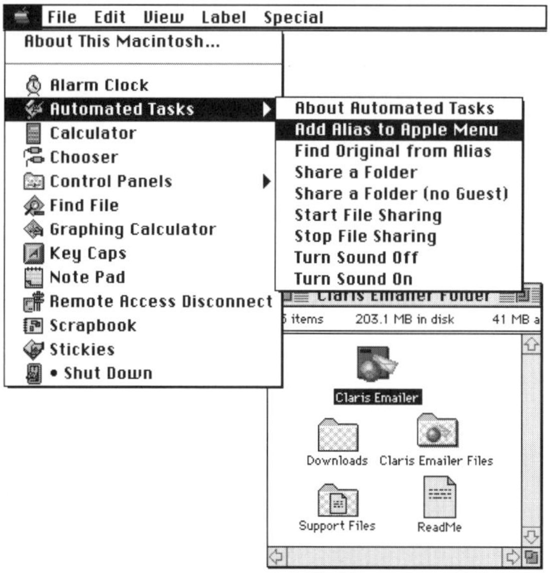

FIGURE 7-15. Using AppleScript to create an alias.

Now, when you want to boot up Claris Emailer you do not have to open a bunch of windows to get to it. Instead, you can just select it under the **Apple** menu bar item.

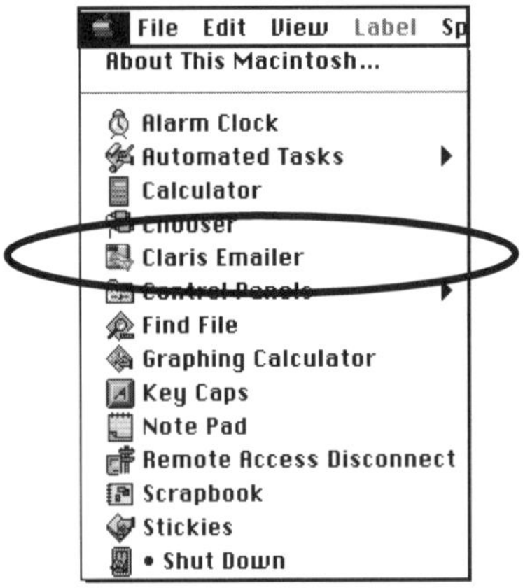

That is one example of what you can do with AppleScript using just the scripts Apple gives you with the MacOS. You can create other scripts of varying complexity yourself. All you need is System 7.0 or higher with AppleScript added, or System 7.5 or higher, which has AppleScript built in.

Again, this is AppleScript at its simplest. Move a little deeper and you will find that AppleScript is a plain-language programming code that enables various applications to communicate with each other and to share resources. To do this it uses a unique MacOS feature called *Apple events*. Any application that is Apple events aware can be extended far beyond what its original designers intended and offers users the ultimate ability to customize their software to meet their own requirements.

Since Claris Emailer is AppleScript savvy, I can use it to illustrate the workings of Apple events. Go to Claris Emailer's **AppleScript** menu bar item and choose the **Go to Claris Emailer Home Page** command.

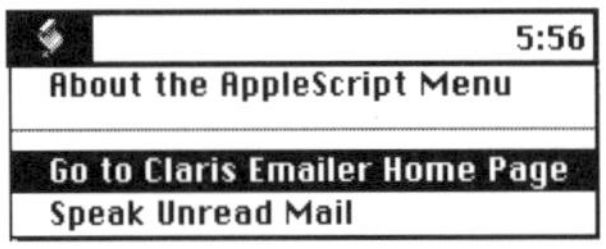

If you have Netscape Navigator on your Macintosh, Claris Emailer will send a URL to it via Apple events. This will cause the browser to launch and take you right to the Claris Corp. WWW site.

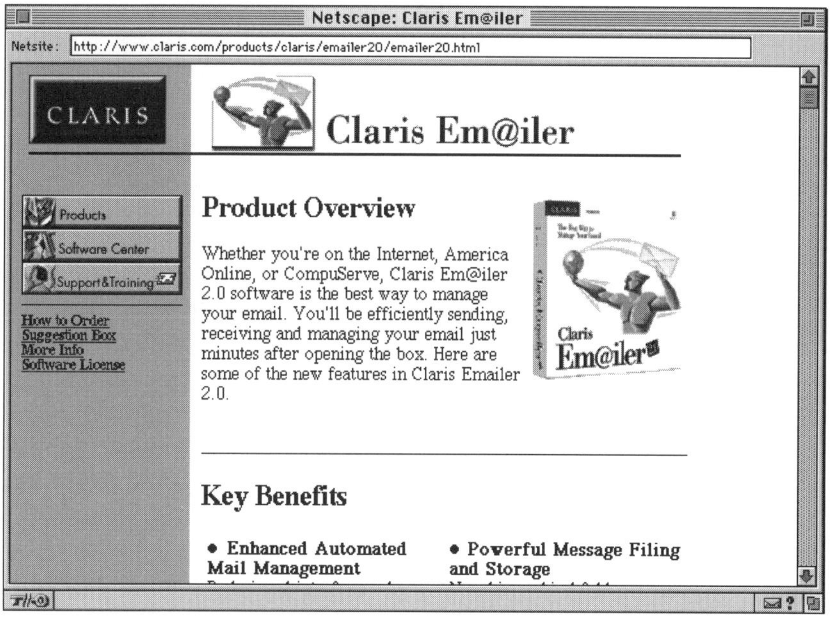

FIGURE 7-16. Logging into the Claris Home Page.

In its original state Claris Emailer shows just two scripts under its **AppleScript** menu bar item, the one just illustrated and the one that uses the MacOS' Speech Manager to tell you verbally how many unread messages you have and in which folders they are stored. Scripts become visible under the **AppleScript** menu bar item when you drop them into the "AppleScripts" folder inside the Claris Emailer Files folder within the Claris Emailer Folder.

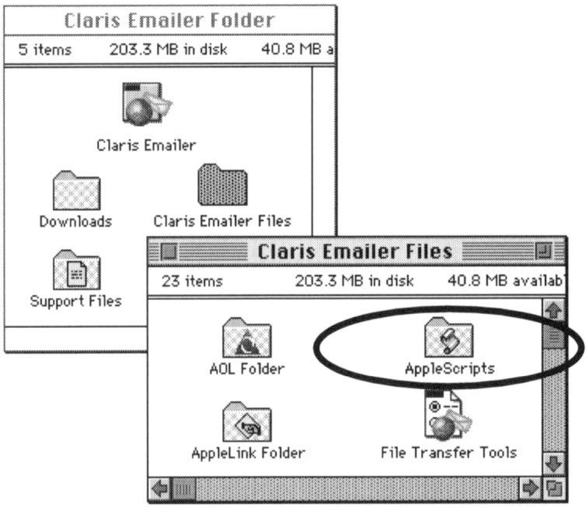

Claris Emailer comes with several more scripts that you might find helpful. These are located in the Support Files folder within the Claris Emailer Folder.

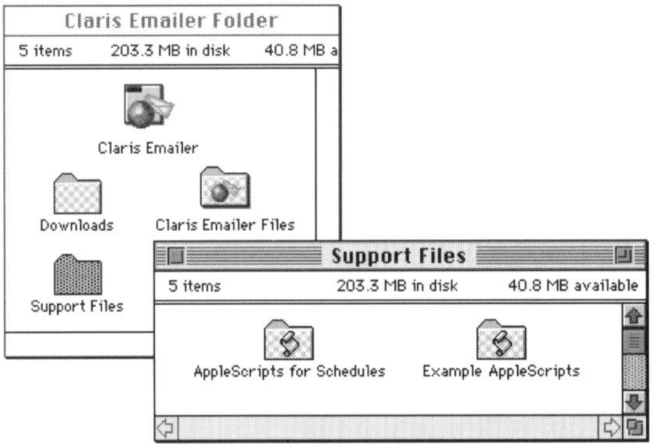

AppleScripts for Schedules

The "AppleScripts for Schedules" folder contains several scripts that give Claris Emailer the ability to open and close MacPPP by itself. (For more information on MacPPP, refer to Chapter 6.)

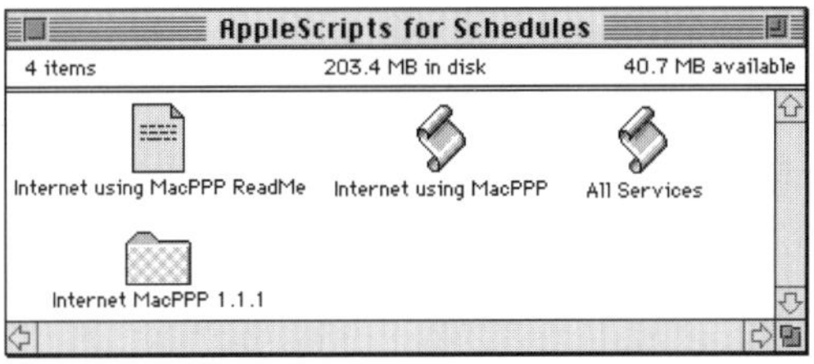

In addition to MacPPP itself, these scripts rely on the MacPPP Control AppleScript Addition available at many sites on the Internet. You install it by dragging it into the "Scripting Additions" folder within the "Extensions" folder of the System Folder.

To use the "Internet using MacPPP" script, just drag it into the AppleScripts folder in the Claris Emailer Files folder. You may then create a schedule as I showed you before, only this time choose the script in the AppleScript pop-up menu of the Schedule Entry window.

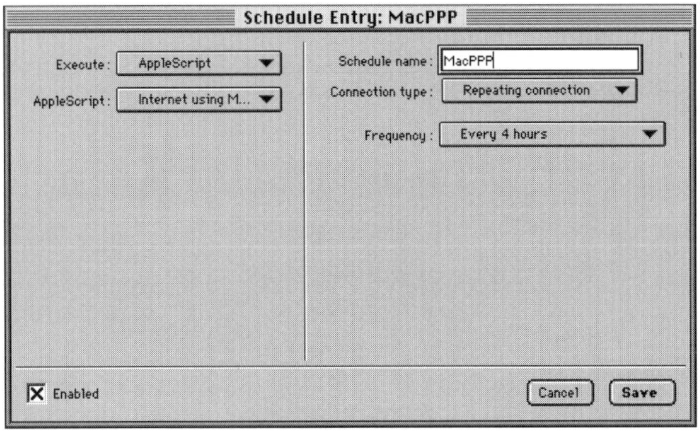

FIGURE 7-17. Using AppleScripts in schedules.

You can use the Script Editor application to modify the behavior of any script. It is found in the "AppleScript™"

folder, which is usually placed in a folder, called "Apple Extras" on your Macintosh hard drive.

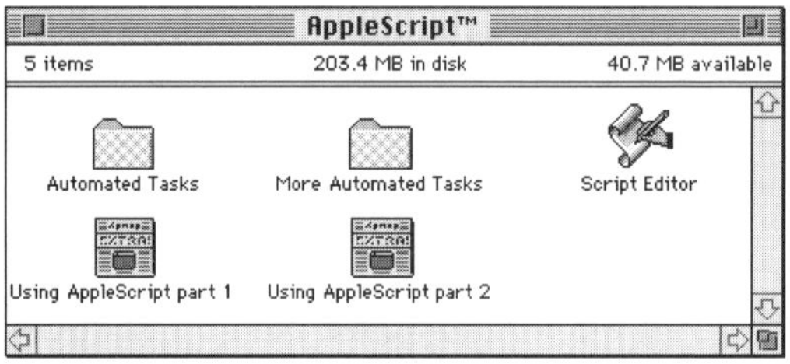

In addition to the "Internet using MacPPP" script, you will find a few other variations on it in the "Internet MacPPP 1.1.1" folder within the AppleScripts for Schedules folder. Besides waiting longer for the MacPPP connection to open (two minutes), these scripts have the following characteristics:

- **Internet MacPPP 1.1 (if open):** Connects only if MacPPP is already open.

- **Internet MacPPP 1.1 (hard):** Performs a hard close after a connection.

- **Internet MacPPP 1.1 (soft):** Performs a soft close after a connection.

All four of these scripts were designed to use MacPPP and to connect only to your default Internet account. To add additional functions you may edit them with Script Editor.

The "All Services" script can be found in the same folder and can be used to check all your accounts. Claris Emailer has this ability built in already, however, so consider this script more of an example than anything immediately useful.

Example AppleScripts

To get to the really fun stuff, you need to open the The "Example AppleScripts" folder. Here you will find many useful scripts that can be used with little or no modification. They are intended only as examples and are not supported by Claris Corp.

- **Convert Emailer1:** Directs Claris Emailer 2.x to convert Claris Emailer 1.x files.
- **Emailer - Create Messages Test:** Creates a batch of test messages. (Mostly useful in troubleshooting connections and verifying email delivery.)
- **Emailer - Get Account List:** Gives you a list of your Claris Emailer accounts.
- **Emailer - Get Folder List:** Gives you a list of your Claris Emailer folders.
- **Emailer - MacSlip Script:** Works in much the same way as the MacPPP scripts, except it is used with MacSLIP.
- **Emailer - Transfer Message:** Moves a message from one folder to another.
- **Emailer USENET news WWW search:** Works in conjunction with Netscape Navigator to search for USENET news about Claris Emailer.
- **Mark as read:** Changes the status of all selected messages to "read."
- **Mark as unread:** Changes the status of all selected messages to "unread."

- **New Mail in the In Box:** This script is used with the New Mail notification preferences I showed you earlier. To make it work, select the **Run AppleScript** check box and choose it in the pop-up menu. Deselect the **Blink icon in menu bar** and **Play sound** check boxes.

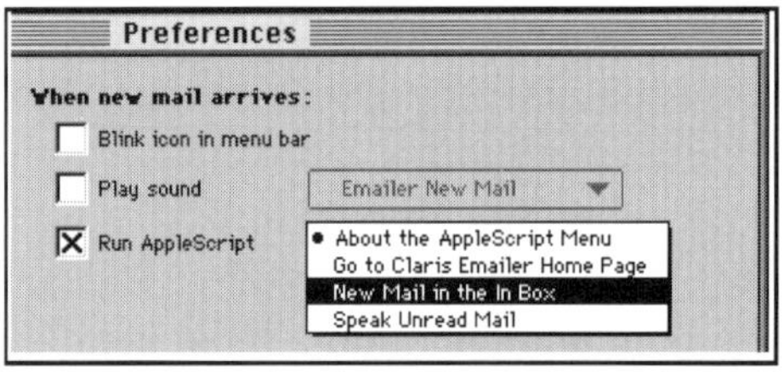

Now Claris Emailer will only notify you if there is new email in your In Box. It will not notify you when an auto-filing Mail Action files a new message. You can modify the script to notify you when email comes in to additional folders as well. For instance, you could create a "family" folder and modify the script to let you know when a message from a relative has been auto-filed.

Some of the examples in this folder are scripts that have been compiled as AppleScript applications. You can place those on the Desktop and use them with Macintosh Drag-and-Drop:

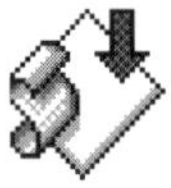

- **Emailer Droplet - Send Files:** Creates a new message and makes enclosures of the files you drag onto it.

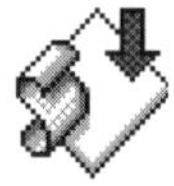

- **Emailer Droplet - Stationery:** Creates a new message and fills the body with the contents of the text file you drag onto it.

- **Emailer Droplet - Bulk Mail:** With this script you don't have to just take bulk email; you can dish it out, too! It uses two files to create new messages. One file must be called "Address List" and contains the addresses of the intended recipients. The second file is the one that is to be the body of your bulk message. Its file name will become the subject.

Do not forget that AppleScripts can also be used to expand the capabilities of your Mail Actions. They can be invoked using the Run AppleScript check box in a Mail Action Entry dialog box.

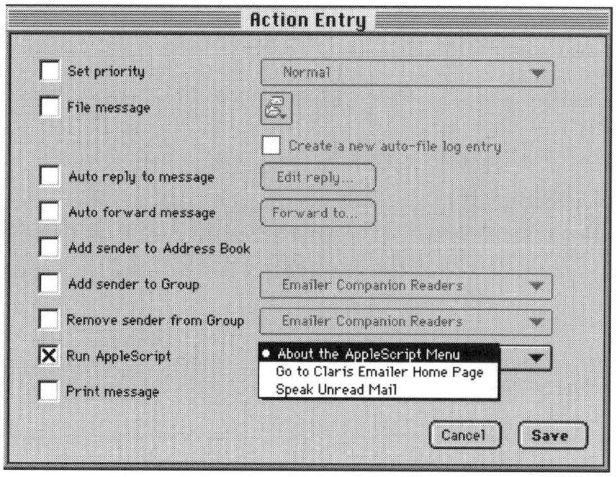

If you find these examples interesting, I recommend that you explore AppleScript more completely. One place to start is Apple's own AppleScript WWW site. You can find it at "http://applescript.infovista.com/."

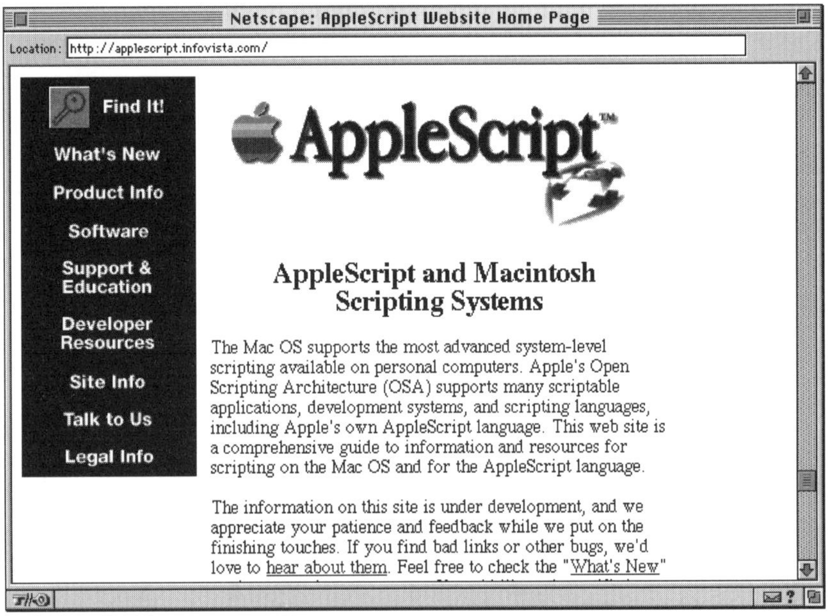

FIGURE 7-18. Logging into the AppleScript Home Page.

Freeware and Shareware AppleScripts

As fun as it is to create your own AppleScripts for extending the capabilities of Claris Emailer, there is not much point in reinventing the wheel. Claris Emailer has an enthusiastic following of developers and users, and they have created a wealth of useful add-ons. Most of these are a quick download from the Internet.

Erik's AppleScripts

Written by Erik C. Thauvin, these AppleScripts for Claris Emailer 2.0 or higher include:

- **Emailer - Talk FAQ:** Retrieves the Emailer-Talk FAQ via email or the WWW.

- **Insert Current URL:** Inserts the front window URL of Netscape Navigator or Microsoft's Internet Explorer into an open outgoing message.

- **Trash Deleted Mail:** Permanently deletes all messages in the Deleted Mail folder.

David's AppleScripts

Written by David Cortright, these AppleScripts include:

- **Bulk Forward:** Forwards selected messages to a single email address.

- **Change Recipient Type:** Changes all unsent recipients in an outgoing message to the selected recipient type.

- **No More Spam:** Replies to an unsolicited message and then deletes it.

- **Send a Copy:** Resends a previously sent message by creating a new copy. This keeps the old message intact.

Will's AppleScripts

Written by Will Mayall, these AppleScripts include:

- **Change Subject:** Changes the text in message subjects.

- **Permanently Delete Messages:** Deletes messages.

- **Replace Subject:** Replaces the text in message subjects.
- **Unsubscribe:** Unsubscribes from mailing lists.
- **Convert from Emailer 1.0:** Forces Claris Emailer 2.x to convert Claris Emailer 1.x folders.
- **Set Print Font:** Changes the font and its size for printing.

Sample Scripts

Written by Dan Crevier, these are described as the definitive sample AppleScripts for Claris Emailer 2.0.

- **DB Stats:** Tells you how many folders and messages there are in the "Mail Database."
- **Resend Message:** Resends an open outgoing message.
- **Decode QP Message:** Decodes an improperly labeled quoted-printable message. To use it you will also need to download the Decode QP AppleScript Addition.
- **Print Selected Messages:** Prints selected messages.
- **eNot AppleScript:** Shows how to use the Mail Agent protocol with AppleScript to be notified of new messages as they arrive.
- **Export Selected Messages:** Saves selected messages in a UNIX mailbox format file.

- **File Replies with Originals:** Moves replies to selected messages to the same folder as the originals.
- **Import UNIX/Eudora Inbox:** Imports an In Box in Eudora's UNIX format.
- **Import UNIX/Eudora Outbox:** Imports an Out Box in Eudora's UNIX format.
- **Insert Explorer URL:** Inserts a URL to Microsoft Internet Explorer in a message.
- **Japanese Scripts:** Shows how to work with incoming messages in Japanese.
- **Save Bookmark Sample:** Shows how to use a save bookmark Apple event.
- **Set Font to Geneva:** Makes the font of an open message Geneva.
- **Set Font to Monaco:** Makes the font of an open message Monaco.
- **Reveal Reply:** Opens the reply to an open message.
- **Toggle Read Status:** Toggles the status of selected messages between read and unread.
- **Toggle Replied To:** Toggles the status of selected messages between replied to and not replied to.
- **Toggle Schedules:** Toggles schedules between enabled and disabled.

Emailer was originally created by Fog City Software. While Claris now owns it, Fog City continues to provide files and information to users on their Web site. All of the Apple-

Scripts I mentioned can be found there. Find the newest ones at "http://www.fogcity.com/em_utilities2.0.html."

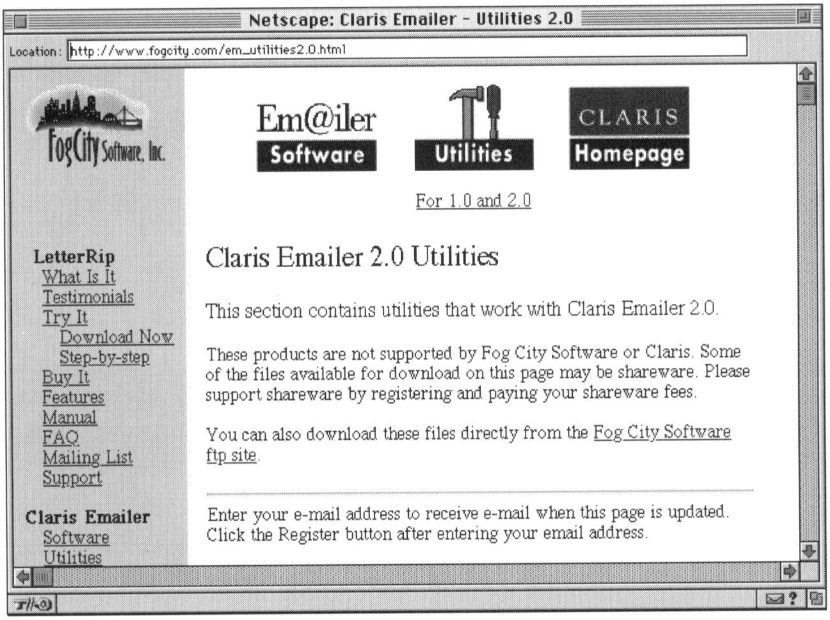

FIGURE 7-19. Logging into the Fog City Software Home Page.

Summary

Many of Claris Emailer's operating behaviors can be customized to meet your individual needs. There are general preferences that can be set for the entire application and more specific preferences that can be set for each account. In addition, Claris Emailer is Apple events-savvy and can make extensive use of AppleScript. Several AppleScripts are shipped with Claris Emailer, and many more are available from third parties on the WWW.

Appendix

The following information is taken from the SimpleText documents that accompany Claris Emailer. For the most up-to-date information visit the Claris WWW site by choosing the **Go to Claris Emailer Home Page** command under the **AppleScript** menu bar item. Alternately, you may visit the Claris forums on America Online (keyword "Claris") and CompuServe ("go Claris").

I did not repeat those items that pertain to material already covered elsewhere in this book.

Upgrading Instructions for Claris Emailer 2.0

For those upgrading from a previous version of Claris Emailer 1.x or Claris Emailer Lite, the following instructions provide a clean install, which will avoid any accidental loss of data.

Simple Upgrading Instructions

1. Verify that the folder that contains your existing Claris Emailer application is named "Claris Emailer Folder."

2. Move the Claris Emailer Folder to the root directory (first level) of your hard disk.

3. Launch the Claris Emailer 2.0 Installer.

4. In the Install Location section of the installer window, press the **Switch Disk** button until you see the disk on which your Claris Emailer Folder resides.

5. Press the **Install** button.

During installation the Installer will ask if you are upgrading from a previous version. If you are, select **Yes**. You may then be asked to identify your Claris Emailer Files folder. If you have multiple Claris Emailer Files folders, select the one that contains your existing Filing Cabinet or Claris Emailer database.

WARNING! *If you create an entirely new Claris Emailer Folder, rather than installing into your existing one as instructed above, Claris Emailer DOES NOT move the Claris Emailer Files folder (including your new mail database) into the new Claris Emailer Folder. The new Claris Emailer application uses the Claris Emailer Files folder in the old Claris Emailer Folder.*

If you want an entirely new Claris Emailer Folder, you need to drag the Claris Emailer Files folder from your old Claris Emailer Folder to the new one after the conversion is complete.

If you delete your older Claris Emailer folder without transferring the Claris Emailer Files folder as described, you will delete all of your previously saved email messages and your new mail database.

Detailed Instructions

An important new feature of Claris Emailer 2.0 is storage of your email documents in a database. The database provides quicker access to your documents and saves hard disk space, because your documents are saved in this new database format.

These instructions will ensure that you safely convert your saved mail from 1.X and 2.0 public beta versions to 2.0 final format.

Please read and follow these instructions carefully.

Before you convert:

Currently in Claris Emailer 1.X, your documents are saved individually in the Filing Cabinet folder of the Claris Emailer Files folder. In the 2.0 version of Claris Emailer, a Mail folder in the Claris Emailer Files folder contains a database, which stores all your messages.

Upgrading Claris Emailer 1.X or a previous beta version of Claris Emailer 2.0 is easiest when the existing Claris Emailer Folder is named "Claris Emailer Folder." If it is not, you should rename it before installation.

When you double-click to install Claris Emailer 2.0, the Installer screen has a panel in the lower left corner labeled "Installation Location." Use the pop-up menu to choose the folder in which the Claris Emailer Folder is located. Be sure to choose the folder that contains the Claris Emailer Folder, NOT the Claris Emailer folder itself. (For Example: If your Claris Emailer Folder resides in a folder named "Applications," select "Applications" as the installation location.)

Then install Claris Emailer 2.0.

A dialog will ask "Are you upgrading from any earlier versions of Claris Emailer or from a beta version of Claris Emailer 2.0?" Click Yes.

The installation will then proceed for a while. If you answered yes to the upgrading question, you might be presented with a dialog asking you to locate the Claris Emailer Files folder from your previous version.

This dialog contains all the Claris Emailer Files folders found on all mounted volumes. When you click on one of them, a pane in the bottom half of the dialog shows the path to that folder. Select the folder you wish to upgrade and click OK.

If you installed into a folder other than the existing Claris Emailer Folder, when you start Claris Emailer 2.0 you see a dialog asking you to locate the Claris Emailer Files folder. Navigate to and choose the Claris Emailer Files folder that you upgraded when you installed. If you installed into the existing Claris Emailer Folder, you will not have this step.

Next, if you are upgrading from Emailer 1.x (including Lite), a dialog asks whether you want to convert your existing messages. Click Yes to convert your messages to the new database format. Depending on how many saved messages you have, the conversion process can take several minutes to several hours.

WARNING!

If you create an entirely new Claris Emailer Folder, rather than installing into your existing one as instructed above, Claris Emailer DOES NOT move the Claris Emailer Files Folder (including your new mail database) into the new Claris Emailer Folder. The new Claris Emailer application uses the Claris Emailer Files Folder in the old Claris Emailer Folder.

If you want to have an entirely new Claris Emailer Folder, you need to drag the Claris Emailer Files Folder from your old Claris Emailer Folder to the new one after the conversion is complete.

If you delete your older Claris Emailer Folder without transferring the Claris Emailer Files Folder as described, you will delete all of your previously saved email messages and your new mail database.

Frequently Asked Questions

Question: My modem is not listed in the pop-up menus for modems. What should I use?

Answer: Try picking a similar model in the pop-up menu. If you own "XYZ Modem 28.8," for example, try "XYZ Modem 14.4."

Try these in the CompuServe modem setup:

- Hayes
- Hayes-Compatible (default)

- Hayes-Compatible (alternate)
- Hayes-Compatible 2400

Try these in the Apple Modem Tool setup:

- Generic MNP / V.32
- Generic 2400
- Hayes-Compatible Modem

These settings work with most modems, although they may not permit the use of some of your particular modem's advanced features. If they do not work, contact the modem's manufacturer and ask if they have their own Apple Modem Tool. Alternately, you can create a custom setup for your modem if you are comfortable configuring modem initialization strings by using the **Custom** item in the **Modem** pop-up menu.

Question: When I am addressing my email, how can I move directly from the recipient field to the body field of the message form without having to tab through all the fields?

Answer: You can use the **Command-Tab** key combination to move the insertion point from the recipient field to the body field.

Question: Why do people who receive email from me via the Internet say that my name is not listed in the reply address?

Answer: You need to make sure your name is entered in the **User name** field for that particular Account. If it is, then you are probably using a service that does not support this convention.

Question: Does Claris Emailer preserve special Macintosh characters?

Answer: Claris Emailer uses a special formatting called *quoted-printable* for email sent via the Internet. This formatting is part of the *Multi-purpose Internet Mail Extension (MIME)* email standard.

When email is sent via one of the commercial online services, Claris Emailer tries to convert the characters to characters that look similar. A "ü" is converted to "u," for example.

Question: Why did I get a message that says my email was not delivered?

Answer: Sometimes email sent via the Internet cannot be delivered. Often these warning messages can be ignored, as your message will eventually get through.

Question: I connected and received email, but some of my outgoing messages were not sent. What happened?

Answer: There are a number of things that might have happened:

- If you are using a schedule, make sure that you have the outgoing email's account selected in the schedule window and that you have enabled the check boxes to both **Send mail** and **Get mail**. Also make sure that the time parameters have been set for the schedule and that the schedule's **Enabled** check box is selected.

- Some services require that there be text in a message's Subject and Body fields and will not accept a message without it.

- Perhaps a connection could not be held or established. Review your Connection Log.

- Look at the status of the message in the first column of the folder window that contains the outgoing message (usually in the Out Box.) It should show the clock icon. If it shows the alert triangle, then there is an error in one of the addressees. If it shows the pencil icon, then the message has been saved as a draft. If it shows a check mark icon, then the message has been sent correctly.

- Sometimes a service may be malfunctioning in such a way that you can receive email but not send it. If you have more than one account, try to send your email from a different one using the **Send via** pop-up menu in the message form. If the problem persists, contact your service provider.

Question: What does a blank Destination field mean?

Answer: A blank Destination field in a message form is treated in the same way as choosing **Internet**.

Question: How can I copy and paste multiple instances of quoted text in an outgoing message?

Answer: Copy the text in the incoming message (or any other application), then use the **Paste As Quotation** command under the **Edit** menu bar item to place quotation marks in front of the text as you paste it.

Question: Why was my message with 100 recipients sent twice?

Answer: Commercial online services and some Internet mail hosts have limits on the number of recipients with one message, so Claris Emailer sends the message to recipients in smaller batches.

Question: Why did Claris Emailer slow down after a file was received?

Answer: Files sometimes need to be processed after they are received. This is very processor intensive and might slow down the computer until it is done.

Question: I received a message that says it was sent after it was received. Why does the sent time seem incorrect?

Answer: Claris Emailer displays the time that the email server observed when sending a message. If an email server is not within the same time zone as the sender, you will see the time that the email server sent the message, not the true time that it was sent.

Question: I received a large message that came in as a file. Why did the message appear as an enclosure?

Answer: Claris Emailer receives and displays messages up to 64,000 characters in length. Anything longer gets saved as a text file.

In addition, large messages are converted to files by some services because they cannot display messages larger than 32 Kbytes with their own software. If the enclosure is a text file formatted as a message, Claris Emailer tries to read it as a message. If this succeeds, the message is converted from an enclosure and presented normally.

Email servers and commercial online services often have limits on message sizes. In addition, online services sometimes have a different limit for messages sent or received via an Internet gateway. When this is the case messages containing less than 64,000 characters might still be truncated.

Question: I received a large text message and Claris Emailer created a file. SimpleText tried to open it, but the file was too large. What should I do?

Answer: You should be able to open the text file with most word processors by choosing its **Open** command from under the **File** menu bar item.

If you have the Internet Configuration System installed, you can assign a file type for these files. Use the **Editor** option accessible via the **Helpers** button.

Files received from other platforms might not have the information a Macintosh needs to open it from the Finder. These appear as blank icons. If the file is in plain text, however, you should still be able to open it with a word processor.

Question: Sometimes there is an address in the text of a message that I would like to add to my Address Book. What is the easiest way to do that?

Answer: If you have Macintosh Drag-and-Drop installed, you can drag addresses from the body of any message form into the Address Book to create a new entry. These address formats are supported:

john_doe@pop.host.com
John Doe, john_doe@pop.host.com
"John Doe" <john_doe@pop.host.com>
John Doe <john_doe@pop.host.com>
"John Doe" john_doe@pop.host.com
john_doe@pop.host.com (John Doe)
<john_doe@pop.host.com> (John Doe)

In short, a full Internet address that contains the @ symbol.

Question: How do I find the address of another subscriber to an online service?

Answer: You need to use the software that came from the service.

Question: Can I put a space in an America Online address?

Answer: Spaces are optional in America Online screen names. A screen name "Jane Doe" could also be written "JaneDoe." When you send a message to someone at America Online via the Internet, however, the address cannot contain a space. Claris Emailer knows to remove any spaces when sending such a message.

Question: Why did the address book I imported not contain names?

Answer: Address books used by other email programs often do not store names. You need to edit such addresses after importing them.

Question: I want to export my Address Book, but I know that groups are not exported. What can I do to save the groups?

Answer: If you have Macintosh Drag-and-Drop you can save groups by selecting them in the Address Book window and dragging them to the Desktop to create Desktop Clippings.

If your Macintosh's Finder does not support Desktop Clippings, select a Group and drag it to any application that supports Macintosh Drag-and-Drop, such as SimpleText. You could also drag it into an outgoing Claris Emailer message.

To put a saved group back in the Address Book, select the Desktop Clipping (or list of addresses if you saved it as text) and drop it into the Address Book. You will need to enter a group name and description.

Groups are not exported because there is no standard for importing groups into other programs.

Question: When I export my Address Book, what happens to the default address for each entry?

Answer: The default entry is exported as the first address, which makes importing the Address Book easy.

Question: Is it OK to save hundreds of messages in a folder?

Answer: Folders can store thousands of messages, although this can slow their initial display.

Question: Why do I sometimes get bad connections and sometimes cannot connect at all?

Answer: The following will cause this:

- You get a busy signal.
- You cannot get a phone line ("All circuits are busy").
- You have bad phone lines (with noise, crosstalk, or other technical problems).
- Your online service or ISP is experiencing difficulty.
- There is a poor connection between your modem and the one on the other end of the call.
- Your computer has too many other programs running and Claris Emailer cannot get enough time from the Macintosh's processor.
- You need to dial a a number or code to get an outside line.

Question: What do I do when I cannot connect?

Answer: Try the following:

- Dial again. Many connection problems are temporary.

- Make sure you have entered the correct phone number. Verify that you are getting an outside line by dialing with a "9," or "8," (make sure to include the comma), then "1" and the area code. To test this, dial the number you are trying to connect through with the regular telephone. If you can't get through, neither can your modem.

- Try a lower speed (Bps).

- If you are using the Apple Modem Tool, disable error correction. The online services use built-in error correction.

- Double-check all settings to be sure the modem type specified is correct.

- If you are not using the Macintosh Comm Toolbox, try it. Sometimes it is more reliable.

- Switch to a "Hayes-compatible" modem string.

- If you are doing lengthy file transfers, try turning off AppleTalk. AppleTalk can compete with your modem for the Macintosh's processing time and cause failures.

- Try a different service to determine if one service's connection is bad or your problem is local.

- Try another telecommunications application besides Claris Emailer, such as a WWW browser or ClarisWorks, to see if the problem is in Claris Emailer or in your setup.

- If you are staying in a hotel, call the hotel operator and ask if you have to do anything special to enable your phone to connect.

Question: I have Call Waiting and it is disconnecting my modem. How do I avoid this?

Answer: You can disable Call Waiting before making a call by entering "*70," before the number (e.g., *70, 555-1212.)

Question: I have the most difficulty getting an America Online connection. What should I do?

Answer: Try switching from **SprintNet** to **AOLNet** in the **Connection type** pop-up menu of the Service Provider Entry dialog box.

Question: Why doesn't the connection terminate immediately when I press the **Stop** button in the Connection Status Window?

Answer: When you press the **Stop** button Claris Emailer tries to terminate the current action, but some interactions with a mail host take some time to cancel.

Question: Why wasn't a file sent by my online service?

Answer: Some online services prevent enclosures from being sent to recipients via the Internet. Try using the **BinHex** encoding option.

Question: Are enclosures deleted when I delete my messages?

Answer: Enclosures remain in the Downloads folder until you "trash" them.

Question: I was receiving a message from America Online when the connection was lost. Now I cannot retrieve the message. What happened?

Answer: America Online's servers mark a message as read as soon as the message begins to be delivered. If the message is interrupted before Claris Emailer can completely read it, the message is still marked as read and Claris Emailer can no longer access it. When this happens Claris Emailer makes a note of it in your Connection Log and directs you to use the America Online client to read the mail.

In the America Online client look in your Read Mail folder. The last message read should be the message that was skipped.

Question: Do I need to use a comma or a period in a CompuServe address?

Answer: You can use either one.

Question: Do I need to schedule RadioMail connections?

Answer: Claris Emailer automatically retrieves email from RadioMail. You may optionally set up a schedule to send RadioMail messages from your Out Box.

Question: Can Claris Emailer read an online service's forum messages?

Answer: Claris Emailer only accesses an online service's primary email systems.

Question: If I have a schedule set to send email only, will Claris Emailer try to connect when I have no email to send?

Answer: Claris Emailer does not connect if there is no email to send.

More Questions?

If you did not find an answer to your question here, refer to the SimpleText documents that came with your copy of Claris Emailer. There may be more up-to-date information there than this book has documented. For the most up-to-date information, visit the Claris Web site at www.claris.com.

Index

Numerics

A

B

C

M

N

O

T

U

V

W

X

Y

Z

About AP PROFESSIONAL

AP PROFESSIONAL, an imprint of Academic Press, a division of Harcourt Brace & Company, was founded in 1993 to provide high quality, innovative products for the computer community. For over 50 years, Academic Press has been a world leader in documenting scientific and technical research.

AP PROFESSIONAL continues this tradition by providing its readers with exemplary publications that bring new topics to light and offer fresh views on prominent topics. Often, today's computer books are underdeveloped clones, published in haste and promoted in series. Readers tend to be neglected by the lack of commitment from other publishers to produce quality products. It is our business to provide you with clearly written, educational publications that contain valuable information you will find truly useful. AP PROFESSIONAL has grown quickly and has established a reputation for fine products because of this commitment to excellence.

Through our strong reputation at Academic Press, and one of the most experienced editorial boards in computer publishing, AP PROFESSIONAL has also contracted many of the best writers in the computer community. Each book undergoes three stages of editing (technical, developmental, and copyediting) before going through the traditional book publishing production process. These extensive measures ensure clear, informative, and accurate publications.

It is our hope that you will be pleased with your decision to purchase this book, and that it will exceed your expectations. We are committed to making the AP PROFESSIONAL logo a sign of excellence for all computer users and hope that you will come to rely on the quality of our publications.

Enjoy!

Jeffrey M. Pepper
Vice President, Editorial Director

Related Titles from AP Professional

Ahuja, *Network and Internet Security*

Ahuja, *Secure Commerce on the Internet*

Campbell, *World Wide Web Pocket Directory*

Casey, *The Hill on the Net*

Connor/Anderson, *Networking The Desktop: NetWare*

Cougias/Dell/Heiberger, *Complete Guide to Mac Backup Management, Second Edition*

Cougias/Dell/Heiberger, *Designing AppleTalk Network Architectures*

Cougias/Dell, *Managing AppleShare & Workgroup Servers*

Cougias/Hessel, *Managing AppleTalk Networks*

Crane, *Mutual Fund Investing on the Internet*

Feiler, *Cyberdog*

Fisher, *CD-ROM Guide to Multimedia Authoring*

Fisher, *Multimedia Authoring*

Foley, *The Microsoft Exchange Guide*

Graham, *TCP/IP Addressing*

Keogh, *Webmaster's Guide to VB Script*

Levine, *Live Java*

Levitus/Evans, *Cheap and Easy Internet Access (Windows Version)*

Levitus/Evans, *Cheap and Easy Internet Access (Macintosh Version)*

Levitus, *WebMaster Macintosh*

Levitus, *WebMaster Windows*

Loshin, *TCP/IP for Everyone*

McKeehan, *Safe Surfing: A Family Tour of the Net*

Ozer, *Publishing Digital Video*

Ozer, *Video Compression for Multimedia*

Pfaffenberger, *Netscape Navigator 3.0 (Macintosh Version)*

Pfaffenberger, *Netscape Navigator 3.0 (Windows Version)*

Pfaffenberger, *Publish it on the Web! (Macintosh Version)*

Pfaffenberger, *Publish it on the Web! (Windows Version)*

Pfaffenberger, *Netscape Navigator Gold*

Pfaffenberger, *The Elements of Hypertext Style*

Ribar, *The Internet with Windows 95*

Schengili-Roberts, *The Advanced HTML Companion*

Shaffer/Simon, *Network Security*

Sinclair/Hale, *Intranets vs. Lotus Notes*

Skardhamar, *Virus: Detection and Elimination*

Sullivan, *Using Internet Explorer to Browse the Internet*

Tittel/Robbins, *E-Mail Essentials*

Tittel/Robbins, *Network Design Essentials*

Tittel, *PC Networking Handbook*